Conversations with Jason Berry

Literary Conversations Series
Monika Gehlawat
General Editor

Conversations with Jason Berry

Edited by Howard Hunter

University Press of Mississippi / Jackson

The University Press of Mississippi is the scholarly publishing agency of
the Mississippi Institutions of Higher Learning: Alcorn State University,
Delta State University, Jackson State University, Mississippi State University,
Mississippi University for Women, Mississippi Valley State University,
University of Mississippi, and University of Southern Mississippi.

www.upress.state.ms.us

The University Press of Mississippi is a member
of the Association of University Presses.

Publisher: University Press of Mississippi, Jackson, USA
Authorised GPSR Safety Representative: Easy Access System Europe -
Mustamäe tee 50, 10621 Tallinn, Estonia, *gpsr.requests@easproject.com*

Library of Congress Cataloging-in-Publication Data

Names: Hunter, Howard (G. Howard) editor
Title: Conversations with Jason Berry / Howard Hunter.
Other titles: Literary conversations series
Description: Jackson : University Press of Mississippi, 2026. |
  Series: Literary conversations series | Includes bibliographical references and index.
Identifiers: LCCN 2025043366 (print) | LCCN 2025043367 (ebook) |
  ISBN 9781496861177 hardback | ISBN 9781496861184 trade paperback |
  ISBN 9781496861191 epub | ISBN 9781496861207 epub |
  ISBN 9781496861214 pdf | ISBN 9781496861221 pdf
Subjects: LCSH: Berry, Jason—Interviews | Journalists—United States—Interviews |
  Journalism—United States | Reporters and reporting—United States—Interviews |
  Investigative reporting—United States | Historians—United States—Interviews
Classification: LCC PS3602.E7637 Z46 2026 (print) | LCC PS3602.E7637 (ebook)
LC record available at https://lccn.loc.gov/2025043366
LC ebook record available at https://lccn.loc.gov/2025043367

British Library Cataloging-in-Publication Data available

Books by Jason Berry

Amazing Grace: With Charles Evers in Mississippi. Saturday
   Review Press, 1973.
Up From the Cradle of Jazz: New Orleans Music Since WWII,
   with Jonathan Foose and Tad Jones. University of Georgia Press, 1986.
   Revised edition, University of Louisiana at Lafayette Press, 2009.
*Lead Us Not Into Temptation: Catholic Priests and the Sexual Abuse of
   Children.* Doubleday, 1992. Revised with a new introduction,
   University of Illinois Press, 2000.
The Spirit of Black Hawk: A Mystery of Africans and Indians.
   University Press of Mississippi, 1995.
Louisiana Faces: Images from a Renaissance. With Philip Gould photographs.
   LSU Press, 2000.
Vows of Silence: The Abuse of Power in the Papacy of John Paul II,
   with Gerald Renner. Free Press, 2004.
Last of the Red Hot Poppas. Chin Music Press, 2006.
Render unto Rome: The Secret Life of Money in the Catholic Church.
   Crown, 2011.
Earl Long in Purgatory. University of Louisiana at Lafayette Press, 2011.
City of a Million Dreams: A History of New Orleans at Year 300.
   University of North Carolina Press, 2018.

Contents

Introduction

On an unseasonable balmy evening in March 2002, Jason Berry stood on Canal Street in front of a truck with a satellite dish for an interview with CNN's Anderson Cooper. It was not the most auspicious location. Canal Street is the major thoroughfare in downtown New Orleans, dividing the French Quarter and the Central Business District. The traffic of streetcars, vehicles, and pedestrians create a din uncongenial for serious conversation. And the subject was fraught. *The Boston Globe* had run a series of articles on Cardinal Bernard Law providing cover for Catholic pedophile priests by moving them from one parish to another. In 1985, Berry reported a story on a priest abusing young boys in Lafayette, Louisiana. Since the publication of his book in 1992, *Lead Us Not Into Temptation: Catholic Priests and the Sexual Abuse of Children*, Berry had become the preeminent talking head on the ongoing scandal in the Catholic Church. While an indoor setting would have been more suitable to the occasion, CNN had no choice but to interview him on the foot of Canal Street, because in just ten minutes and fifty yards away, Berry's play *Earl Long in Purgatory* was about to open at the Southern Rep. The one-man show, starring local actor John "Spud" McConnell, is about one man's (in Berry's words) "salvation quest." Earl Long, who served as Governor of Louisiana on three occasions, could be an outrageous figure; he was known for hurling colorful invectives at his opponents and publicly cavorting with the New Orleans stripper Blaze Starr. Yet, in the 1950s, by going against convention and publicly espousing the idea that Black people should be treated fairly, he was ahead of his time. Uncle Earl, as he liked to be called, was the perfect imperfect character to wrestle with his demons on stage. That Berry pulled off the interview and enjoyed an opening night with a packed house and favorable reviews is impressive in its own right, yet the occasion is also representative of a larger gestalt, a body of work that has probed the human condition through journalism, theater, cultural criticism, the novel, film, and history for over half a century.

Berry's exposure of the clerical abuse scandal bore witness to the rights of victims and served as an indictment of the institutional Catholic Church.

In *Vows of Silence: The Abuse of Power in the Papacy of John Paul II*, written with Gerald Renner, another Catholic journalist, the authors make the case that the Vatican protected Father Marcial Maciel, founder of the Legion of Christ and serial abuser of young seminarians. The theological revanchism of the Legion appealed to John Paul's conservative instincts. He "found a triumphal force in the militant spirituality of Opus Dei and the Legion, their cultivation of traditional Catholics, their ability to raise funds, and their stance against moral relativism."[1] As Berry has argued in his trio of works on the church, the tendency to protect abusive priests is all tied to an inner institutional struggle with modernity specifically on the question of clerical celibacy. In Berry's third book of the series, *Render unto Rome: The Secret Life of Money in the Catholic Church*, he argues that the medieval structure of the church hierarchy not only allowed bishops to cover up abuses, but also to liquidate parish assets to settle lawsuits filed by victims of abuse and close churches with little laity involvement.[2] The financial malfeasance of the Vatican itself comes from that same structure that operates under a shroud of secrecy. Content gleaned from both books figures prominently in a *Frontline* documentary, *Secrets of the Vatican*, which Berry coproduced.

Nevertheless, to assume the church trilogy and numerous articles written on church corruption (including over eighty pieces for outlets like the *National Catholic Reporter*) constitutes the major stream of Berry's work with the occasional diversion or tributary like *Earl Long in Purgatory* would be a mistake. His initial passions—politics and Louisiana culture—have fueled works in print and film that have formed their own distinct but congruent stream. It was young writers like Berry and photographers like Michael P. Smith who contributed to a cultural renaissance in New Orleans and southern Louisiana in the 1970s and 1980s, breaking through the bounds of cultural segregation. His 1980 film coproduced and written with Jonathan Foose, *Up From the Cradle of Jazz*, highlights two musical families, the Lasties and Nevilles, who were well known in the music community but not necessarily public figures at the time. The film inspired a book on New Orleans music written with Foose and Tad Jones, *Up From the Cradle of Jazz: New Orleans Music Since World War II*. The work features well-known musical artists like Fats Domino, Irma Thomas, and Allen Toussaint. It also connects New Orleans music to African traditions, with a thread that runs from the city's Congo Square to Mardi Gras Indians through groups such as the Meters (it's not a coincidence that the Nevilles' uncle was Big Chief Jolley, who founded the Wild Tchoupitoulas).

A common goal of Berry's work as reporter and historian is introducing readers to people who are not household names but who are worth knowing. For example, in all three books of the church trilogy, there is Thomas Doyle, a former Dominican priest, canon lawyer, and military chaplain who put himself in the service of clerical abuse victims; in *City of a Million Dreams* (arguably Berry's magnum opus), there is Pierre Casanave—a free man of color and undertaker in antebellum New Orleans who formalized the structure of the funeral procession with music that would later morph into a storied tradition; and there is Mother Catherine Seals, the Spiritualist minister, healer, and founder of the Manger, a shelter in the New Orleans Lower Ninth Ward that cared for pregnant girls, children, and homeless and battered women.

A coherent thread running through Berry's work is what priest and writer Andrew Greely called the "Catholic imagination." It's a worldview that finds the sacramental in both the extraordinary and ordinary things. It is not limited to Catholic teachings and practices per se, but is more of a leitmotif that finds beauty and strength in ritual with a spiritual connectedness in both the formal and informal. For example, in *Louisiana Faces: Images of a Renaissance*, a book in which he wrote the text to complement Phillip Gould's photographs, Berry points out: "A good many of those who appear in these pages are not artists or musicians, but everyday people whose moments in the lens convey nuances of a social fabric, rhythms of a daily life that rise to their own level of art and inspire others with quotidian joys, a precious sense of time and rootedness."[3] Berry's own childhood was one full of small graces through a close-knit family and a joyous Latin Catholicism that came out of a Mexican heritage on his mother's side. His grandmother took him to Mass at St. Stephen's, a majestic neo-Gothic church in their Uptown neighborhood. On Napoleon Avenue's sidewalk, in front of the church, he also was introduced to the aesthetics of Mardi Gras parades, a phantasmagoria of color and sounds that assault the senses of a young child in wondrous ways.

Hence it makes sense that as a writer and historian Berry would be drawn to the jazz funeral as ritual, sacrament, and spectacle. In 1990, he was the recipient of a grant from the National Endowment for the Humanities and, in 2001, a Guggenheim Fellowship, both of which he used to research and film jazz funerals. As he avers in *City of a Million Dreams*, the tradition's roots are both European and African. While the New Orleans funeral procession of King Carlos III in 1789 (five months after his death in Spain) was the first known funeral parade to include musicians. Berry also includes an account of the 1622 funeral procession of King Alfonso I of Kongo; its trumpeters and drummers "foreshadow the Illustrious Body procession for Carlos III in 1789."[4] The jazz funeral is also a metaphor for the city itself—like death and rebirth in the Christian rite, New Orleans has had to survive setbacks and disasters, including yellow fever, hurricanes, corruption, racism, poverty, and urban violence. Whether the city can endure these vicissitudes, Berry leaves open to question in *City of a Million Dreams*. In his life's work, New Orleans and the Catholic Church figure most prominently as characters in a Greek drama of tragedy, pathos, and hope.

As a public intellectual, Jason Berry has been a moralist in the tradition of his hero Albert Camus. In an essay "Albert Camus and Civil Rights: A Journalist's Brief," Berry credits Camus, an atheist, for bringing him back to the church after his faith was blown off its moorings by the scandals: "In time, an older impulse drew me back to the liturgy, the notion of church as a big tent. I kept on thinking of Camus's idea of absurdity defined a 'human need and the unreasonable silence of the world.' Faith, for me, changed from a source of solace to a search for God's voice in human suffering—a way to fill that absurd silence and the awful mystery of why people suffer. Words are central to the search; words to fill the silence, words in order to believe."[5]

Yet in spite of the existential struggle that moralists face, the following interviews are hardly devoid of a comic sensibility or a light touch. After all, Berry's novel *Last of the Red Hot Poppas* is an outrageously funny book, even though it came out of his work as an environmental reporter in the 1980s, when Louisiana was used as a toxic dumping ground for petrochemical companies. In New Orleans, profundity will always be balanced by irony simply because things are seldom what they seem. The Mardi Gras mask is an apt metaphor even if hackneyed. And Jason Berry's aperçu that New Orleans is a city of both laws and spectacle with the two forever in conflict underscores the notion that for this scion and chronicler of the city, the weight of history is both a burden and a blessing.

HH

Notes

1. Jason Berry and Gerald Renner, *Vows of Silence: The Abuse of Power in the Papacy of John Paul II* (Free Press, 2004), 297.

2. Jason Berry, *Render Unto Rome: The Secret Life of Money in the Catholic Church*, (New York, 2011), 4–9.

3. Phillip Gould and Jason Berry, *Louisiana Faces: Images from a Renaissance* (LSU Press, 2000), 4.

4. Jason Berry, *City of a Million Dreams: A History of New Orleans at Year 300* (UNC Press, 2018), 59, 70.

5. This was a paper that Jason Berry gave at a conference. Jason Berry, "A Life Worth Living: Albert Camus 100 years Later," (Lecture, University of Houston, November 22, 2013).

Chronology

1949   Born February 20, 1949, in New Orleans, Louisiana, to Mary Frances Devine Berry and Jason F. Berry Sr. Attended neighborhood public and Catholic schools. Graduated from Jesuit High School in 1967.

1968   Transferred from Loyola University New Orleans to Georgetown University. Studied Shakespeare, Dante, the Romantic poets, T. S. Eliot, James Joyce, and the theology of Theillard de Chardin. Active in protesting the Vietnam War. Reviewed films and plays for upstart weekly The Georgetown Voice. Cofounded a literary magazine, the Georgetown Quarterly. Graduated cum laude in 1971 with a degree in English.

1971   In Jackson, Mississippi, volunteered for the gubernatorial campaign of Charles Evers, mayor of Fayette and brother of Medgar Evers, a civil rights leader assassinated in 1963. As press secretary, wrote news releases and interacted with journalists on the campaign. Evers lost, but fifty-two African Americans were elected to public office.

1972   Worked on a book about the Evers campaign. Walker Percy, impressed by a piece on Southern politics in the *Vieux Carre Courier*, offered a referral to Judith Sachs of Saturday Review Press in New York. Upon reading the manuscript for *Amazing Grace: With Charles Evers in Mississippi*, she offered a contract. Book published in 1973 to good reviews.

1974–77 As a freelance journalist, published reports on IRS abuses targeting civil rights activists in Mississippi in the *Delta Democrat-Times* and *South Mississippi Sun*. With support from the Fund for Investigative Journalism in Washington, DC, the reporting continued in *The Nation, The Washington Star*, and *Atlanta Gazette*. Wrote an op-ed in *The New York Times*. Published book reviews in *The New Republic* and *The Washington Post*, and wrote numerous articles for New Orleans outlets.

1978   With Jonathan Foose, a Delta folklorist, he conducted oral history interviews with New Orleans musicians David and Walter Lastie of the Ninth Ward and Charles Neville of the Thirteenth Ward. With a grant from the Louisiana Committee of the Humanities, the duo used the oral histories as foundation for a video documentary. *Up From the Cradle of Jazz* aired in 1980 on Louisiana public television affiliates.

1980   Began work on history of New Orleans popular music with Foose and film consultant Tad Jones, supported by a National Endowment for the Humanities grant.

1982–83   Accepted to Journalists in Europe program and relocated to Paris. Published articles in *The International Herald Tribune*, *Passion*, and *Reader's Digest*. In 1983, took travel assignments in London, the Netherlands, and West Africa. Gave lectures with screenings of *Up From the Cradle of Jazz* at US Information Service Cultural Centers in Nigeria, Cameroon, Benin, and Togo. Published a *New York Times Magazine* profile of Nigerian activist and playwright Wole Soyinka, who later won the Nobel Prize in Literature. Received the New Orleans Press Club 1983 award for his investigative reporting in *Gambit Weekly* on oil waste pollution in Cajun country.

1985   Gained access to legal documents on church officials and Gilbert Gauthe, a Catholic priest in the Lafayette, Louisiana diocese, indicted for sexually abusing young boys. Led to a joint assignment with the *Times of Acadiana* and the *National Catholic Reporter*.

1986   Published the book *Up From the Cradle of Jazz: New Orleans Music Since World War II*, with Jonathan Foose and Tad Jones with University of Georgia Press.

1990   Received National Endowment for the Humanities, Independent Scholar Fellowship for research on jazz funerals.

1992   Published *Lead Us Not Into Temptation: Catholic Priests and the Sexual Abuse of Children* with Doubleday. Served as off-air correspondent for PBS *Frontline* episode, "Who is David Duke?"

1993   Won Wilber Award from Religion Communicators Council for *Lead Us Not Into Temptation* for Catholic Press Best Book.

1994   Began working as music columnist for *New Orleans Magazine*. Continued in role until 2019.

1995   Published *The Spirit of Black Hawk: A Mystery of Africans and Indians* with University Press of Mississippi.

1996–98   Served as director of oral history video project on jazz funerals at Tulane University's Hogan Jazz Archives and Payson Center. Received Ford Foundation grant for $110,000.

1998   *When the Saints Go Marching In*, a nine-minute film on jazz funerals produced with Tulane University.

2000   Published *Louisiana Faces: Images from a Renaissance* with Louisiana State University Press. Wrote the text to accompany photographs by Philip Gould.

2001   John Simon Guggenheim Memorial Foundation, fellowship for research on jazz funerals.

2002   Named Humanist of the Year by the Louisiana Endowment for the Humanities.

2002   Berry's play *Earl Long in Purgatory*, a one-man play starring John McConnell, debuted. Directed by Perry Martin. Won a Big Easy Award for Best Original Drama in 2003.

2004   Published *Vows of Silence: The Abuse of Power in the Papacy of John Paul II* with Gerald Renner and Free Press.

2006   Published novel, *Last of the Red Hot Poppas*, with Chin Music Press.

2007   Served as Distinguished Visiting Writer-in-Residence at Tulane University.

2008   Produced, directed, and narrated *Vows of Silence*, which was named Best Television Documentary, Docs D. F. Mexico City international documentary film festival 2008. The film had air dates in Ireland, Spain, Italy, with sequences on *ABC News* and PBS's *Frontline*.

2009   Received Voice of the Faithful, St. Catherine of Sienna Distinguished Layman Award.

2010   Received Moses Berkman Memorial Journalism Award for Career Achievement from Trinity College Program on Public Values.

2011   Published *Render unto Rome: The Secret Life of Money in the Catholic Church* with Crown. Won Best Book Award by Investigative Reporters and Editors 2011. Received Casey Medal for Meritorious Journalism for article "Money and Influence Peddling at the Vatican" part of a *National Catholic Reporter* series.

2014   Served as coproducer and interviewee on PBS *Frontline* documentary *Secrets of the Vatican*. Produced and directed by Antony Thomas.

2018   Published *City of a Million Dreams: A History of New Orleans at Year 300* with University of North Carolina Press.

2021   Producer-director of *City of a Million Dreams: Dancing for the Dead in New Orleans,* based on the book. Released for film festivals and outreach screenings.

2022   Received ChildUSA, Sean P. McIlmail Hero Award for reporting on the church.

2024   Served as Visiting Fellow at Civitella Ranieri Foundation in Umbria, Italy.

Conversations with Jason Berry

Berry: Press Aide to Charles Evers

Mike Winship / 1971

From *Georgetown Today*, November 1971. Reprinted by permission.

The campaign of Charles Evers, the first Black man to run for governor of Mississippi, is a landmark in American political history. There's another landmark, too. His press secretary, twenty-two-year-old Jason Berry (College '71), is perhaps the youngest person to hold such a position of responsibility on a major campaign. He handles press statements and appointments for the nationally known mayor of Fayette, Miss.

Berry, who majored in English at Georgetown, doesn't think his youth has created any problems. "No one seems to care as long as you get the job done," he remarked.

Berry, a white Louisianan, became involved in Evers's gubernatorial race last summer, shortly after his graduation from Georgetown in May. He wrote to a family friend who knows Charles Evers's secretary in Fayette, where Evers has attracted national attention as mayor since 1969. As a result, Berry was invited to do volunteer work and wrote some press releases. They received good play in the media, and Evers offered him a job as his press secretary.

The young New Orleans native finds working for Evers "an adventure. He's very overt with his emotions, spontaneous, and warm. It's incredible to go into Black churches with him and see people's eyes and hearts lifted."

Berry is one of five whites (the only one from the Deep South) working on Evers's paid staff, now busy with last-minute details before the November 2 election. Evers often points to Berry as an example of white Southerners supporting his election. "The mayor sees a great deal of hope in white Southern young people, as I do," Berry said. "The hate-mongering image is changing."

What's more, there is little divisiveness on the biracial campaign staff, he added. "We have had our run-ins, but that's to be expected when you're working with someone fifteen hours a day."

Evers, Mississippi's Democratic National Committeeman and brother of Medgar Evers, the murdered civil rights leader, is running as an independent against state Democratic candidate Bill Waller. Most experts concede the election to Waller, but Berry is not so sure.

"I think Evers's chances are better than most people realize. If we can get 250,000 of the possible 310,000 Black votes in a massive canvass effort, 45,000 from white college students, and another 45,000 white votes from across the state, we could do it."

Berry believes strongly in his boss. "His record in Fayette has been phenomenal. He has built that town up from nothing. He can very obviously do that for Mississippi."

But there have been problems. The campaign budget has been at a constant low ebb, and Berry estimates that 60 percent of the press releases he writes are "edited to the bone so that they say nothing. They are buried somewhere in the comic pages or ignored completely."

Reaction to Charles Evers's candidacy has been mixed. "Sometimes you can feel the dirty looks," Berry said. "Some people won't accept him as a candidate because he's a Black man." At the same time, he recalls many occasions where white Mississippians have listened openly and with fair mindedness to Evers's message.

Berry is keeping an extensive journal and tapes of Evers's speeches. He hopes to hole up on his family's Mississippi farm and write a book on the campaign following the election. After that he's not sure where he's headed, although he wants to go to Europe and plans to become a writer.

One result of his work on the Evers campaign has been self-disenchantment with involvement in politics. "The whole refinement of politics is going down the drain. It's become too systematized. In addition, I'm too candid and quick to react. The sophistications needed to politically woo people irritate me.

But win or lose, Berry is very hopeful about the South's future. "This campaign has given me a different attitude about what the South can be. In thirty years, Mississippi could be a model for racial harmony throughout the United States."

—Mike Winship, C '73.

The Catholic Quandary

Don Lee Keith / 1992

From *Gambit*, October 6, 1992. Reprinted by permission of Judi Terzotis for *The Advocate* / *The Times Picayune* / NOLA.COM

Jason Berry, author of *Lead Us Not Into Temptation*, talks about the Catholic Church's sex scandal and how it affected his own faith.

In 1984, when New Orleans freelance journalist Jason Berry first heard about a situation in Cajun country involving a Catholic priest who had been accused of molesting a number of young boys, he knew right off that there was bound to be a story that demanded news coverage. What the New Orleans-born, Catholic-educated writer did not know was that covering the progressively controversial case would form the basis for a book exposing a subject that's already being called the Watergate of the Catholic Church. *Lead Us Not Into Temptation*, with the subtitle, *Catholic Priests and the Sexual Abuse of Children*, came out of the publishing mill at Doubleday only last week, but early returns from retailers seem to indicate that it's on its way to the bestseller charts. Berry, having launched a promotional tour with a special appearance on *The Today Show*, spent seven years seeking answers to his own questions about the complexities of his subject. He shared those questions—and some answers—in a recent *Gambit* interview.

Don Lee Keith: As a Catholic, did you not face a conflict within yourself in writing a book that is obviously going to place the Catholic Church in an unfavorable light?

Jason Berry: I've never been the kind of person who wears religion on his sleeve. I didn't go to church for a number of years. When I was a bachelor, I was unable to reconcile myself with the heavy yoke of guilt. After I got married, however, I felt sort of like, well, all of a sudden—it was legal! Then, when we began our family, I found myself being drawn back to the core of the faith, which I think has more substance than a church made of rules.

It was evident to me very early in my research—when I was writing newspaper articles on the first case, long before I actually started on the book—that the situation there in Vermilion Parish wasn't just a story about a sick priest who had sexually abused children, but it's a story about the abuse of power by the bishop, an ecclesiastical mindset that kept recycling that priest from one parish to another. My own memories of priests happened to be very benevolent, and the events that I began to piece together in my first year of reporting in Lafayette stood out in stark contrast. The deeper I probed, the more clearly I saw that the larger picture was one of institutional corruption.

I kept thinking about moral behavior. I easily understood, in a clinical sense, that what many of these aberrant priests had done could be analyzed and explained pathologically, but what the bishops had done in their deliberate cover-ups, this really cut to the heart of moral thinking. There they were, bishops trained in ethics and scripture, acting like Nixon in the bowels of Watergate.

Learning such things meant that I had to deal with a lot of anger on my part. The only way I could do it was by talking with priests I trusted. And it was in dealing with my anger that I came to realize that the institution and its leadership might be corrupt but that the faith itself transcended the foible and follies of mere mortals, the bishops.

DLK: How much cooperation did you get from people associated with the church?

JB: I tried to get interviews with various church officials, but few would agree to be interviewed. This might have proved to be quite a problem had I not had copies of legal depositions by almost all these persons, statements they had made under oath. These sworn testimonies were a very potent set of primary sources of information. When they are considered collectively, it is undeniable that from one end of the country to the other, the systemic pattern of the church in addressing the problem of sexual abuse of children has been to stonewall the press—and, for the most part, legal inquiries. The result was, of course, a series of autonomous cover-ups—one sordid cover-up after another—played out across the map of the domestic church.

DLK: And what, in the meantime, has been the response from Rome to this whole controversy?

JB: Rome has been very, very silent, and that has become part of the overall problem. The bishops are caught in a quandary—between a restive and depressed clerical culture in this country that is becoming progressively more homosexual, and at the other end, a Vatican administration that is on a campaign to impose orthodoxy upon theologians who are seeking insight into the Catholic intellectual tradition. The combination of those two forces has created a historically fragile position for the bishops. They simply don't know what to do. In the first place, they're having enough trouble just keeping the priesthood together without any guidance from Rome. And without any sense from Rome that there is a need for reform, they can't put forth their own reform agenda. Meanwhile, they're unable to attract new men to the priesthood, and the number of men in seminaries is way, way down.

DLK: The traditional policy of self-protection by institutions, including the church, notwithstanding, were you able to find any moral justification at all for action on the part of the Catholic hierarchy in trying to cover up pedophilic abuse cases?

JB: None whatsoever. And it saddens me to know that this is the church that proclaims the dignity of the human family, the church that proclaims the sanctity of unborn life, and yet, at the same time, it is the church that treats abused children and their families with the most callous disregard.

Throughout the seven years that it took to put this book together, I kept returning to thoughts of the three women who had influenced me so indelibly—my mother, my grandmother and my great-grandmother. They were all three very religious, very devout, and they each had their own impact on my sense of values.

It was perhaps through thinking about these three women that I arrived at this ultimate conclusion: All these unseemly cover-ups, the reprehensible actions and attitudes forthcoming from church authorities, the disgusting dismissal of the feelings of the victims and victims' families—none of it would have happened if there had been biological mothers among the bishops, women who had born children. Bishops are a sexually segregated society who, because of celibacy, are unlettered in the vocabulary of child raising, cut off from the experiences of effective bonding. That life has desensitized these men to the full impact of what has happened to these kids and to these families.

As the scandals widened, I started getting phone calls from people who had seen my articles. Some of them had their own stories of this priest or that priest who had been guilty of sexual abuse. For those persons, this was a heavy burden, one they had to carry, and I kept being reminded of the image of Sisyphus, who was condemned by fate to forever push a large rock up a hill. I was also reminded of the essay by Camus on the absurdity of the world's unreasonable silence. Camus was, of course, an atheist, but to me, there was a message in the Christian tradition, in Christian witness, and I think it is that we struggle to give voice to the meanings of God. Certainly, that is the fundamental message of the gospels, that a voice in times of great struggle, suffering, and hardship can fill the silence of the world. I don't want to over-intellectualize, but I felt that the families of the victims in these child abuse cases needed a voice, wanted a voice, and I chose to be that voice.

DLK: Still, the book's attitude seems markedly more constructive than most of the criticism leveled at the church in recent years. How do you feel about the newfound freedom of such critics?

JB: Some of the church-bashing—and there's a lot of it that goes on these days—is for unjust reasons. The church has weathered twenty centuries of often stormy moments and has achieved a great amount of good. In recent times, it played a major role in toppling such tyrants as Marcos and Duvalier. There's an awful lot of good that goes on across the Catholic landscape.

I think the bishops are certainly within their religious rights in resisting abortion and in opposing the death penalty; a public ethos to this effect is very consistent. On the other hand, I believe such action as the Vatican's condemnation of birth control, and the harsh treatment of gay people by Vatican documents—all of that runs counter to the better impulses of the Catholic Church.

Similarly, I found it sadly disappointing that Archbishop (Philip) Hannan handled the recent Dino Cinel situation so poorly. I have always liked Hannan, though I've not known him really well. I admired him for what he did about a housing program for the elderly, and as a civil rights advocate, he was a very progressive figure in the community. He played a key role in the Lafayette situation that I wrote about—made a major effort in trying to get the district attorney and the other attorneys to agree to plea bargaining, in an attempt to keep the thing from having to come to trial. And then, three years later, when there's a sex scandal involving a priest from right here in New Orleans, he calls up Cinel in Rome, tells him to stay there, which Cinel didn't do. The right thing would have been for the archbishop to go to the people, at some point, to have been direct and tell them what they deserved to know. I had somehow expected more of Hannan, had expected him to be more upright and straightforward, and when he wasn't, well, I felt disappointment. Profound disappointment.

DLK: Your two previous books have been on fairly safe subjects—civil rights and New Orleans music. Any fear that with this one you're liable to get to be known as a muckraker?

JB: I happen to think that muckraking is an honorable profession if it is done with a true, moral sensibility. I didn't set out to write lurid stories about bad priests, and my God, I could easily have larded this book with graphic sexual passages so revolting that nobody would have bought it. I really wanted to keep the sexual content to as much of a minimum as possible, using clinical language, using legal testimony, so that the larger thematic current would be more powerful. After all, it is essentially a book about corruption of power. Sexual abuse may be a leitmotif coursing through the narrative, but it's actually about the abuse of ecclesiastical authority.

DLK: Your book makes an unmistakable point that the pedophilia cases you've written about are merely symptomatic of a larger sexual conflict within clerical life. Please elaborate.

JB: While statistics show that from 5 to 10 percent of men are gay—most of whom are of course not child molesters—the number of gay men who join the priesthood is far higher, 30 or 40 percent. There's no definitive study on this, naturally, but the ratio is way out of proportion. Some critics, in fact, have gone so far as to insist that the priesthood has become a "haven" for homosexuals. Nevertheless, it was the church that recently sent out those letters from Rome calling homosexuality "an objectionable disorder" and "a moral evil." To gay people, that was hostile language, and they were right; it was indeed hostile. They were also right in insisting that they have the right to be accepted, to be welcome, in all Christian churches. So—on one hand, the church attacks gays, and on the other, it employs a rigid celibacy requirement that refuses to allow married men and women to serve as priests, while in the meantime the institution continues to draw gay men into the clergy in numbers far out of proportion to the population. You've got to wonder what's wrong with any institution, particularly one as powerful as the church, that can't even follow its own pronouncement.

DLK: What accounts for the attraction of gays to the priesthood?

JB: I don't want to sound cynical, but the church, for them, is a good place to hide. There they have the respectability of the clerical collar, and none of the demands by society to be married.

I also found a real cynicism among gay priests regarding celibacy. It would make sense that any priest, gay or straight, who insists on being sexually active, leave the clergy. And many of them do leave to get married—1,300 a year.

DLK: How much pressure to change the celibacy rule is being exerted on the church as a result of the recent sex scandals?

JB: The real pressure has only begun to be felt, and that pressure is financial.

Celibacy became part of church law during the Middle Ages because of concern that children of priests would inherit ecclesiastical property.

Tolerating homosexuality was sort of a by-product of enforcing the celibacy restriction, because while homosexuals might do things the church didn't approve of, at least they wouldn't produce children who through inheritance could diminish the church's holdings.

The situation today is that huge amounts of money—at least $400 million in the last few years—have had to be paid out due to these pedophilia cases. At the same time, the amount of monetary contributions from parishioners has gone down 50 percent in the last generation. The church is taking in less money, and it's paying out more. And it is this financial dilemma that is going to affect the celibacy requirement.

If that requirement were optional, those priests who wanted to remain celibate could do so, and those who wished to marry could marry. By setting an admirable example in family life, those married priests might very well engender greater financial contributions from parishioners who would be inspired by the kind of Christian witness they observe in these priests.

Regardless of any pressure that results from the sex scandals, however, the Catholic Church won't be able to wait too much longer before moving away from the premise that only unmarried males can be priests. It is a dangerously unhealthy view of family dynamics.

Point of Contact

The Dallas Morning News / 2006

From *The Dallas Morning News*, February 26, 2006. Reprinted by permission of Erin Sood, research editor at *The Dallas Morning News*.

Question: Is it really a good idea to observe Mardi Gras this year?

Answer: I think it's understandable. It's kind of a gasping effort to kick start the economy. You know, considering how badly the city has been broken, anything that will start the money flowing to small businesses has got to be seen in a positive light.

Q: Did you ever imagine the city would be in as bad a shape as it is six months after Katrina?

A: I had no idea. We are not the country that put men on the moon. We don't have the same infrastructure; we don't have the same level of preparedness. We've been stiff-armed by President Bush. He's absolutely turned his back on us, and I think what happened here could happen in different ways to other cities.

Literally everyone I know who has a house and who is in a position to make a fairly rational decision about the future is just numb. We're in a state of limbo. We don't know if we'll get the levee protection. This is a great city, and it needs to rebuild.

Q: You've written a lot about New Orleans culture. What do you foresee as the greatest cultural loss in all of this?

A: I think a lot of the working poor who make up the Mardi Gras Indians, the social and pleasure clubs, have been displaced and dispersed. Many of them will not come back.

And the writers, it's going to be very hard to capture the sensibility of the city in novels and plays and fiction, a city that's been so traumatized. The whole image of the Big Easy, the good-time town, becomes almost trite now. There'll always be the quick, easy shots of Bourbon Street the entertainment channels can give us, but this is a city that's going to go through a long, painful struggle of redefinition.

I've never seen the city as polarized racially, politically and socially as it is now. It is not a pretty place to live. I don't know what Mardi Gras will be like, to tell you the truth. I don't think it's going to be a very joyous experience.

Unholy Trinities

Clancy DuBos / 2006

From *Gambit*, September 12, 2006. Reprinted by permission of Judi Terzotis for *The Advocate* / *The Times Picayune* / *NOLA.COM*.

Clancy Dubos: This is your first novel. What made you decide to try your hand at fiction after six nonfiction books?

Jason Berry: I love literature and have read heavily since childhood. I review many novels, so the work itself was not alien to me. It's been sixty years since *All the King's Men* focused on the world of Huey Long—or Willie Stark, as Robert Penn Warren called his man. I wanted to capture the era after the Long dynasty, as politics became a form of show business and people snored at the gigantic environmental damage. In the 1980s, I did a lot of political writing and investigative reports on politicians and waste pit deals. I was struck by the surreal politics—so many extremes, such outrageous exaggerations, as if in a novel by Gabriel García Márquez. In 1991, I spent stretches at Jimmy Swaggart's defamation trial, and then went out following the governor's race between David Duke against Edwin Edwards. Swaggart, Duke, and Edwards—the unholy trinity! I wanted to capture this bizarre outback of democracy by flavoring the narrative with rhythms of the music and the poetic way people speak. The big change between the Long era and the time of Edwards was the oil industry's power in bankrolling campaigns and getting elected officials to yawn at destruction of the environment. That's why the wetlands eroded: political cynicism. More than anyone else, Edwards personified that era now passing. There are a few surface affinities between Edwards and the fictional governor Rex LaSalle. I'm confident that Rex stands out on his own. I would never accuse Edwards of wearing disguises in zydeco clubs, or telling a gal pal, "I'm just a Roman from Ville Platte."

CD: You've written many articles and op-ed pieces about Louisiana politics and politicians. Several real-life characters clearly inspired some of the characters in your book. Who have been the main inspirations for your characters and storyline?

JB: Actually, I'm not sure I'd agree that many real people are thinly disguised here. The novel began with an image that came to me one day: the regal First Lady wakes up, crosses the hall, and finds Rex dead in the spare bedroom, with lipstick traces just south of his equator. I wasn't sure where the story was leading me or who killed Rex for a time. I kept working at it slowly, and more characters came to me.

The initial, surface similarities between Edwards and Rex faded as LaSalle came into his own. Music is central to his character, and in that sense, he's a little like the Bill Clinton, who played saxophone in his 1992 campaign. In the end, though, how do you explain a governor who wears disguises in zydeco clubs? Edwards and Clinton are much too vain to do something like that. Now Reverend Christian Fraux is a composite drawn from several African American preachers I have known, here and in Mississippi. Fraux's eulogy in the capitol borrows a few lines from a sermon that Bishop Paul Morton gave at the funeral of Raymond Myles, the gospel singer. Jerry Lee Lewis has a walk-on moment in the novel as himself. Doctor Nobby, the rock promoter turned toxic waste dealer, is drawn from a gaggle of people I met in back rooms of music clubs. Some of those boys swagger around like cowboys and have such rippling music lingo.

Now as far as the crooked legislators scheming to get rid of the alcoholic lieutenant governor, I think I should shut up lest future phone calls not get returned.

CD: Who is your favorite character in the book, besides Rex?

JB: The state of Louisiana is the central character. Otherwise, I love them all. [Rex's girlfriend] Sophie Thibodeaux's spiritual quest was influenced by clergy abuse survivors I interviewed for *Lead Us Not Into Temptation.* Henry Hubbell, the protagonist, has certain overtones of me in my thirties, all that idealism and outrage mixed together like Maker's Mark and Peychaud's bitters. What I learned about the Catholic hierarchy concealing pedophiles has rendered me more stoic, taking a longer view of the human experiment. I feel closer, ironically, to Christian Fraux, the Black preacher, undertaker, and moral intelligence of the novel. Reverend Fraux's crisis—unable to pray as he takes charge of the governor's body, with the FBI chasing him—comes closer to my own stumbling spiritual quest, learning to pray all over again through all that muckraking. Writing this novel was a way of reaffirming my belief in comedy, and the music that has given me such mooring in life. First Lady Amelia LaSalle reminds me of any number of Southern ladies who combine elegance and toughness. As the father of a daughter in college, I'd have to say that Mayor Bobby Broussard—Amelia's daddy—became more real to me in the final stages of composition.

CD: Who are your favorite real-life political characters in Louisiana? And why?

JB: Earl Long. His madness mirrored the racial insanity of the 1950s, when I was a kid, and watched his meltdown on TV at my father's urging. My play, *Earl Long in Purgatory*, dealt with certain matters that mark the novel—the quest for salvation, life after the fall. The main characters in the novel at one point or another end up talking to God. These Catholic themes rather stalk me. I blame it on the Jesuits.

Until Katrina, Aaron Broussard never meant much to me either way—I live in Orleans, he's the president of Jefferson Parish. We talked on the phone once, but I didn't really know him. On the news, he seemed adroit; then I saw him break down on that CNN interview during the hurricane and suddenly wanted to bear-hug him. We know now he got some of his facts confused in the interview, but he spoke from his soul, and it moved me. I realize many Jefferson voters resent him for sending the pump operators to Washington Parish before the flood. I'm not excusing that. I only mean to say that on CNN he was so deeply human, broken up, sobbing, and his agony captured a deep reality.

Nagin is different. It's easier to forgive his blunders during Katrina than to swallow his preening in the national media now. He oozes charm but just has no clue how to run a city. And so he perfectly mirrors the schizophrenia of the body politic: All these closet Confederates voted for him because they hate the Landrieus for being too liberal—and then all those Blacks voted for Nagin *as their guy*, despite his rank failure to deliver a plan for rebuilding Black neighborhoods. It's like jury nullification, voting against your own interests. If I were God, I'd order Ray Nagin to sit down in a room with Moon Landrieu and take notes for four days.

Interview with Jason Berry

Charles Henry Rowell / 2006

From *Callaloo* 29, no. 4 (Fall 2006): 1239–51. Reprinted by permission.

Charles Henry Rowell: It is extraordinary to be able to visit you at your home here in New Orleans after Hurricane Katrina. Before we came to your home, we drove through the area called Lakeview, and I was surprised to see so much devastation there. Our drive from Baton Rouge also revealed to us a lot of destruction as soon as we started approaching New Orleans. But it is another experience to enter your home where there is order and tranquility—an overwhelming experience in contrast to what we just saw in some parts of the city. Will you talk about the physical and emotional impact of the hurricane on you and your family?

Jason Berry: We were fortunate that the house did not flood. And that's the line of demarcation in most people's lives here today, the degree of damage and devastation that one has to deal with, or not, as the case may be. As I say, I was lucky. One neighbor took about two feet of water. My house is raised so none of the flooding got inside, though the yard was trashed. You can actually see the water line on the fence; the garage was a science project for quite a stretch, though it's finally clean now. Insurance covered most of the damage. Our losses were mild compared to people in the deeply flooded neighborhoods.

My wife, my mother, and I went to my brother's house in Covington, Louisiana, about thirty miles across Lake Pontchartrain. We evacuated there, as we had in the past, to ride out the storm, thinking as most people did, that we would come back in a few days. I did not pack much—a few days' clothing, just one laptop of the two that we have. And so there were six of us there, Lamar and Ellen and their son Zachary, Melanie and me and my mother Mary Frances. My two daughters from my first marriage went with their mother to Abbeville, Cajun country, where they have family. We were in close touch by cell phone all the way until the hurricane actually hit that

Monday morning. Then I lost contact with my kids for several days, which was upsetting. But I knew they were in a safe place, and I heard on the radio that there had been no power outages in that part of the state. I knew where they were with family out there. We spent five days in Covington. The tree damage was so heavy that the road out was impassable. We were trapped.

CHR: It seems as if you were going into another area that had been affected by the hurricane. This is moving away from the Gulf Coast, yes?

JB: That's right. Covington is north of Lake Pontchartrain. So you're going north toward I-55 that heads up eventually to Jackson, Mississippi. The area across the lake is called the North Shore and includes towns like Mandeville, Ponchatoula, and Hammond. When I was a kid we referred to it, generically, as "across the lake." Now people call New Orleans "the south shore."

I'm trying to think of a single word to describe the hurricane. Terrifying might be too strong, but the wind was an awesome thing to behold. The winds from Katrina were so powerful, that these enormous trees were being uprooted, as if this cosmic giant was pulling teeth out of the jaw of the earth. I saw these enormous trees coming out, being uprooted and then pounded down on the ground as if someone was flailing the earth. I've never seen anything like that. The bay window shattered, it happened when I was sitting there and I jumped back. We had to get a tarpaulin to keep the wind and the water from pouring into the living room. After the storm passed that afternoon, there were trees everywhere. The electricity was out but the telephone started working after a while. I walked out into this shimmering mist over the whole area, and the trees were so big that you had to walk around or crawl over the smaller ones, and forge your way through thickets of brush and vine to climb over the next tree. It was like a flattened forest; I could see the Bogue Falaya River down the slope, draped in that gray afternoon mist. It was some spectacle. And I was curious about who was left in this neighborhood. I heard a faint humming and climbed over a good sized tree and moved on, walking and climbing, toward that sound. And I see this guy in the distance, standing there with a saw, one of those gas-powered chain saws, and he's carving through the tree. I said, "Hello," and he turns around and says, "Helloooo." He was a French, the first man I saw. It was sort of like Robinson Crusoe finding Friday except he's from Paris. This guy's name was Bruno. He was a yoga instructor, about thirty years old, a Buddhist by faith I soon learned, and he was built for action, biceps much larger than mine. He was a generation younger, about thirty. Turns out he was married to the daughter of the state's leading criminal defense attorney, Mike Fawer, who lived down the lane.

CHR: Down the lane from you?

JB: Down the lane from my brother Lamar's house. Fawer's daughter, Melanie, was married to Bruno. Bruno became the leader of our upscale chain gang. We had a veterinarian, a guy did some sort of financial services work, my brother does corporate marketing, and then a fellow who showed up with a tractor; we spent four days hacking and carving, while others traipsed through the back lanes to a neighboring cul-de-sac and caught rides to Home Depot to get more chainsaws, as the ones we used kept breaking. They weren't made for trees of the size we had to cut. Somebody had a golf cart and kept us in cold water. The scene reminded me of the Walker Percy novel, *Love in the Ruins*—all these people in a country club subdivision, trying to reclaim their little swath of civilization. The subtitle of that novel is *The Adventures of a Bad Catholic at a Time Near the End of the World.* I don't consider myself a bad Catholic, though I imagine a lot of people who resent the books I've done on the clergy abuse crisis might take that view. Anyway, it took us four days to carve out of there, with a big final boost from the St. Tammany Parish Fire Department. I ended up with a terrible case of poison ivy for which a doctor subsequently put me on steroids. I understand why those things are illegal now. I was bug-eyed and unable to sleep for about a week. That Friday—while I was itching, before I saw the doctor—we drove from Covington to Baton Rouge. We wanted to get my mother reunited with her community; she had lived at Chateau Notre Dame, an assisted living facility run by the archdiocese, just a block from my home in New Orleans. The place had flooded out, and the people working there had evacuated to Baton Rouge, taking care of the elderly residents. Those who did not have family with whom they could evacuate were taken by bus to a gymnasium next to a Catholic school in Baton Rouge. They were in the large gym sleeping on cots; but it was air conditioned, and they were well cared for. We arrived about noon on that Friday and hadn't seen any television during this time. We had been listening to the radio and getting scattered reports, and from those we knew that there had been epic devastation in New Orleans. Listening to the radio, the stress on the radio announcers of WWL AM, was wrenching. You could hear it in their voices and the scenes and the descriptions that they were giving and other people who were giving as they called in—a world going down in dirty water.

In any event, we got to Baton Rouge, and from there got mom situated in a good facility in New Iberia, a brand-new facility where several of the people from her retirement home, the Chateau Notre Dame, also ended up being placed. The administration of the Chateau found locations around the state since they couldn't get back to New Orleans. When that work was done, the administration fired the staffers who had worked so hard helping through the evacuation. They gave them some severance pay, which was good, but I think they could have handled it in a more decent way. I managed to keep track of one of the Black women on the help staff who had been close to my mother before the storm. We kept in touch by cell phone as she evacuated to a Red Cross shelter in Hammond, and then headed to Houston. I put $500 in her bank account.

Back to New Iberia: It was Friday afternoon after we got mother situated, and the realization came down on Melanie and me that we had no place to go. We went to eat at Taco Bell—this was Friday afternoon of the first week—and that's when we saw the footage from the Convention Center and the Superdome, all the squalor and suffering of those poor folk who had stayed behind. And the totality finally hit me—remember, we were out in Covington, carving with chainsaws, and no TV. It's one thing to hear radio reports, but when you see pictures of the people in those public spaces, with the polluted water and bodies on the street, you realize this is the city you love, the city where we live. Melanie started crying and I got blistering angry and cursed that TV set—cursing George W. Bush in point of fact—with these Cajuns sitting there looking at us, they knew we were from New Orleans, they could tell. We walked out of there and never in my life have I been overpowered by such an abject feeling of powerlessness. That's my town going to hell on TV and this wretched president who sends National Guardsmen to Iraq can't get the boats and trucks in to rescue people engulfed in one of our cities.

At that moment we faced the question: Where do we go now? One of the WWL radio announcers, the news director Dave Cohen, had said, "New Orleans is over. Where do I live?" His words stayed with me. I kept thinking New Orleans is over—and I just could not get myself around that. Your town, your place, the life as you knew it, over, what does that do to a man, to all the people from that place? We'll be dealing with these after-shocks for years to come. Obviously as I sit here today, in an interview, the city is not "over"—but the city as we knew it before Katrina, is over. More than half the population is gone.

There we were, driving around New Iberia, trying to find a room, feeling like nomads. I called a B&B, the people were very cautious at first. They wanted to know where we lived and who we were. And it occurred to me that with so many people fleeing New Orleans the smaller towns and cities around the state were uneasy about people wearing that stranger tag. Look, there is a criminal class in New Orleans and I understand human fear. The owners of the B&B knew we were white, yet they still wanted assurances. You've certainly read the media accounts of the people crossing the bridge into Gretna, coming out of New Orleans, and how they were driven back. And out in Cajun country there were similar fears by whites toward whites. I'm not at all trying to suggest that it was harder for us than those thirsty, exhausted people trying to cross the Crescent City Connection—we were in a good car and not destitute—but the parallel does suggest how the cleavages of class and race kept surfacing throughout the crisis. I explained to the owner of the B&B, I'm a writer, my wife's a college professor. We just put my mother in this town—you know, we just need a place for a night or two, so they let us in. Next morning we got up and started driving around New Iberia, looking for an apartment, and that was surreal. I got on the phone and someone at the newspaper I had cold-called gave me the name of some real estate guy and he says, "Well, there are no apartments, but I can put you in a trailer park for $14,000 and the water's free." I thanked him. My wife is not the kind to live in a trailer park. So here we were, casting lines, trying to figure out where to stay that night—*New Orleans is over. Where do I go?* I called a friend in Lafayette, Jackie Lyle, whom I had known years ago when I did some reporting with the *Times of Acadiana*, a weekly newspaper there. Jackie and her husband, Conrad Comeaux, were friends of mine from twenty years back. I'd seen them occasionally over the years. On the phone I said, "I'm like everybody else in New Orleans looking for a place to live, do you have any leads?" And she said, "Well, why don't you come to our house and we can put you here and we'll go from there." Lafayette had gotten so quickly overcrowded by day five that the rental units were filled. We ended up staying a month at Conrad and Jackie's house with three other couples. I must say that the meaning of hospitality was exemplified by those people. Conrad is the tax assessor of Lafayette Parish so he knew a lot about real estate. And we couldn't find anything to rent. People were buying houses right and left amidst this diaspora of well-heeled New Orleanians in Baton Rouge and Lafayette.

CHR: Your movement is a bit puzzling to me: you first went north to Covington and then west to New Iberia. Why didn't you return directly to your home in New Orleans from Covington.

JB: We couldn't.

CHR: Are you saying that you were not allowed at that time by the authorities to reenter the city?

JB: Exactly. Mayor Nagin was telling people that the city was not safe, that it lacked basic services, because of the flooding, And you have to remember that Hurricane Rita came along on the heels of Katrina and the city flooded again. This neighborhood had standing water of a foot and a half or so.

CHR: Can you give me some context about this neighborhood where you live?

JB: Certainly. We are in the Carrollton neighborhood, which is on the western fringes of the city, near the Uptown area, where Loyola and Tulane universities are located. One block from this house is the New Orleans Archdiocese, and the large seminary complex which occupies most of a city block with the big green lawn and the pastoral oak trees. The archbishop's mansion is part of the complex. Directly across the street from the seminary, an entire city block on Carrollton Avenue burned to the ground. I don't know precisely what happened, but one story has it that people ended up getting into those houses to escape the storm. I've heard that someone, a squatter perhaps, intentionally set fire to one house and the others were soon caught in the blaze. This could be an urban myth. Much later, I called the fire department, but they had no report—the fire happened a day or so after the hurricane. It could have been a broken gas main, which happened in other parts of the city, leading to fires. Whatever happened, it's quite a stark scene today—bricks, the front steps, the twisted iron now dark as bacon crisps, left over from the grillwork on the porch of what used to be a huge house. The entire block burned down. That is what I saw when I came back a few days later.

I got in on day ten with rising frustration by that point. For years I've taken solace in the fact that I didn't have to report to an editor in a newspaper office, that as an independent writer, I could pursue my own focus in books, articles, and the documentary film work. For the first time in my life, I wished then that I'd had an assignment. I wanted to be in New Orleans to interview people, to be covering the crisis, to learn what was happening. But the town was crawling with reporters, and I was dealing with some complicated family issues, between my wife, worried about her grandchildren displaced to Houston, and my older daughter who needed to find a college for the semester since Tulane had shut down, and then my former wife, whose house was wrecked in the flood. She was living with her mother out in Cajun country, with my younger daughter who has Down syndrome. I had responsibility for a lot of women. So getting back into work as a journalist was not an easy thing. I did land some consulting work for ABC News; but it was day ten when I finally got in. I paid an off-duty cop to go in with me and we got past the roadblocks. I met the guy through Chris Wiltz and her husband Joe Pecot. Actually, another writer, Moira Crone, went in the car with the cop and I followed. We wanted to see the condition or existence of our houses. Moira and her husband, a writer named Rodger Kamenetz, live close to Tulane, in an area that didn't flood. My house is farther down, in Carrollton, which I knew had flooded, though at that time I didn't know how high the water had gotten. At that point, I didn't know whether my entire archives or all my files had been destroyed. I've got forty, fifty boxes of material on the Catholic clergy abuse books I've done [*Lead Us Not Into Temptation* (1992) and *Vows of Silence* (2004)]. I had a large collection of interviews, tapes, and the like for a work in progress, a history of the city that uses brass band funerals as the prism. And, I had the manuscript of my novel, *Last of the Red Hot Poppas*. [Editor's note: The book was published in September 2006 by Chin Music Press.]

Along about the sixth or seventh day after the flooding, as we watched the horrific coverage on TV, I told myself, well, if the house is wrecked and everything I've worked on is gone, and you can't go back and recover it, then go to Washington or New York or Boston and get a job in the media. I didn't want to do that, obviously. I'd worked years to establish myself as an author and writer, but if all you've got goes down in the muck, you have to start anew. All of that was swimming through my thought field in those early days; but I managed to get in and determine that the house was okay. We hadn't suffered any looting, the art collection was intact, and so I pulled a bunch of the files with me and took my laptop, Melanie's jewelry, and some other things. I also looked in the garage, where I had stored some of my files. The boxes on the lower level were trashed completely. I also lost a lot of books I had put in storage out there.

CHR: Did you stay a while in your home on that visit?

JB: Oh, no! I was in the house less than four hours. The electricity wasn't on until the end of October and then the gas didn't come on until the end of November. We spent a month in Lafayette, staying with those good folks and then we drove to the outskirts of Dallas to stay with Melanie's sister and her husband. Among other things we had to get a second car, my Taurus had flooded and I filed for insurance based on the home inspection that one day. I had to buy a car and we felt we could get a better deal if we went to the Dallas area. Lafayette was a gold rush for car dealers and people who had houses to sell. We got to Dallas and it was surreal, so big and new and spanking bright, all those strip malls with the same Starbucks and McDonalds and Blockbusters, the same spread in town after town. I'll probably get in trouble with some of my relatives in Texas if they read this, but you know, New Orleans had only independent bookstores, there was no Barnes & Noble or

Borders within the city proper because they couldn't find sufficient space. The city was old and I loved that quality of timelessness about it. Anyway, we got to Dallas and stayed there for about a week. We were still bugged-eyed and trying to figure out what we were going to do; but it was becoming clear to me that the city in some form would soon, more or less, be habitable. Melanie has tenure at Loyola in the English Department, so her salary continued. I had gotten a few assignments, and with the ABC work, I was doing okay. So by the time I got to Texas, it was October. I bought a Volvo over there and finally got back the second week of October.

The loss and wreckage was numbing, yet sections of the city were getting back to normal. I wanted to put my own sense of order on things, however I could, so I resumed work on the jazz funerals book, realizing that I would have to make certain changes to take into account the devastation of the flooding. One of my best friends here in town, Michael White, is a clarinetist, a gifted man. He has an endowed chair at Xavier University. Michael has generated a string of CDs and has done substantial compositional work in the traditional idiom. I had already interviewed him at length. His profile opens the book, and by the time I got to Dallas, I had no idea where he was. I finally connected with him by emailing Basin Street Records and included my cell phone number. I was sitting on my sister-in-law's porch at the far edge of the Dallas metro area in a town called Allen, Texas. Michael was in Houston as we spoke on cell phone. We talked about an hour and a half. He told me about evacuating with his mother and his aunt. He was pretty certain that his house had been destroyed. He had a huge collection of books and CDs. I later went with him to the house and in fact hired a cameraman to videotape it, as I was working on a film about the funerals. But as I sat there on that porch in Texas, looking out at this sparkling suburban street, talking to him, picturing what he was going through, I realized that this guy had suffered an enormous loss way larger than my own. I can't imagine what my life would be like if everything in this house had been destroyed. I later went into Michael's house on two occasions, and retrieved a lot of his art works and got several of them with a place that conserves and preserves pieces like that. I have a lot of his African pieces in storage, in fact. He lost five thousand books and as many CDs, and a great many original compositions. All of this was sinking in as I began working on my manuscript again, this time with a new focus.

CHR: You were writing a book on the hurricane?

JB: No, I knew by then that there were at least four people with contracts working on books about the hurricane, and I didn't want to write a disaster narrative or a perfect storm book because I figured there would be more than enough books like that. I knew I had to revise my book, which follows the history of the city through the evolution of the burial traditions. And I had to account for the devastation from the flooding and the hurricane as it affected the musicians, like Michael White, who already figured into my narrative, men whose musical experiences go back many years. The theme of resurrection that is so central to the jazz funeral tradition would find a dramatic direction, I sensed, as time passed after the flood. I use the word flood rather than Katrina, because the greater damage was from the flooding, not the hurricane per se. The wind damage was enormous yes, but the flooding was epic, scriptural if you will. In any event that's how I sort of centered myself—emotional, spiritually, professionally—by going back to that manuscript and engaging myself in the history of the funerals and the city, continuing the work I had begun long before the hurricane. I also played a great deal of rhythm-and-blues music on the CD player in the car during the long trips back and forth to Cajun country to spend time with my mother and my little girl, Ariel. My older daughter Simonette, a student at Tulane, had gone off to Boston University for her fall semester.

CHR: What did you find in relation to what your feelings were while you were away?

JB: Well, I came back the second time to help Melanie pack and then take her to the airport. She was going to Houston to spend time with her grandchildren. This was in early October. We drove around the neighborhood, and she was quite upset, and we got into the house and got some things that she wanted to take. Of course, we had no energy so there were no lights or anything like that. I had to come back and deal with the issue of the refrigerators that had to be emptied and discarded; those spent refrigerators became part of the post-Katrina iconography, a leitmotif in the lives of so many of us now. But to answer your question, the processing of the pain as it affected me was gradual. I had my house, many other people did not. I can't say it was like a war zone, but the feeling of loss cut hard and deep. In late October, my friend Adam Nossiter, a journalist here who had been working with the Associated Press, invited me to stay in his house. He's got a pretty big place over in the Garden District. And he was just in the process of leaving the AP to join *The New York Times* as the New Orleans bureau chief. His wife and two sons were in Jackson, Mississippi, because there was no school here for kids to go to. So I stayed there several weeks. Got up early and worked on my laptop at Adam's house then I would come over here, in the afternoons, to my house, working in gloves with a shovel and bags to dig out the muck in the garage. I lost a lot of books, some files, but fortunately in comparison to what could have been lost, it was not as huge. I had issues with this house—meeting with insurance adjustors, arranging with the contractor to repair the roof. Fortunately, the contractor we had that did some work for us a year ago was doing some work in the neighborhood and he was able to put patches on the roof very quickly. I didn't have to deal with FEMA for the roof, thank God. You see right across the street my neighbor has a blue tarp on top of her roof and she's been dealing with FEMA. I spent that first month at Adam's, coming here in the afternoons, and every ten or twelve days driving over to Cajun country to see my mother and little girl. . . . Finally we moved back in here, I guess it was the beginning of November.

CHR: You had no running water, and your water heater did not work.

JB: I had running water but it was not hot until the gas was turned on, and that was just before Thanksgiving. But compared to what happened to so many other people my personal experience was not extreme. I don't think there was anything terribly traumatizing about it, but where it hurt the most was just driving around the city, seeing the loss and debris, all those homes and communities, and thinking of so many people I knew whose lives had been upended. It still hurts to think about them.

CHR: Without these basics—running water, electricity, and the other modern conveniences to which we've all become accustomed—you were in a state of helplessness.

JB: It was hard, yes. But I'm not trying to portray myself as some kind of Harrison Ford hero. I wept often during those weeks. I missed my little girl, Ariel. I missed both of my kids. My older daughter Simonette was situated well with friends I have in Boston, and she was going to B.U. But I missed Ariel, and it was hard on my mother being uprooted, and of course I missed her as well. What hurt more than anything was the devastation of the city—streets I had followed in funeral parades, the music clubs in back neighborhoods, places in City Park and the whole fabric of neighborhoods between Freret Street and the Lake—a huge area of the city—all these areas that were so badly inundated. I am a native son, I grew up here and the city is in my bones, in my soul. And to see a place that you love as much as a woman or your children so battered and flooded and pulled apart just brings you down, damn hard. And in response, you see the callousness of those Social Darwinists in Congress, like Dennis Hastert (the House Speaker) who said that maybe people shouldn't live there because it's under sea level. I'd like to put him on a boat to Venezuela with a one-way ticket.

And then this idiot we have in the White House, I wonder how the hell he got out of those Ivy League schools. I know how he got in; he had pull. You know I've never been so ashamed of the political establishment. We've got a legendary history of corruption in this state; I've written about it. One of the reasons I ended up coming back here is because it was so rich in culture. And then as a muckraker, you couldn't find so many political specimens as corrupt as they are here. I guess if I did time in Washington, I wouldn't find it much of a place to live. The place is rootless, and the only jazz is played by people moving through. Everybody wears their resume in that town. The American political system failed, from Bush to Blanco and Nagin, like a row of falling dominoes. Blanco has recovered better than the two men. I had a lot of sympathy for Nagin at first. He was overwhelmed during that first week. I admired him for getting on the radio and speaking angrily as he did, demanding help for the city. What bothered me in the weeks following the disaster was that he didn't use his position to rally the public, to call on the nation to pressure Congress to provide transitional housing, to help get people back. Instead, he relied on Joe Canizaro, the biggest land developer in town, and the ULI [Urban Land Institute] in Washington DC. It was very strange. Here were all the urban designers and urban planners, descending on this broken city like the gods from Olympus, coming down the mountain, telling us how we should remake our town. And what they recommended, as we all have read about now, is reducing the footprint of the city, letting the Lower Ninth Ward become a swamp, letting some of these people of New Orleans East sacrifice their homes. I understand the issue from an infrastructure standpoint; the levees failed and the area was jeopardized to begin with. Yet, with all of that said, I must say the idea that these areas should be written off and the people who live there should be expected to sacrifice their homes seems harsh and Malthusian to me. Doesn't the government owe us a levee system that works? Even if they do get some kind of compensation, forced removal is tough to swallow. You know, the Dutch were able to build a system, and it works.

CHR: The Dutch built the same system in the Guyana in South America. They created very strong seawalls to protect Georgetown, the capital, to protect the city from the violence of the Atlantic Ocean.

JB: That comparison is quite to the point. Consider the politics here. I want to be careful what I say here because I don't think Canizaro is a bad man. You know, he's conservative, a Republican, he's given a ton of money to Bush. He flies in the plane with Bush when he makes appearances out here. Now this is all pre-Katrina. But the idea that you can simply rebuild a glittering city by wiping away the poor folk, by ridding the underclass, is elitist and offensive to me. Richard Baker, the congressman from Baton Rouge, made a comment along the lines that Katrina did what society could not, by getting rid of all these poor people. That comment was heartless. I'm not ashamed to speak as a liberal on these things. Look at the moral erosion we have had under this Republican regime with all of these would-be Christians, rushing to war, tolerating forms of torture that would make Jesus scream bloody hell, and then when a great city drowns, they can't get the military to rescue people on time. New Orleans is a great city, in spite of the poverty and political failures. This is one of the richest cultural places on the continent. We had a string of African American mayors during the time when the population of the city got smaller. The tax base eroded, Washington cut more and more funds for basic services, and a whole swath of the population was hanging on by a thread. Nevertheless, this was their home, and those folks had a right to come back. The idea that you can simply take a broom in the form of a hurricane, and a flood that was caused by human error, and sweep out a whole piece of the population, is just immoral. I hate it when people say, "Now we can get it right." As if we couldn't get it right before because *they* were in the way. I thought democracy held more potential than giving up on those in need. This sloppy, sentimental elitism cuts against my grain. A *New Orleans Magazine* cover in the November 2005 issue featured a gold statue of Joan of Arc, a gift from the French government from years ago, with a headline saying, "And now, the Renaissance." I saw that cover, and I must admit that I write the music column in that publication, and the whole thing made me embarrassed. It was so wrongheaded. Because we had a rich cultural renaissance from the 1970s, after the racial barriers came down, well into the 1990s, despite the crime. The city was a culturally exciting place with a great range of expression in literature and painting, in music and sculpture, the parades and folk art, and then some. It will be years before this city has anything approaching that level of creative intensity because so many people are gone. Much of the musical culture drew from working-class Black neighborhoods. I guess the bigger question now is whether the working poor will return, to kick start the hospitality industry. Then you ask, will the drug gangs return too? I hope not. But you know, for this city to work, to function, we need a good police force. And we need social services to bolster the schools. We need programs for these kids who don't have the kind of family structure that they need. One of the things that haunts me about the whole Social Darwinism mentality in Washington is the notion of, I've got mine Jack, I'm on the boat and the rope ladder is up, sorry you're down there in the waves. That is the mentality of this grubby, greedy Republican majority in Congress under Bush and during the crisis of Katrina, they showed their shameful colors.

This was a small city that could have been much more manageable had there been a concentrated effort to eradicate blighted housing and restore the housing stock and create a genuine safety net for these kids traumatized by violence and drugs. Look at the Seventh Ward, where Andrew Young was born, where Dutch Morial and Sidney Bechet were born, albeit many years apart. The first three Black mayors of post–civil rights New Orleans were Creoles from the Seventh Ward. That neighborhood had a storied history and before Katrina it was a basket case, bombed out, a drug zone. You can't just blame Washington or bad cops for that. There was a breakdown in responsibility by Black political leadership too. It takes an enlightened housing policy and money and the political will to decide if you're going to bring back these houses and then try to provide some kind of infrastructure for the young people to put their lives in order. I don't know if the politics of this country or of this state is moving that direction.

CHR: Could it be done by the city? Through the politics of the city?

JB: Not the way things are now. Perhaps if public outrage continues to build, but at present, most people I talk to see the problems, but have retreated into their own lives. I think there is a collective numbness. The political class seems leaderless.

CHR: Before we arrived here at your home, Dave and I drove through an area called Lakeview, which sustained a lot of damage from Hurricane Katrina. But the national media told us nothing about that area. What do you think accounts for that? The press focused only on the Superdome, the Ninth Ward, and the Convention Center.

JB: A lot of the media attention has focused on poor neighborhoods, especially the Lower Ninth Ward. And indeed the devastation there was stunning. Many upper- and middle-income areas had extraordinary damage as well. The Lakeview area—Harrison Avenue to the lake, standard issue, middle, upper-middle class, block after block—those homes were destroyed. Some I think can be rebuilt, but you know the city is in a catch-22 as to whether the levees will be restored, and as a consequence, what people will do about home ownership here. There has already been a substantial brain drain, with physicians, nurses, college professors, journalists, and others leaving the city for other places to live. This is especially the case among professionals who have young children to raise. I don't know whether writers or painters have left in the same numbers, but I suspect that is the case.

A lot of the musicians are displaced right now, although many of them want to come back. I just saw Wynton Marsalis's subcommittee report on the Bring New Orleans Back commission, which estimated that only about 250 of 2,000 musicians were able to come back. Whatever the numbers may be, they are grim. So if we don't get adequate levee protection, and, as it seems apparently, we are in an era of ferocious hurricanes in this age of global warming, how many times do you tempt the gods? How many times do you gamble with your own faith in where you live? This house wasn't destroyed this time. Will it be the next? I don't know. But I'm spending extra money every month to store files in a place on higher ground. And my wife and I talk often about whether to buy a home out West. There are moments in my daytime, working hours, when the image rolls into my head of water breaking through the wall and my books being toppled and the floodwater soaking the paintings I so cherish.

CHR: How do you think writers will respond to this disaster?

JB: Well, Charles, I think what will unfold is a memory of the flood that permeates the literary and cultural psyche. The persona of the good time town with the roguish politicians who have a certain charm is a part of this place—the novel I've written (*Last of the Red Hot Poppas*) explores that comedic persona that serves as a mask for decay and even evil. We have, too, the dissolute, charmingly batty aristocrats, the wild figures, and then the raffish, bohemian characters in the human parade that gives these latitudes such life, such melody, such off-beat diversity. All of that I think has to be weighed in the creative undertakings against the damage that has been done and what the flood really means. Has the city been irrevocably changed? Will its comic essence come back? I don't know the answer to those questions. I know what I'd like the answer to be, but we live in an unforgiving world. Hurricanes have had a long history here, and so do floods. There was terrible flooding here with Hurricane Betsy in 1965, but it was mostly in the Lower Ninth. In 2005, when 80 percent of the city floods, it does something to the common mind. That "something" is bound to register artistically.

There may be blues songs and expressions in music and drama to match what we have seen in the visual arts, in the paintings and photography and documentaries that have come out already. But I believe that with literature we face quite a struggle as writers seek to find a means of interpreting the deeper consciousness caused by the flood and shared because of the flood. How these revelations mesh with the older, comedic character and the personality of the town that we know through the works of everyone from Tennessee Williams to Walker Percy, from John Kennedy Toole to

Valerie Martin and others—well, who can say? How does a novelist, how does a writer deal with that devastating moment of destruction and what the place becomes as a consequence? Answers like that, in the form of literary art, take time.

CHR: What you're saying invokes the title of that new anthology, whose title is from a song—*Do You Know What It Means to Miss New Orleans?* Will you talk about that collection?

JB: I'd be happy to. And thank you for the question. Well, the book is an anthology and I was invited to contribute an article. Bruce Rutledge and his brother David of Chin Music Press in Seattle gathered a group of writers by telephone, email, that kind of thing, and invited us to contribute. The piece I did is called "The Holy City of New Orleans," and it's an autobiographical essay much along the lines of some of the things I've talked about today. . . where we ended up after the flood and what it was like. The many contributors sound a similar chord in reflecting on what was lost, how it was lost, and what that loss means. I think collectively we are all struggling to understand the loss as it is with us yet and it is hard to see ahead with any measure of hope.

I went to Naples, Florida, last week to give a speech and I got off the airplane in this gleaming new airport, Fort Myers. It was Florida, it was sunny, it was warm, it was the middle of the winter, it had actually been chilly back here when I got on the plane. And I thought, This is how other people live. I'm back in the rest of America now. And it happens every time I go to an airport or another city. I've been to New York twice in the last month, in January, once for a meeting and again for a conference. And you know, going into Midtown Manhattan, walking the streets, it all seemed so normal like the last time I'd been to New York. And yet I couldn't help thinking about the broken town back home. And maybe it is me more than others, but that memory of the flood I think will haunt me and track me probably until the day I die. That's not to say I won't be happy. I've done a fairly good job at achieving that. But a lot of people here are depressed. You hear terms like Katrina fatigue, Katrina cough, Katrina talk; some people can't remember what they said a minute ago or an hour ago, so they will repeat themselves or babble sometimes. I'm sure cigarette sales are up, and that antidepressants are being used in greater volume than before. I imagine more people are drinking more heavily. This is just an educated guess. But as far as that sweet little book goes, those of us who have contributed are trying to express how we dealt with the events in our lives surrounding the storm. It's a sort of chronicle of the hurricane and the brief period afterward. I suppose where I am in my own life is trying to figure out where I'm going as a citizen of this city. The reason I called that essay "The Holy City of New Orleans" is because whenever I watched these reports from the Middle East, they keep talking about the holy city of Quam, or the holy city of Iran, and you know I can imagine for the Muslims and the Islamic devout to go to a city that had profound religious significance, that's why they call it a holy city. America, I'm afraid, is a garage sale. We forget what we bought yesterday because we want to buy something new tomorrow. There's just this appalling absence of memory about our culture, maybe television does it. But I think this city is holy. This is where jazz began, this is where the native art form emerged, and for all of our conflicts and our problems, for all of the sinful poverty, the legacy of racial domination that haunted the city for so long and in some way still does, with all of that said, nonetheless, I find a quaking spirituality about this place. You find it in the churches Sunday after Sunday, with those gospel choirs radiating that music across the town like a long accordion. You get in in the Mardi Gras Indians dramatizing the memory of a line of big chiefs and urban warriors stretching back to the 1880s. You find it in the St. Jude Novenas and in so many of the folk art expressions. I could go on. There is an essence of holiness in this city that offsets the violence, crime, and sprawling hedonism. I think if you're from here or live here long enough, you learn to carry that spiritual intensity with you, that rare spiritual aura, that balance between what we do to endure, and how we celebrate the essence of humankind, the ways in which the mores of daily life in these latitudes manage to color us, mark us, and endow us with a sensibility that makes you miss the city each time you leave it.

Maciel, a Sexual Predator

Marisa Iglesias / 2007

Translated from Spanish by Ellen Cohen. From *Milenio*, February 25, 2007. Reprinted by permission of Victor Hugo Michel, Editorial Director of Milenio Television/Channel 6.

It has been ten years since Jason Berry and Gerald Renner published the first report in the *Hartford Courant* about the abuses of the founder and Superior of the Legion of Christ, an article that marked the collapse of a myth.

At the end of 1994, the journalist Jason Berry received a call from Arturo Jurado, former Legion of Christ, who lived in California. He spoke with him about the very grave acts committed by the founder and hierarchy of the order, Father Marcial Maciel. Barely a year before, Berry had published his book, *Lead Us Not Into Temptation*, an investigation about pedophilia in the Catholic Church in the United States. Berry told Jurado that he would read what he sent him, but there was no guarantee of publication. The topic had left him exhausted.

Chronicler of the cultural life of New Orleans, Berry was occupied by documenting the jazz funerals of that city, when in 1995, another call finally convinced him. It was from José Barba, a university professor who led an implacable battle denouncing Maciel's abuses. Berry received the judicial complaints of nine of Maciel's victims, and he searched, without luck, for an outlet to take an interest in the matter. Two years later, Gerald Renner, a journalist specializing in religious topics who had already published a pair of articles about the Legionaries of Christ in the United States, contacted Berry. His newspaper, the *Hartford Courant* would publish the story on February 23, 1997. Nine years later, Maciel would be reassigned by the Vatican.

Marisa Iglesias: That article changed the course of Maciel's case. You uncovered his biography.

Jason Berry: I believe that we have the responsibility, as moral beings, to demand the truth from the powerful. The Greeks were right: Character is destiny. Maciel was a sexual predator. But Mexico, like the greater part of the world, was late in realizing the harm caused by pedophiles. Latin Americans seem less able to understand dual personalities, pathological conduct behind prominent facades.

MI: Did you imagine ten years ago that the events would take this course?

JB: After the first interviews, and the negative things we heard about Maciel, it seemed to Renner and me that the evidence was overwhelming. I believed that our 1997 report would have a greater effect in Rome and that Maciel would be stopped. I underestimated the depth of the denial of the crisis on the part of Pope John Paul II and the astuteness with which Maciel manipulated him. When Cardinal Ratzinger ordered the investigation, I thought that Maciel would be punished, even though I didn't know what form that would take. And even though the final decision was much less harsh than it should have been, at least deposing him was achieved.

MI: Is this the defeat/ruin of Father Maciel?

JB: Yes, but it is not a complete victory for the Mexicans who won in the ecclesiastical courts: The Vatican did not acknowledge their bravery. Even so, Maciel fell into disgrace and was humiliated. And the investigators and journalists unearthed more information, and it will go down in history as one of the greatest frauds in the history of religion.

MI: Do you believe that having opened the Maciel case served to detonate other stories of sexual corruption in the Catholic Church, like those in the United States in 2002?

JB: No. *The Boston Globe*'s investigation in 2002 focused exclusively on the acts of Cardinal Bernard Law in Boston. Maciel was not a topic of interest for the United States or European press, until Ratzinger was elected pope in 2005.

MI: How much did the United States media occupy itself with the case when the Vatican reopened the investigation into Maciel?

JB: The American newspapers covered the Vatican's decision of the downfall of Maciel substantively. On the other hand, the television news did not give it much coverage. The Vatican sent out a communication but did not hold a press conference. Its intention to manage the information discreetly was evident, as there was embarrassment/shame for the legacy of John Paul II. The United States media treated the matter as an external issue—a decision made in Rome about a Mexican religious leader. If the Vatican had condemned the Legion or the Regnum Christi, the coverage would have focused on their schools in the United States.

MI: Have you declared that the media should have focused on sexual abuse in the Church sooner? How much has changed in the last ten years?

JB: There has been a seismic change. Until the end of the 1990s, the cover up of the sex abuse cases weren't relevant. But the coverage of the Boston case, in January 2002, set off a chain reaction that put pressure on the Vatican. Since then, the topic has cooled considerably in the media, at least in the United States. But that is the nature of news cycles. And except for war, politics, celebrities, and sports, no topic holds the interest of the press for so much time. However, I don't believe that a relevant case of concealment on the part of a bishop or cardinal would be ignored by the media at this point.

MI: How many Father Marciels are there still in the Catholic Church of the United States?

JB: A figure of such size or power with as many victims as Maciel doesn't exist in the American Church. The statutes of North American bishops from 2002 establish an immediate removal of those priests who have received even one accusation. And even though the statutes don't always work, many priests have been deposed. The Mexican bishops need a similar rule. The Vatican does too. According to a study by John Jay College of Criminal Justice of New York, paid for by bishops, the number of predatory priests in the United States is 4 percent. Dozens of aggressors have been removed, have died, or on a lesser scale, have been incarcerated.

MI: And in Latin America?

JB: In general, there is not sufficient information about how the church has concealed these scandals. When the lawyer Jeffrey Anderson was expelled from Mexico City, after giving a press conference on the presumed cover-up of Father Nicolas Aguilar-Rívera by Cardinal Norberto Rivera, who, after abusing more than ninety children, was sent to the Diocese of Los Angeles where he violated many more, then to be accepted once again into the Mexican Church, I realized that the [Vincente] Fox administration was helping the cardinal in his concealment. I don't know if attacks on lawyers in other countries in Latin America would be as shameless, but I would say that, too frequently, the Church sees itself to be above the law.

MI: How important has Marcial Maciel been to your professional life?

JB: If José Barba had not been so persuasive on that telephone call in 1995, I doubt that I would have continued that investigation. Despite having known many impressive people from Mexico, the country in which my great-grandmother was born and where I have many very dear cousins, I could not say that investigating Maciel would have made me happy. But I am happy that Gerald Renner and I have been able to do what we did. Martin Luther King used to say, "True peace is the presence of justice." And I continue to search for that peace.

Thinking About New Orleans #9: Jason Berry (Part I)

Jane Ciabattari / 2007

From *Critical Mass*, June 13, 2007. Reprinted by permission.

This is the ninth in our occasional series about New Orleans writers. It's hard to judge how many writers have been displaced, dislocated, and disoriented by Katrina and aftermath. A New Orleans native, Jason Berry went to Jesuit High School and Georgetown University. His first book, published with an assist from Walker Percy, was *Amazing Grace: With Charles Evers in Mississippi*, based on his time as a volunteer in Evers's gubernatorial campaign. After a stretch in Europe, he moved into a $75-a-month apartment in the Irish Channel in 1973 and began freelancing. He has spent most of the time since then in New Orleans, writing about local politics and culture. In 1992, his third book, *Lead Us Not Into Temptation* (Doubleday), an investigation of clergy child sexual abuse, generated national attention. He describes his seventh book and first novel, *Last of the Red Hot Poppas*, as "a story of the petrochemical age, the era from the end of civil rights through the resurging oil wealth of the 1990s." Rex LaSalle, the governor in the novel, he says, was inspired by Edwin Edwards, the flashy Cajun who was elected four times and now holds an endowed chair in a federal penitentiary (casinos: extortion). "But had there never been an Edwards, I would have invented a character with similar traits—the roguish charm, flamboyance, and telegenic skills—to personify the evolution of demagoguery since the days of those country warhorses before TV. I wrote a fair number of magazine and newspaper pieces about various politicians and the legislature, which in the 1980s would have tested Fellini's imagination. Most of the characters in the novel are not based on real people. The state of Louisiana is the central character."

Berry wrote of his Katrina experiences for the *National Catholic Reporter*: "Hemingway called courage 'grace under pressure.' I have seen that grace in great display these terrifying days, grace entwined with another kind of valor: the realization that in order to be brave, you must first be afraid. My wife, Melanie McKay, and I left our house in the Carrollton neighborhood of New Orleans to ride out the storm with my brother, Lamar, and his family in Covington, Louisiana, a leafy town across Lake Pontchartrain, fifty miles north of the city." I talked with Jason about what has happened since then.

Jane Ciabattari: Two days before Katrina, you and your wife headed to Covington, then spent seven weeks in Louisiana and Texas before returning home in late October. When you think back now, what were those months like for you? Personally, professionally?

Jason Berry: It was surreal agony. In Covington, I didn't see TV for five days, though I heard a lot of radio. I spent most of that time cutting trees where we were hemmed in. When we finally saw TV, in New Iberia, I felt a fathomless anger at the sight of the city beaten and trashed—the abandonment of those people in the flood and nothing I could do. We were stuck like nomads in the other places you mention. I had responsibilities to help my mother, my wife, and my daughter get situated. Even before I learned that our house had not flooded, watching the destruction on TV made me feel powerless. I landed some work for ABC News. I also had bad poison ivy after the chainsaw work in Covington. Soon along a doctor put me on steroids. It killed the rash but I couldn't sleep. I was a zombie, drinking too much to try to sleep, waking up at 4 a.m. after dreaming about bloated corpses, then glued to the internet, trying to reconnect with friends. It was a nightmare.

JC: What are your living and working conditions like compared to pre-Katrina?

JB: My house did not flood, and that's the line of demarcation. My working conditions are fine; the home office is in good shape. I pay $225 a month for a storage unit and still haven't gotten all of the priest files out there. I have so much material for the work in progress that it would take three days to box and move all that should another hurricane hit. We're going to California for vacation this summer and I'm praying we don't get hit again. That is the biggest change, the mental vistas, the anxiety in following weather news. I get up at 5:30, make coffee, read the papers in the solarium, look at the green plants outside, and wonder if a flood will come. Every day I wonder. People all over the city think the same thing. For a year or so, I had these daydream interruptions—water breaking through the wall, the books and artworks going down. Yet I can't underscore how fortunate we are to have a house intact. Everyone is dealing with skyrocketing home insurance costs. Life here has gotten much more expensive.

Just about every night, I hear police sirens out there, somewhere. Our neighborhood has not had a serious crime, but New Orleans leads America in homicides; young drug dealers fight for shrinking turf. The police department is a mess. So is Mayor Nagin's recovery plan. Half of the population is gone, and many of those people did not live in the Lower Ninth Ward. Whole areas of Gentilly and Lakeview—standard-issue middle- and upper middle-class neighborhoods—are shells, houses with waterlines yet to be repaired. It's a national scandal, though the media have tired of pointing the finger at Bush and Congress. The media backed off when Nagin won his reelection by snookering Blacks into supporting him as a born-again African American. Nagin lunged from one recovery plan to another, failed to bring in the funds we need to rebuild, and blames everyone but himself. Now, with a big boost from Jesse Jackson, he is reinventing himself as a Black liberal, when in fact he's a Social Darwinist toward his own folk. Jackson played a big role in getting displaced Blacks to come back and vote for Nagin. I watch all this amidst and try to stay focused on my work. It is not easy.

My wife Melanie McKay is a professor of English at Loyola; many of her friends and colleagues have left, which has been hard on her and others, including me. It's sad to see those people and others I know move on. My buddy Michael Tisserand, the *Gambit Weekly* editor, moved to Evanston; his wife, a pediatrician, worked here for a guy whose Uptown practice was wiped out. The guy committed suicide. I played baseball as a kid with that fellow. Stevenson Palfi, a filmmaker I knew, killed himself too. These losses add up. And yet on the other side, the music continues, and each time I see people in a restaurant or the park or at some cultural event, one feels the common soul, a commitment to the great texture of this city, a place betrayed by politicians yet alive with culture because of the social mosaic.

There is also a more genuine civic activism, people across lines of class and race pitching in and trying to help than ever before and such little political leadership. The vacuum of politics here will become a case study in postdisaster response literature. That is the hardest part of living here, the collective feeling of drift, the stupidity of governance.

Thinking About New Orleans #9: Jason Berry (Part II)

Jane Ciabattari / 2007

From *Critical Mass*, June 14, 2007. Reprinted by permission of Jane Ciabattari.

This is the second and last installment of the ninth in our occasional series about New Orleans writers. It's hard to judge how many writers have been displaced, dislocated, and disoriented by Katrina and aftermath. As we approach the second anniversary of Katrina, we spoke with a New Orleans native, Jason Berry, a jazz historian and author of *Up From the Cradle of Jazz*, a history of local R&B and jazz. In 1984, he got information about a priest who had abused altar boys in Cajun country. He took an apartment in Lafayette and commuted on a joint assignment for two weeklies, the *Times of Acadiana* and *National Catholic Reporter*, an investigation that became national in scope and formed the basis for his book *Lead Us Not Into Temptation* (Doubleday, 1992). More on his books, including his essay in the Chin Music Press anthology *Do You Know What It Means to Miss New Orleans?* and his newly published first novel, *Last of the Red Hot Poppas*, here.

Jane Ciabattari: A few months after Katrina you called New Orleans the "Pompei on the Mississippi." Do you believe it will come back to life in the long run?

Jason Berry: If we don't flood in the next five years the city will endure at half to three-quarters its previous size. The recovery is stillborn. People wait for federal funds, bottle-necked in the state-administered Road Home program, to reach them so they can repair. These delays have done incalculable damage.

There are also encouraging signs. Downtown apartments are being built or renovated. The public schools are undergoing a transformation via a charter movement; young people are moving here for teaching jobs and to work in the rebuilding. In some ways, this will become a city of the young. My daughter Simonette, an artist who just graduated from Tulane, is committed to living here, which gives me hope as well as pride. The museums have come back; the music infrastructure lags greatly. The pity of where we are is that there is so much goodwill nationally and this emerging civic ethos, and then these political dunces are pushing down, blunting the energy trying to work up. Historically, people here are passive and cynical about politics, nothing like the high-octane activist cultures of New York or Boston or San Francisco. This is a Latin and African city with jaded assumptions of power to begin with.

In my travels, people always ask about the Ninth Ward, with little realization of the destruction elsewhere. It saddens me to see performance artists drawing crowds to gutted houses in Lakeview; I mean that in no criticism of the dancers. Artists go to places that yearn for truths to be expressed. It's the need, the continuing loss, that sickens me. The long run? That's a tough one. With climate change, we're a target for another deluge. It is in our history, many times over. Yet the city has endured. I know good, capable people pushing hard to make restoration of the wetlands and upgraded levee design a front-burner issue. I want them to succeed. I'd like to think the better impulses of humankind will have a resurgence. The birds are still a symphony outside my window each morning, which makes me think that God may yet smile on us. I do pray for that.

JC: This series focuses on New Orleans writers. But you also know the musicians of New Orleans. How are they doing now? How many have been able to maintain residence in New Orleans?

JB: Many musicians are displaced and return irregularly. Henry Butler is in Denver. Michael White commutes between here and Houston. Aaron Neville bought a home near Nashville and has been back only once, briefly, for his wife's funeral. Cyril Neville moved to Austin. Joe Lastie, a drummer with the Preservation Hall band, lives outside of Atlanta. The list goes on. My guess is that about a third of the musicians are back, which is less than the 45 percent of the general populace returned, and that's because more musicians lived in downtown wards that were hit heaviest in the flooding. A lot of the parading clubs and Mardi Gras Indian members have been dispersed. Many groups are working hard to help bring them back: Habitat for Humanity is building a musician's village in the Upper Ninth Ward with help from Harry Connick Jr. and Branford Marsalis. The Tipitina's Foundation raised $100,000 to restore Fats Domino's house, among many other projects; the Jazz and Heritage Festival Foundation has given grants to many gospel and neighborhood groups; the Musician's Clinic is involved in major projects. Wynton Marsalis spearheaded projects that have raised nearly $3 million, with $100,000 grants to several museums and $15,000 grants to a number of musicians. This is quite a remarkable effort, totally outside politics.

Although they're not music-focused, I should mention Brad Pitt and Angelina Jolie, who bought a large home in the French Quarter and have been contributing to a green-friendly rebuilding effort. They've been good citizens in the best sense. How far all of this collective energy goes toward rerooting musicians is hard to quantify, but the efforts are an encouraging sign of this emerging civic ethos.

JC: How do you respond to the death of Alvin Batiste during Jazz Fest this year?

JB: Alvin Batiste's death was a great loss indeed, though the two-day funeral ceremony was a graceful mirror on his life. I did a profile of him and a follow-up on the funeral in *Gambit Weekly*, which can be accessed on their website, bestofneworleans.com. Whenever an artist and a teacher of his stature passes, it leaves quite a space, but the musicians he educated—Donald Harrison Jr., Wess Warmdaddy Anderson, Marlon Jordan, Stephanie Jordan, let me not go on—are a tribute to his legacy. He was a wonderful man, and as he often said, "Jazz is a continuum." His own recordings are part of that continuum.

JC: What are you working on now?

JB: I'm writing a history of New Orleans, using burial traditions as the narrative prism. In 2001, I had a Guggenheim Fellowship, which allowed me to get about a hundred pages done. I've nearly doubled the length in the last year. This narrative has taken shape gradually as I followed jazz funerals, filmed them, and watched them change. The flood forced me to make some changes to the structure and scope of the book. Katrina caused a diaspora of musicians that I had to confront—and with it the idea that the city might be in its death throes. This is not a book about the hurricane, but in the final section, I follow a small constellation of artists, picking up with their lives, trying to return. Through them the narrative will dramatize a quest for the city's resurrection by those who perform burial traditions that are famous the world over.

JC: You have done environmental reporting in New Orleans and in Cajun country. How would you describe the ultimate causes of the devastation of Katrina and Rita and the possibilities for the future? What solutions and preventive measures do you think could keep another disaster from happening?

JB: New Orleans flooded for several reasons. The levees were badly designed and maintained by the Army Corps of Engineers, a federal agency. The wetlands south of New Orleans—historically, a buffer to storm surges from hurricanes—eroded because of thousands of miles of finger canals carved by the oil industry, and because of a huge canal dug in 1965 as an alternate shipping lane from the river through St. Bernard Parish out to the Gulf: the Mississippi River Gulf Outlet. MRGO, as it's known, went right through St. Bernard, just below the Lower Ninth Ward. MRGO destroyed the wetlands there, creating an open alley for Katrina's storm surges, which were twenty feet or more. Congress and the Corps are now moving to close MRGO, a project that Senator David Vitter, a Republican and no friend of the environment, has supported. Even he realized that something was wrong in the marsh down here. The larger issue is repairing the wetlands and fortifying the levees at a stronger, higher level. How that happens depends on whether this emerging civic ethos puts pressure on the legislature and the next governor, presumably Congressman Bobby Jindal, a very intelligent Republican.

Hurricane Rita drove water up the dead wetlands too, but Rita came down harder on the coastal parishes west of the city, wiping out several towns. I don't know that one can prepare for a storm of that intensity; several communities are not rebuilding, which is sad, but a grim bow to reality in the age of climate change.

Quite a number of well-informed people across the socioeconomic spectrum want the levee upgrading and wetlands rebuilding to happen. The state legislation will pass; the wild card is cost. It is going to be a gigantic undertaking. The state will have a guaranteed revenue stream for part of it through recent legislation in Washington pegged to a portion of offshore oil profits in the Gulf of Mexico. But it will take a much larger federal infusion, on a regular basis. We need the equivalent of a Tennessee Valley Authority for climate change defense along the Gulf and Atlantic coasts. That cost will run into the trillions. I suspect it will take another major storm devastating another area—Tampa, Charleston, Manhattan, or Rhode Island, which is quite vulnerable—before Congress embraces the big planning it will take.

Politicians don't act unless forced to.

Jason Berry with Allan Turner

Allan Turner / 2008

This research interview was conducted for the Briscoe Center for American History at the University of Texas. July 4, 2008. Reprinted by permission.

Allan Turner: We're talking with Jason Berry in New Orleans, Louisiana, on July 4, 2008. Mr. Berry is an author and filmmaker, quite knowledgeable about New Orleans culture. He is coauthor of *Up From the Cradle of Jazz*, a study of New Orleans music post–World War II period. He has also written, as an investigative reporter, two books on pederasty and the Catholic Church and has recently completed a documentary film on the same subject. Jason, I would like to talk to you about how you're a native New Orleanian. Tell us a little bit about yourself. Why don't we just start with some basic biographical material.

Jason Berry: I was born here, February 20, 1949. I grew up in the uptown area of New Orleans, not far from Audubon Park. Went to a public school through the fifth grade. And then we moved, and I attended a parochial school, Saint Francis of Assisi, and then went to Christian Brothers School, and from there to Jesuit High School. Graduated in 1967. And I would say that there were sort of three strands that sort of came together during those years, as an adolescent. One was the realization that the Catholic Church was undergoing a great change as a result of the Second Vatican Council. The other was the impact of watching the civil rights movement on television. And the third was my exposure to the music of the city. I would drive home from football practice in the afternoons, and there was a radio program by a DJ named Shelley Pope. He called himself Black Pope. This was on the soul station. And he would always end the program by saying, "My darling, the cocktail hour has come to an end," and you'd hear the shimmer of ice in the background. And then he'd say, "And so we must say goodbye once again. You know, I'll be seeing you soon. I would do anything for you, my darling. I would even swim the gasoline river with torches held high in both of my hands for your love." And there'd be a drumroll and we'd get the news. And I'd go inside, there'd be *The Huntley-Brinkley Report* (NBC News) and I'd watch the South change before my eyes. So, the reason I mentioned these three confluences is because I think what I carry with me in not exactly a conscious way at first, but it became more conscious during the years I spent at Georgetown, was the realization that a society, even one encrusted with segregation, can change in just the way that a church 2,000 years old can change. And running through all that was a grand experience with the music and popular culture of the city, even though at that point in my life, I was barely exposed to it. I grew up on the fringes, you might say, of old pedigree. I mean, I got invited to some of the debutante parties and went, but my parents were not members of the carnival social organizations, although, you know, they had opportunities to travel. My mother was a rather everyday woman who was going through graduate school after my brothers and I were old enough to be in school. And my dad was an executive with a cafeteria chain.

AT: I was going to say the Carnival Society, the Boston Club, the Pickwick, the kind of quintessential elitist . . .

JB: Oh, I have never been inside the Boston Club. Nor the Pickwick Club. I have been to some of the balls. More of them when I was younger. Because, you know, you're dating girls, you get invited on some list, that sort of thing. But by the time I was, I guess, nineteen or twenty, I really had no desire to return. I was living in Washington. The antiwar movement was in full sweep. Nixon was president. Reading *The Washington Post* was an education in itself. And I was immersed. I mean, I had one foot in the antiwar movement and the other foot was planted in the great books canon. So I was a voracious reader. And I did some articles for the college publications, things like that. But by the time I was a senior at Georgetown, I had an experience that set me in another direction. I had sort of assumed I would go to graduate school and get a PhD.

AT: What were your studies? English?

JB: English literature and I had a minor in history and philosophy. But I had a very bad experience with a professor. My senior year I had been nominated for a Rhodes Scholarship, which I ultimately did not get. But one of the professors I got to recommend to me was a man named Robert Ayers, who had taught a course in Dante and a T. S. Eliot seminar I had taken in the spring of my junior year. And I had done a paper on T. S. Eliot's *Murder In the Cathedral*, the drama as mass. And over the summer I did a little more work on it because I was thinking about graduate school and how good it would be to have some sort of essay published. And so I sent it to the *New Orleans Review*, which is edited at Loyola University, and, you know, a respectable academic little magazine of poetry and essays. And they liked it and the editor accepted it. And so I went back that fall and I went to Professor Ayers rather thrilled that I had this accepted, and of course I was hoping I would get my Rhodes Scholarship. I told him I had it accepted. He looked at me rather sternly and said, "Well, you can't do that." And I was a bit taken aback as he explained that since he had given me the idea as an assignment, and I had gleaned information from others in a seminar, that the work really wasn't sufficiently original to bear my singular name. Crestfallen to say the least, I went to see the man who was sort of my mentor at the time, John Glavin, who has since become a good friend. John did not have tenure himself at that time, and he was mortified and told me that this was a terrible thing, but he didn't really know what he could do. And I began to size up academic politics at that point. I knew I'd gotten shafted. And there's another piece to this that's kind of worth mentioning. In my junior year, I had taken a terrific course on modern British literature by a young professor named McKenna, John McKenna, who lived for the written word and just made it come alive. And I read *Ulysses* in that class under his tutelage, and, well, I'm sure he was gay, although the word wasn't used much then. It would be hard not to imagine that he was going through a brutal tenure battle, and we later learned that Ayers was opposing him. Ayers had been an Air Force pilot during the war, and I wouldn't exactly say he had the demeanor of a military man, but there was a brusqueness about him. And, you know, he and McKenna were as opposite personalities as you could find. Anyway, McKenna committed suicide. I think he died maybe in the spring of junior year. I don't remember the exact sequence of that, but I knew that Ayers had done something wrong to me, and I had already submitted his name. I probably should have written to the Rhodes people and said, "Look, this guy did this to me, I'm withdrawing," or something like that, but I didn't. I just went through with it. And I don't think it had any real effect. Well, I never saw what he wrote about me. Maybe he wrote a bad letter, and I didn't know about it.

AT: So, did you retract your article from the review?

JB: Oh, yeah, I pulled it.

AT: But that was not enough, seemingly, to placate him.

JB: Well, he seemed placated. I don't know what he wrote because I never saw the letter. And I never had any sense that he was going to stab me in the back in that regard. But I really soured on the idea of going to graduate school at that point. So, when I graduated in the spring of '71, I went to Mississippi and volunteered for the Charles Evers campaign for governor and worked there the summer and fall through the election, which was in November. And then went to my family's place out in the woods, in Mississippi in Pearl River County, a town called Poplarville, and holed up for about a year and worked on a book about the campaign.

AT: Like, you say, that was your first.

JB: I got my first book. I was quite fortunate to get it accepted. In fact, how it got accepted is an interesting tale. I had met Walker Percy in the late summer or early fall of 1971 through a family friend, a woman named Berry Morgan. No kin, no relation to me, but she was a writer of short stories and had done a novel. She wrote a lot for *The New Yorker*. And she was a friend of my mother, and I knew Berry not well, but you know, she was sort of like an aunt-like figure. So she telephoned Percy and said, "Would you be kind enough to meet with this young man?" So he agreed, and I spent a long afternoon talking with him, sitting on the banks. He had a patio right out on the bayou. And it was brilliant, I mean, an inspiring afternoon. I said, "Well, I'm thinking about doing a book on the campaign." He said, "Well, you really should. You know, you've got quite a vantage point. A young white Southerner." Well, jump cut. I guess it was in '72 that I did an article for an alternative weekly here, the *Vieux Carre Courier*, on the emergence of progressive Southern governors. It was sort of an across-the-board piece about different states and these guys like Reuben Askew and Jimmy Carter. Percy read it and called me. I was at the farm. I guess he'd gotten a number from my mother. Anyway, the phone rings and it's him. He said, "How are you coming with that book?" And I said, "Well, you know, it's just about done." And he said, "Well, I've been offered a contract to do a book on politics by an editor in New York City." And he said, "But that's not my bag. Maybe you'd be interested." I said, "Yeah, I sure am interested." So, he gave me the name of the editor, Judith Sachs. Judith was with Saturday Review Press, and I had just gotten a literary agent who was interested and had the manuscript. A couple of weeks later, I had a contract.

AT: That's serendipity.

JB: Of the first rank.

AT: Let me ask you, when you went to Georgetown and when you were, I guess, exposed to the larger world, was this sort of a feeling that you had finally come home, or did you have some anxiety or difficulty relating to the Washington world in a time that certainly was a period of political ferment in the country on a number of fronts?

JB: Well, I would answer the question this way, Allan. By the end of my sophomore year or my junior year, I had really turned my back on the South. I did not want to come back. I was almost embarrassed on one level about being from the South. Although I love New Orleans and I thought it was a special place, I had, you know, a lot of galloping ambivalence on that level. I wanted to go to England to study literature, or to a good graduate school in the United States. I was also getting more involved in a modest way in politics. I had gotten a job on Capitol Hill my senior year. Someone in the public relations office at Georgetown had a friend you know, someone who knows someone. Anyway, I got a job working for Lee Metcalf, who was the junior senator from Montana under, well, Mike Mansfield, who was the senior senator. Metcalf was an old school prairie populist, very nice guy. And I worked fifteen or twenty hours a week. My main job was to read the Montana newspapers and cut all of the announcements of young newlyweds. The senator would then send them a little packet with greetings.

AT: Reaching out to the constituents.

JB: The constituents. And every time I typed out the addresses, I imagined these young people back in Montana. I don't know what it was, FHA loans, how to get a house and, I would take the lunch hour late, like, around one, so I could go down and watch the Senate, during debates. And it was quite an education, politically in that sense, just being in such proximity to people making laws and having debates. I remember as the war became more of an impassioned story and issue of the day. One night, I went to a church downtown in Washington. I think it may have been the National Methodist Church, that is, I have forgotten which church it was. I don't think it was a Catholic church. Al Lowenstein spoke, William Sloan Coffin from Yale, and they had Ted Kennedy. I remember Kennedy saying, "Dear God, this war must end!" And it was such a moral cause and crusade that appealed to me. And, of course, I was reading a lot about Vietnam. I understood the collision of positions on that issue. Anyway, by the spring of my senior year, I got interested in the fact that Charles Evers was running for governor. I think I read an article in the *Post* and again, through Berry Morgan, I was put in touch. Berry Morgan had lived in Port Gibson, Mississippi, which is right up the road from Fayette. And she knew a woman named Marge Baroni, whose family had been with the Natchez movement. I think you find people like this in many of these medium-to-small Southern towns during that period of history that were quite allied with Black activists. And she had gone to work in 1969 as Mayor Evers's assistant when he became mayor of Fayette. So I had an entree through her, and I also met

Hodding Carter III, and he was at an event in Washington. In fact, I picked him up at the airport. I was doing volunteer work for Edmund Muskie at that point and was really thinking about staying in Washington. I just sort of wrangled my way into giving him a ride because I was curious about Evers and met him, spent the day with him, and, soon thereafter, I think I wrote a letter, called. And then I went down right after graduation and got the job for seventy-five bucks a week. So anyway, that's how I got the job.

AT: Very well. So, after publication of the book.

JB: *Amazing Grace.*

AT: Yeah. What do you do next?

JB: Book was published in 1973 in the fall. But I finished it in August or September of '72. I got the advance money, which was $2,500, and, on that princely sum, I went to Europe. I mean, that was pretty decent money for someone who's twenty-three years old and single without responsibilities. So, I bought a Eurail pass for $300, and I had a bunch of American Express traveler's checks. I didn't even have a credit card. I traveled for about eight months and spent the last three months of that period in Paris. And I had the most serene sensation when I arrived in Paris. It was a very foggy morning, and I felt immediately as if I had been there before, almost in another incarnation or something like that. I got a little room, a servant's room in a big, elegant apartment building right near Invalides and Napoleon's tomb. It's located on the Rue Bixio, I remember was the name of it. And so I had my little room with the toilet down the hall. For three months I got to know the city and went to the Alliance Francaise where I was making pretty good strides in learning French. I fell in with a group of young Americans. There was also a Portuguese guy, or a guy from Brazil who spoke Portuguese, and a guy from Ireland—just a group of us who went on picnics and hung out and did things together. Then came back in late summer of '73. The book came out that fall and I did some speaking engagements at places where I knew people. I had a berth at Georgetown, and I knew a guy at Boston U. And then I started freelancing and I came back to New Orleans. Many years later, my second wife Melanie had told me when we first started dating, the fateful decision in your life was moving back to New Orleans rather than getting a job in Washington or New York, which is absolutely true. It would have made much more sense, in terms of a career path, to have tried to get on with *The Times* or *The Post* or one of the networks.

AT: Well, and certainly this was a period, and I may be off just a few years, but I'm thinking of a period of Southern expatriates in the literary field gaining some ground. There was Willie Morris at *Harper's* and William

Styron. Of course, Styron was creating quite a bit of controversy with *The Confessions of Nat Turner*. But a number of Southern writers and editors were getting a lot of attention during this period.

JB: That's true. I was not one of the lucky ones [*laughter*]. I didn't get serious attention.

AT: So you came back to New Orleans. Came back, with what type of feelings at that point?

JB: I came back partly because I wanted to write fiction. I knew I could live here inexpensively. I also came back because wherever I traveled in Europe, as young Americans, well you start exchanging the bio details, where you're from. And every time I said New Orleans, people's eyes would light up. And I didn't quite know what it was about New Orleans that so intrigued them or entranced them. And so I realized that as much as I had enjoyed my childhood and adolescence, I didn't really know that much about where I was from. You know, I grew up in a middle-class home, went to a very good high school, but it was also a Catholic military high school, Jesuit High School. And, although I liked it, I didn't really get exposed to what you might call an artistic milieu. My older daughter Simonette, in contrast, went to the New Orleans Center for the Creative Arts, NOCCA, the school the Marsalises and Harry Connick attended. I'm sure there's a novelist who will come out of there if one hasn't already. Now, that school didn't exist when I was a kid. But all that said, the main reason was that I wanted to write fiction, and I was just very curious about the place. And so for the next seven or eight years, I had a wonderfully thumping bohemian life here. I moved into an apartment in the Irish Channel, 1017 Third Street. I had the top floor of an old house, a big room with a balcony, a second room, which had a small bed and a table if I had people, and I used the front room to work. I had my typewriter in there, and it's a pretty good-sized kitchen and a long kind of angular bathroom with a bathtub. And I lived there for several years, enjoying it greatly. I think I paid seventy-five bucks a month.

AT: Oh, really?

JB: Oh, that's an amazing deal. And I started freelancing. I did a lot for the alternative papers. There were two of them at the time: *Figaro* and the *Vieux Carre Courier*. And then I worked for *New Orleans Magazine*, for which I still write, they pay about the same [*laughter*]. It's never been a full-time gig, I tell you that. I also started getting published pretty early on in some good places. I did some reviews in *The New Republic* and in *The Nation*. I guess the real turn professionally came when Evers was indicted in 1975, on income tax evasion. And I got very curious about what that meant.

Truth be told, I thought, Well, gee, if this guy goes to prison and I've written this book that was rather celebratory of him. Look, in retrospect, the book is really more about me than him because it's written all about a young Southerner waking up to racial realities, but he is sort of the key figure. So I wanted to figure out what was going on. Well, I started interviewing other civil rights leaders, and I remember Aaron Henry, who I think may have been elected to the legislature at the time, or if not, it was right before, but he told me, they come after me all the time. They used to audit me all the time. So I just started calling people, and I got one name after another of people who had been active, people I'd met through the campaign work. And I got a grant from the fund for Investigative Journalism. It wasn't much, and it was about $400. In fact, I called Hodding to ask him, and he said that the newspaper (*Greenville Delta-Democrat Times*) had been audited every year for, I don't know, twenty years. And he said we always assumed that Senator James Eastland was behind it because Eastland had hated his father, who had stood up against the Klan, as a courageous editor, before he got ill toward the end of his life. And so I got the grant and I did two long articles, one for the *South Mississippi Sun* on the Gulf Coast, and the other one was for the *Delta Democrat Times*. And then I decided I wanted to see if this was a pattern across the South, and I got a pretty substantial grant from the Southern Regional Council in Atlanta. And I spent about two months driving across the South interviewing a lot of people, who, by this time, were becoming elected officials, political organizers, or power brokers. That piece eventually ran in *The Nation*. And then I did a couple of others on the IRS in the 1970s. I got a larger grant from the Fund for Investigative Journalism and did two articles for *The Washington Star*, which was the respectable afternoon paper. So I was working on my brilliant fiction at night, which somehow eluded the New York publishers, or at least they didn't want it. I think I did one novel and then a second novel, neither of which got published, but I was getting a lot of my journalism published. In fact, a congressional committee under Congressman Rangel from New York did an investigation where they got the GAO, or the General Accounting Office, to do an investigation of the Mississippi IRS. And they eventually concluded that the people audited didn't do anything wrong and I thought it was horseshit. Of course, audit twenty-six people from the same political movement? Go figure. Anyway, I guess, the reporting did have some impact. But I was not able to get a book contract, I think part of that had to do with my inexperience, or I should say lack of sophistication in writing book proposals. I was working really hard in journalism and doing fiction at night. I wasn't really, shall we say, polishing myself, presenting myself to editors and learning how to politic in a literary sense. I did some of that. In those years, I was my own force of nature, I guess, and not really worried about networking.

AT: There is a degree of skill required for that, obviously.

JB: There is, yes, I have to say. So I kind of stumbled along for some years, I guess four or five years. And then I became very serious about the music and, with a colleague, Jonathan Foose, who is originally from Yazoo City, began interviewing musicians in a much more targeted way.

AT: If I might, let me ask you to back up and speak to how you began becoming acquainted with the music.

JB: Well, I was going to a lot of the clubs, you know, I was twenty-five, twenty-six years old. I grew up on rhythm and blues, the Nevilles, Irma Thomas, people like that. And these people who in my adolescence were performing at the proms and dances and concerts were now becoming, via the Jazz Fest, pretty substantial emerging artists, if you will. I was really intrigued with the cultural world of the musicians. The fact that so many of these musicians were either related to one another or knew people—I became aware that there were a great many musical families. Some of these people, two or three generations going back, had you know, music in the bloodstream. So, Jon was spending a lot of time in the Lower Ninth Ward interviewing musicians there, particularly the Lastie family. He'd become very close with David and "Popee" Walter Lastie. David was a saxophone player and Popee was a drummer. And sometimes we just spent afternoons driving around through the Ninth Ward, the tape recorder running, and they were telling stories, and I thought, This is such rich material, these neighborhoods have a folklore, an oral history about them. So we managed to land a grant from what's now LEH (Louisiana Endowment for the Humanities), which at the time was called the Louisiana Committee for the Humanities. And basically, I proposed doing a film on two families, the Nevilles and the Lasties. I'd taken some classes at Novak, the New Orleans Video Access Center, and realized that I needed a good cameraman and someone who could edit. There's a guy named Gene Fredericks who was very interested. So we got Gene on board and wrote the proposal. We got a $36,000 grant, which was a lot of money. That was in 1978, and then, went to work on the film. From the outtakes, it really became apparent that we had far more material than we could possibly synthesize into a one-hour program. More than that, I began to see the outlines of an ambitious, cultural narrative. And so Tad Jones, who had been a historical consultant on the project, joined us. Over the next several years, we did a book together, *Up From the Cradle of Jazz*. We finished the film Jon and I, which was broadcast in 1980. And by that time, the three of us were working full tilt on the book, and I learned about an NEH cycle, with an oral history focus. I think we may have had two chapters done by then sent to several houses in New York, but it wasn't getting anywhere. And the NEH grant office in Washington told me that if we had an academic press behind it, we would have a very good chance of getting the grant. And I thought, Well, what do you get for a book advance? I mean I realize it would be unlikely that we would get a large advance for this book. The grant I think we got was $33,200 if I'm not mistaken. So we contacted the LSU Press. They were interested. They wrote us a very supportive letter saying based on what we've seen, we're interested, but we can't quite offer the contract yet. You need to finish the manuscript. Anyway, that was good enough for NEH. So we got the money and finished the manuscript. First draft in 1982.

AT: And it was ultimately published by the University of Georgia, was it not?

JB: Yeah. And this is a very interesting story. So I got married in 1981. And in 1982, on finishing the first draft of the book, my wife and I had saved some money, and I applied to a program in Paris called Journalists in Europe, which was sponsored by the European Union. We decided to take the money we had saved and spend three months in Europe as sort of a delayed extended honeymoon. And I had really been working very hard on that book, long hours. I probably wrote half of the book, I guess. And Jon and Tad did other pieces, and then, I'm not keeping score, but I edited their pages as well, so that we had a singular prose. Anyway, I was pretty much out of gas by the spring of '82. Then I was accepted to a program in Paris, Journalists in Europe, a kind of fellowship with twenty-nine other reporters. And so Lisa and I went to Paris, and we submitted the manuscript to LSU. I can't remember at which point we signed the contract, but we had the contract when I was in Paris. So then they said, "Well, you've got to cut the book. It's too long." So we ended up staying in Paris for about sixteen or seventeen months, during which time I cut the manuscript down. I did a lot of work on that book over there. I also did about ninety pages on what became, years later, the novel, *Last of the Red Hot Poppas*. But, anyway, in Paris, I was going to these seminars on economics, public policy, and things like that. And they funded full travel assignments. I managed to get the State Department to send me to Africa so I could show my film, *Up From the Cradle of Jazz*; it was quite a global experience for me. And, when I got back in the summer of 1983, we were still working on the book. I was still doing some revising. Anyway, I remember we wanted to get it out for the World's Fair in 1984, so we finally submitted it sometime that fall. And the editor then returned the manuscript after she had done a lot of work on it and it was a disaster. It was just one . . .

AT: Hatchet job?

JB: She did not have much experience as an editor. And I'll give you a few examples. I had a line in there where I said, Little Richard came to New Orleans a one-man sideshow of energy and dazzle. He cut Tutti Frutti, a badass song that fit the temper of the time. You can check those words against the text. I think it's pretty close. And she cut "badass" and put "naughty" [*laughter*]. Well, come on, give me badass or give me life. And the chapter on Professor Longhair ends, the coffin is going into the ground all these photographers surrounding it. And it said after that all you could hear was the cameras clicking. Pop pop pop pop. She changed it. After that, "there was only the sound of cameras in the air." She had a disarming . . .

AT: [*Laughter*] Tin ear.

JB: That's a charitable understatement. She had a disarming habit of switching from the active to the passive rather than the other way around. Anyway, the language was being melted down into this academese. And you know, in those years, I wasn't as diplomatic as I am today. Time does kind of teach us certain things. And I wrote this huge memo. It was actually one hundred pages long, and I even included whole sections in how they should've been edited. And I sent it back to them. I finally was summoned to Baton Rouge. I was sitting in a room with these three women, and I knew going in, I just had this bad feeling. And I finally said, "Look, I know we've had disagreements on this, but I bet if we just spend a week and work over the table, I know we could work this out." And brother, you could have taken a champagne bottle and broken it on the floor with those expressions I got for that. "Well, we don't edit over at the table. That's not the way we do things at LSU Press." Well, okay. So I said, "Look, Jon and Tad and I caucused back in New Orleans, and we figured, okay, how do we salvage this? We want to get it out for the World's Fair." One of the other things she'd done, she systematically changed all of the song titles so that instead, this is before CDs, and if you look at the music histories from those years or just music books in general, pop music, journalism . . . the singles, the 45s are encased in quotation marks like a short story, and the albums are italicized like a novel or like a collection of stories. Well, she changed everything. She had italicized everything, and one of the things I said was, "Look, you're going against your own stylebook you guys published last year." They did a book on Beale Street, *Beale Black and Blue*, and I said, "Go back and look at the Beale Street book and ask yourself if you're doing it the way that book was done." Well, it was obvious that they were circling the wagons. This was a young editor. I later learned that she'd just come from a job at one of the smaller colleges. And so she was mortified. And then I got a letter from Les Phillabaum, who was the publisher, saying that he had read my memo. We sent them a letter and what we proposed was: Okay, look, we'll swallow, I don't know, whatever it was forty, fifty pages of you know, cuts. But in exchange, we want to have the style book the way it should be. There were two other things we requested, and I can't today remember what they were, but they were pretty modest requests. She wanted to put two chapters and make them one, and we wanted to keep the chapters. . . . Oh, this stuff could have been worked out. Anyway, it became this power struggle. And, you know, Jean-Paul Sartre has a line somewhere. *I look back on the young man I was, I look back and I laugh today.* I'm not that young man, brother. Along the way, I learned that it's very, very important to be the polite young man you were taught to be growing up as a kid. Anyway, not that I've ever really been a rude person, but I was upset, to be honest, because I felt we had produced a very fine book, and it was being mishandled, manhandled, just editorially bludgeoned. And so this whole nightmare finally came to an end when Phillabaum wrote us a letter saying, "Well, I've read your proposal for how the book should be edited, and I have reviewed enough." He started out by saying, "Now that I'm a publisher, I don't have the hands-on experience with the authors and I miss that," you know, a sort of wistful, autumn-of-life deal. I mean, I could feel the stiletto coming a mile away, and then he said, "But I must say that I believe the authority of the editing is sound. And what may appear to you as blue pen markings on the page, to a seasoned editor. . . ." All this and all that. And then he finally said, "You can, of course, choose to take your work elsewhere, but it will not bear the imprimatur of the Louisiana State University Press." And when I read that, I said, "You're right, Jack, it won't. Let's get out of here." And so we pulled it. We signed a letter of agreement that their lawyer drew up in Baton Rouge, nullifying the agreement. And three or four months later, the new marketing director at Georgia called. He had been at LSU when all this happened, and he said, "What's going on in your book?" And I said, "Well, we submitted it to the University of Illinois, but we haven't done a deal." And we FedExed it to him, and they made us an offer and paid us in advance. So we finally got the contract with University of Georgia Press, and the book came out in 1986 instead of 1984.

AT: At this juncture, I want to roll back just a little bit and interject a couple of questions. You've kind of described the ordeal of the editing process and what it took to get your work into print. But I'd like to roll back to the research. You had mentioned driving around the Ninth Ward with these guys with a tape recorder running. I'm wondering, Jason, I read the book when it came out. It's been a while, but I definitely recall the portraits you had on the Lastie family. And I'm wondering, you obviously got really close to these people and got them to open up. And I'm wondering how you did that across the racial divide. Were they open to this type of thing? What was required to gain their confidence and to get them to feel comfortable talking with you like this?

JB: That's truly quite a probing question, Alan. Well, in some cases, we spent either together or individually a lot of time with the people we interviewed and got to know them fairly well in a casual way, hanging in clubs and going to events. The Mardi Gras Indian gatherings. . . . And when people become comfortable with you, you know they feel they can be in their skin when there's a tape recorder there and not worry about getting burned. And I think there was another factor. This was the late seventies, early eighties, so not quite a generation since the civil rights upheavals. A lot of these artists recognized that we were genuinely curious about where they had come from. We approached them as artists, and we wanted to know the influences on their lives. And as you know, I'm sure from the many interviews you've done, when you persuade a person, as we're doing today, to block out some time to sit down and talk about life and the influences on one's craft and work and career, people start to take you seriously. And I think we were there at a very favorable moment, if you will, in the life of the city. The 1970s were so exciting in a cultural sense because the racial barriers were coming down.

AT: Was Dutch [Morial] mayor then?

JB: Moon [Landrieu] went out I think in '78 and Dutch had just come in. So, you know, it was right during that political transition. And the city was opening up. I mean, you know you could go to the Contemporary Arts Center. I remember it opened in 1977, and within a year, you could go to events there and you had people in their twenties and thirties, Blacks and whites, Mardi Gras Indians on stage, people second lining. It was truly a galvanizing social experience. And I think the musicians recognized that we were serious about doing right by them. I had started to do articles on some musicians and, you know, people would see the articles and realized that it was a way for them to get publicity. And so all of that converged in a way that helped us a good deal.

AT: I'd like you to speak about your Black Hawk book and how you gained access to that insular world because Kaslow had done a book about that time, but certainly yours was . . .

JB: Well, Andy Kaslow and Claude Jacob had done a book on the Spiritual churches, academic book, you know, very, solid scholarship. I got to know Jules Anderson, who was one of the Black Hawk ministers, during the time that Jon and I were working on the film *Up From the Cradle of Jazz*. We filmed the Black Hawk ceremony, and I started going to the Spiritual churches, I guess, in '78. And, of course, there was a period when I was out of the country, and then when I got back in the mid-eighties, I started going back. There was a fairly long stretch, however, I got involved in the investigative work on the Catholic Church in late '84. And so for a period of almost eight years, I was really drawn heavily into that. Now, I did periodically go to a Spiritual church. Especially after my second child was born with Down syndrome. I mean, I was trying to get as much prayer power as I could. But I really resumed that research in a serious way in '93 and '94. I got a Ford Foundation grant through Tulane to film jazz funerals and also to film a Spiritual church service. I just started going back and interviewing different people. I had published *Lead Us Not Into Temptation* in '92. And I'd gotten a lot of exposure on national television. I had a younger daughter who had Down syndrome and was really in struggling health. Ariel had heart surgery when she was two. And my older daughter Simonette I guess was ten or eleven at the time. Anyway, it was just a very painful period in my life. My wife and I eventually parted. And I was deeply involved with my children thereafter. In any event, I wrote that book as a kind of recovery if you will, from the joint experience of all those years of research about the abusive priests, and then the coming off of this painful dissolution of my marriage. The book, in a sense, was just my own sort of spiritual affirmation. And, as with the musicians, fifteen years before, I found the Spiritual church folk, some were initially a little standoffish. But once I got to know them and spent time with them . . . they had had the experience of dealing with Andy Kaslow, Claude Jacob; David Estes had done a couple of academic articles, so it wasn't as though I was the first pioneer. I'm just fascinated by the varieties of the Spiritual imagination. Coming out of this Catholic background, where I had studied mysticism in college, I've never claimed to be one myself, but I think I understand what it is. At the same time, Jimmy Swaggart was having his meltdown dramas on TV in those years. And you watch these Sunday TV preachers, I mean they're straight out of Mark Twain or Sinclair Lewis as well. And I just found in the Spiritual churches, there's a little bit of that kind of show business quality, but there was also a very powerful current of trance-like surrender by people in the pews that touched me and moved me and made me wonder, because I've never been the kind of person to fall into trances. But I believe that people who have those trances experience the spirit in a way that I, a more meditative or contemplative person, do not. Every time I see people like Christopher Hitchens on TV who did the book (*God Is Not Great*), trying to berate everybody who believes, I think, come on, open the window. Let the bad air out. What an impoverished world we would be if there were no belief in the deity? So, you know, yes, it was exotic. It certainly had patterns of show business to it. But at the same time, watching the people in the pews and how they respond to this and the eclecticism of the altars, the presence of food, the fruit feasts, the beauty of the candles, the way in which people moved around the altars, in the circular dances, the rhythms and cadences of the people at the pulpits, the presence of so many women as bishops. All of this, taken together for me, was quite a different interpretation of the religious experience, much more so than anything I'd really seen before. I wrote that book in the upstairs of my parents' house. They don't own it anymore. It was just a block from here on Fontainebleau. I had queried an editor at Harper San Francisco, which at the time was their main religious books line, and thought I was going to get a contract there, but it didn't come through. And then I happened to have a conversation with Willie Morris's wife, JoAnne Prichard of the University Press of Mississippi. I mentioned it to her. We were having a drink at the Monteleone Hotel. I think it was the Tennessee Williams Festival. We were just talking, and she asked me what I was working on, and I said, well, I'll tell you about doing this book and she said it sounds like a wonderful book. That's it. So I wrote her a two- or three-page letter proposal. She said yes. I think they paid me a $4,000 advance. It wasn't very much, but I wrote the book in maybe four or five weeks. It's not a long book, but as I say, it was a way of getting my own spiritual moorings back in place.

AT: A couple of questions come to mind. One, we were talking earlier about how you were accepted and how you were able to gain the confidence of these people. Certainly a situation where you have the anthropologist syndrome, where you have the danger of making the people you are observing feel as if they are some exotic species under the microscope. And I'm wondering how you avoided that. And then secondly, let me piggyback this question, although it's really not related. You know, I've read about the Spiritual churches and Mother Catherine and so forth, but I'm wondering if you associate some of the things you saw in these Black Hawk ceremonies with the Afro-Caribbean syncretic religions, Santeria, voodoo, the various trances. Seeing those if you see any relation between that.

JB: Oh, I absolutely do. And I think it's reflected in the text. I do make references to those. I don't really take the classical approach of the anthropologist. You know, the sort of fly on the wall. I go in and get to know people and try to win confidences by being honest and aboveboard. And I hang out with people and get to know them, and especially when you're dealing with unlettered people, you develop your own kind of moral sensibility on what is on or off the record. You don't want to burden people. You don't want to embarrass them. On the other hand, if there's something that really jumps out at you that you think must be in there, you have to put it in.

AT: What I'd like to ask you to do briefly, Jason, since it is quite possible that those unseen people in the future have not read the book or are not that familiar with the spiritual churches or the Black Hawk cult. Tell us who Black Hawk is and then tell us about the big money.

JB: Right. Well, Black Hawk was the leader of a rebellious Indian community in Illinois in the late 1820s, 1830s, Rock Island, Illinois, the Sauk and Fox Indians. He was the holdout, who became a chief and a resistance fighter, if you will. Almost by default. He got mad. He saw a land grab going on and didn't like it. And so he fought back and was captured. In fact, Jefferson Davis, a young soldier, escorted him to prison. He was corralled for a while. And then with a couple of other Indians, he was taken to the White House for a meeting with President Andrew Jackson, the purpose of which was to demonstrate to him that the westward movement of the settlers was a momentum that could not be stopped. And we want you to see Baltimore. We want you to see Philadelphia. We want you to see what the world is going to become. Then go back home and, you know, join the program. Don't get in the way. And, of course, he becomes a celebrity when he goes to Washington and Baltimore in these places, because the idea of the noble savage is now spreading. And he would go out on the balcony, these are all historical accounts cited in the book, wearing his formal garb, and people were cheering. He went back to Wisconsin or Illinois, lived his last years in Wisconsin, and dictated a long autobiography, if memory serves, in 1834 and then died in 1838. And that autobiography was very helpful to me writing this short book. He came to New Orleans, if you will, in the ceremonies of a woman named Leafy Anderson, who founded the Spiritual church movement here. The Spiritual churches were proliferating across the southwest in the early years of the twentieth century. They are in some ways akin to the Holiness churches, the Sanctified churches. Zora Neale Hurston did a short book on the Sanctified church. And she lived for a time with Mother Catherine Seals, who was a disciple of Leafy Anderson. The Leafy Anderson founded the local Spiritual Church movement in 1920 and would conduct these Black Hawk . . .

AT: Now these are women of color?

JB: Oh absolutely. They would conduct these skits or tableaux. They were ceremonies in which she would summon Black Hawk, and you sort of read between the lines. And you see, here are poor folk who've come in from the plantations outside the city. These are people from whom the blues sensibility flowed like a mighty river. People who did not know how to read, people who were struggling in the void of the city. And these services where they could have these ecstasies and exaltations of the spirit allowed them to find a certain grounding. So she introduced Black Hawk as a presence in these ceremonies. She died in 1927. And the Black Hawk services continued with different ministers down the line. And, you know, when I discovered it, I guess in '78, '79, unbeknownst to me at that time, this had been going on for what, fifty or more years. And I don't know if there are Black Hawk services since the hurricane. Many of these small vernacular churches were wiped out in the flood. The Ninth Ward was devastated. So, one of the things I just have not done is make a few calls and figure out if any of these ministers are still doing it.

AT: So how did Black Hawk, the spirit of Black Hawk travel from. . . ?

JB: Well, Leafy Anderson spent time in Chicago. And as you know, I explain in the book that there is a certain sort of missing link there. I mean, we can't pinpoint how precisely Black Hawk entered her life. She may have read the memoir. She may have been exposed to people who knew about it from when she started doing these ceremonies in New Orleans. She knew who Black Hawk was, and, if you will, was kind of channeling him.

AT: So, you were attending one of these services? You had gotten a grant.

JB: Anyway, so here we are. This is 1978. We got the grant for $36,000 for the documentary. It was a very muggy winter night, a warm night. And I drove over the Industrial Canal Bridge to this small, small church in an old one-time laundromat. And I walked in there, only about eight or nine people in the church. The minister welcomed me. I think I had called beforehand, and this young guy, Jules Anderson, I later learned his name, was the same guy I'd seen before. So he comes out and he starts. He has a teepee, he starts hitting the tambourine, and he's singing the praises of Black Hawk. He is a watchman. He will fight your battles. And then he starts talking to different people in the audience. And he says, "Now you, to this little lady, I know you're waiting for that money, and when the money comes, put it on the bureau and don't open it. Leave it there for three days." And then he says to another, "You, you're waiting for someone who's far away who will be coming back." Well, all of this was general enough. I mean, you can imagine someone waiting for Social Security, what have you. And yet there was a kind of tenderness about it, even though he had this rather dynamic, charismatic personality. Well, in the middle of the ceremony—and the rain is just beating down like drums on this tiny roof—the door to the church blows open, and this guy comes in off the street soaking wet. I mean, his eyes lit up like red coals. He was obviously high as a kite on something not legal. And he's kind of, you know, shaking in the background when the minister says, "We pray for people behind bars and people in the night." Or something like that. And everybody goes, "Yes, Lord." You know, this is one of the things I love about the Black tradition in churches, the African American tradition. It is so embracing. I mean, if you can imagine going to Holy Name Parish on Saint Charles Avenue or even Mater Dolorosa where I go over on Oak Street, if you're in there in the middle of mass and some guy walks in high as a kite saying, I want to testify, you know, a couple of the ushers would probably say, "Look, why don't you go back here and sit down? You know, we don't want to call the cops if you behave." Hey, this approach, it's just a very different approach to the human condition, to human struggle, to sorrow, because Black folks have dealt with it in ways that we on the other side of the racial divide have . . . most of us have not. Anyway, I remember, Jules Anderson said, he says to the guy who's just come in, "Beatrice, the name Beatrice has come to me," and we're all kind of looking around wondering where he's going to go with this. And the guy says, "That's my mama, bro." "Yeah, and your mom is worried about you, because you're out in the streets, you're walking around." He starts yelling at this guy to basically step up. You got to behave. And of course, I'm sitting there thinking, Well, he probably knows the guy and knows who his mom is or something's going on here. Well, this is really quite a performance. And then he starts walking around and he says, "Now I'm not going to call any names, but there is money in this room. There is *big* money in this room." And we had just gotten the grant, $36,000, to make a film. I think for the record, my salary was about $900 per month for seven or eight months of that. Of course, that was pretty good money back in 1978–79, when you consider that I only had to make a bit more to get by. But, anyway, he starts dancing around the altar, around the teepee. Of course, by this time the lights are out, the candles are up. It was quite exotic. And then he turns and points to me and says, "If you want to know Black Hawk, you must come forward." So I kind of walked up and I just started following him and danced around the teepee for a while. I don't think your anthropologists would do that. You know, maybe I'm a participant journalist or something. I don't know where the lines cross, but. So I did that and then went back to my pew and at the end made a contribution to the church. I went back and reinterviewed him in '94, I guess it was sixteen years later. And, you know, I used that interview as part of the book. The book is, I guess, four episodes, maybe one hundred pages. And I'll tell you something funny. Many years later, I would have been in 2000, 2001, I was having lunch with Tom Cahill. He wrote the book *How the Irish Saved Civilization*. He had been my editor at Doubleday. He was the guy who acquired *Lead Us Not Into Temptation*. He was the head of the religious books line, and the book had been to thirty publishers, and everybody had said no. They were all afraid of litigation at the time. Even though, I mean, Cahill is a very smart man. He read the book and immediately understood from the source notes that it was grounded in legal documents. It's not as though you're libeling people, you know, when you're using it as fact. Yeah, newspapers understand that. But publishers are not as swift as you might think. So that was in 1992. He had since left Doubleday, with the success of his book, and had come down here for a conference, and we peeled off and were having lunch at Mr. B's and we were just talking, and I happened to mention the Black Hawk book. And he looked at me with this expression on his face and said, "What an interesting idea for a book." And I thought to myself, Why the hell didn't I go back to him first? Boy, if we could second guess our decisions.

AT: *Lead Us Not Into Temptation*: Tell us how you got into that project and how that came about.

JB: In late 1984 I saw the news that a priest named Gilbert Gauthe was indicted in Lafayette for abusing altar boys. I got on the telephone, spoke with several lawyers including Gauthe's defense attorney Ray Mouton, whom I had met through my brother-in-law. I could tell he was frustrated at how much he didn't know about how the diocese handled these cases. He was a very mercurial attorney, brilliant lawyer, and one of those personalities who just comes in and fills up a room. Loved bullfighting and went to Pamplona every summer. The first lawyer in south Louisiana to defend drug dealers, and he made a lot of money on oil field accidents. A man of many parts. Meanwhile, I connected with one of the attorneys here in town, a guy I'd actually gone to high school with named Raul Bencomo. I think he'd been a year behind me at Jesuit. Raul was representing several of the families with abused youngsters from Vermilion Parish. There was a lawyer there named

Paul Hebert who had gone to law school with Raul and called him. Paul was really a civil attorney. He had never taken on cases of this kind. And Raul was really moving up the ladder as a high-stakes plaintiff attorney. And so, Raul let me read the bishop's deposition. And when I read the deposition, I realized that this was not just the story of one sick priest who had been so pathological as to commit these criminal acts. It was a story of a cover up. First reference was Watergate. What did the bishop know? And when did he know it? So I started reading as many documents as I could, and I started casting lines to try to get an assignment. And hit one brick wall after another. Tried *The New York Times Magazine*. I had just done a piece for them the year before when I was living in France.

AT: And this was just too hot to handle.

JB: Yeah. That's really what it was. That's exactly what it was. But you got to remember at this time, in 1984, child sexual abuse was just becoming an issue on the national radars, so to speak. I remember in conversations I used the word pedophilia. Several people did not know what it meant. I mean that's how blank the slate was in terms of society back then. So I tried the *Times Magazine*, I think I tried *Vanity Fair, Mother Jones, Rolling Stone, The Nation*, I don't know, *Washington Post Magazine*, I think, I have all this in the book. Anyway, I couldn't even get the Fund for Investigative Journalism to give me money, and they had been rather loyal to me over the years. I think I've gotten more money from them than just about anybody else. I don't know whether that speaks well to them or not. . . . I got a joint assignment with the *Times of Acadiana*, the weekly paper in Lafayette, whose editor, Linda Matys, had previously been the editor of *New Orleans Magazine* and had moved to Lafayette to take over the paper there, and the *National Catholic Reporter*, whose editor Tom Fox was interested. So between those two papers, I had enough running money to do the first three months of pretty hard digging. The series started running in the spring of '85. And then I started getting more and more information about other priests. Finally, the first leg of that reporting culminated in January of '86 when I did a big final sort of summa-tion article, you might say, or culminating piece that traced the movements of seven priests over a period of years and was highly critical of the bishop. Linda by then had moved on to start a weekly paper in San Antonio, with financial backing from the publisher of the *Times of Acadiana*, Steve May. Richard Baudouin had come in to take over as editor. He and I knew one another. We'd gone to the same high school, although he was several years younger. And anyway, Richard wrote a very highly principled and effective editorial calling on the bishop to resign. The paper got hit with an advertiser boycott fomented by a very prominent monsignor and a retired judge from Crowley, Edmund Reggie, whose daughter later married Ted Kennedy. And is his wife today. In fact, Reggie called Steve May at home, the publisher. Steve's a pretty feisty fellow as publishers of alternative weeklies go. Reggie called him at home and said, "You got to retract that editorial." And he said, "Why?" He said, "You just can't do that." He said, "Oh, it's already out." And then he said, "You just got to retract it." "Was there anything wrong? Factually?" "No, no, but you just can't call on the bishop to resign." "Well, we've already done it." And they're going back and forth. And finally, Reggie says to him, "Boy, you just shit in your mess kit." And within several days, five of the biggest advertisers had pulled [out]. I think it was ten that pulled ads. By the end of the week, he would have had quite a civil case had he chosen to pursue it. He eventually lost about $20,000 in ad revenues. And that's a paper that at the time was billing at about a million a year. You know, that's the salary of an ad person who would then rely on commissions. Eventually Ray Mouton, in fact, played quite a role in cooling tempers and getting people to pull off, all of which I recounted in the book. So, I had finished the first year's worth of reporting, and I had quite a substantial baseline of information. I understood how a given community had responded. I had interviewed a great many priests. Cold called most of them. Some of whom talked, many of whom did not. I really was able to sort of create, in my own mind, this community that I eventually wrote about when I got into writing the book a little farther down the line. As I began to hear about cases in other parts of the country, I started sending my clips to other reporters. And I built up a file of newspaper articles and then started casting lines to attorneys, many of whom began to send me depositions, legal documents and the like. And I amassed a fairly substantial archive in doing that. I signed a contract with a publisher in the summer of '85. A new company in Washington called Adler and Adler. And I think I turned in the first 150 pages the following summer of '86. And then the editor got cold feet. It really got under his skin, the deep Rome stuff. . . . He was a Catholic. I'm really having trouble remembering his name. . . . He stiffed me, is what happened. But anyway, I got to keep some money, but he just, I think he thought it was going to be the story of this one community and how it had responded. And in fairness to myself, I should say that the original proposal said there are other cases in other parts of this country. And I'm going to figure out where this is. And I was moving in that direction and had pretty much finished much of the Louisiana section . . .

AT: And it was just too much.

JB: Yeah, it was too much. Well, so what happened was then here it is, the middle of '86. And instead of getting the next $15,000 of the advance, I'm out there trying to figure out how I'm going to make rent the next month. And, so I just started doing more and more articles, and, gradually, you know, I look back and it took seven years to do that book, and I did a lot of extraneous journalism on the side. David Duke happened in 1989, and I had a cottage industry going against him for about three years. Adler went out of business. In fact, it's rather poetic how they went out of business. It was a startup company. And, you know, with small publishers you rely on moving the stock. They published Kurt Waldheim's memoir a couple of months before he was unmasked as a Nazi. Needless to say, that was not in the book. I rest my case. [*Laughter*]

AT: How unfortunate.

JB: Yeah, well.

AT: Or how just.

JB: Maybe. I think maybe God winked at that one. So I kept working on the book, and I moved at a much slower pace. But when Cahill got it in, summer of '91, the book was done. I'd finished the book, and I had to cut, I guess, about 150 pages. But Cahill got it. He understood that it was not just an investigative book, but an attempt to explain why the Catholic Church . . .

AT: Responded as they did.

JB: Yes, exactly. I mean, the book is kind of a psychological profile of the hierarchy.

AT: So what was happening to you psychologically at this point? Because you're looking at this as an investigative reporter on a human level, you must be absolutely appalled by the egregious instances you're unearthing. But then thirdly, you're a Catholic. So how did those elements combine or not?

JB: They combined very painfully. I was living at the time in a very large apartment on Napoleon Avenue. Actually, the entrance was on Liberty Street. You know, about 2,500 square feet and a big balcony overlooking the parades on Napoleon, during Mardi Gras. And I would go out on the balcony at night. And, I was still smoking cigarettes at the time. And I kept thinking about everything I was learning, and I kept thinking about the benevolent experiences I had had with priests in high school. I did a lot of praying on that balcony. I kept telling myself, there is a reason for this. I don't know what that reason is, but there's a reason why I'm in the middle of all this. There was a lot about it that was hard. There was some financial struggle in there that got pretty rocky at times, but I managed to pull through that. But the real difficulty was dealing with all the rejections from the publishing companies. You know, at any point, if somebody offered me twenty-five or thirty grand in '88, '89, I would have taken it in a second, and gotten out of debt. I got a $50,000 advance in '91 and I walked into the Whitney Bank and immediately paid off loans of $12,000. That's a lot of money. When you think back almost twenty years ago, I don't know what it would be today, maybe $25,000 or $30,000.

AT: It's measurable today.

JB: It is measurable today. But the deeper struggle was a spiritual one. I had a lot of anger toward those bishops, and I went to see a therapist, who was quite good, and she got me to sort of focus on what I expected of myself and what my spirituality entailed. And I came to realize that a lot of who I was, in a spiritual sense, had been shaped by my mother, my grandmother, and my great-grandmother, who in their own way, carried this Latin American or Mexican form of Christianity, which was quite joyous and festive. And one of the things I learned in doing that book was how overwhelmingly Irish the American church is. And there's a whole other wing of my family that's Irish American. I've got all these Irish Texans in the gene pool, and they tend to drink a lot [*laughter*]. I dealt with the anger. I had a lot of conversations with priests I trusted, several of whom kept saying, do it. Get it out. I think, in a way, living here was very important to that whole struggle because I was quite rooted in this city, and having that feel of terra firma beneath the feet was important to me. When the book came out, I did a lot of television. I mean, I got more than the fifteen minutes Warhol says we all get. I'd come back from these promotional trips and things, and I'd see people who just gave this kind of vague wave from the side. There were some people who would cross the street and shake my hand. A lot of people didn't quite know. Well, okay, you're out there doing it, you know? You know, what does this all mean? And ten years later, when *The Boston Globe* began its big series, I was suddenly getting thirty, forty calls a day. I was on *Nightline* three times in six weeks, I think. And I had people who before had not really wanted to acknowledge what I did, coming up and shaking my hand congratulating me. I'm not saying that to be vain. The whole experience in doing that work, and it's still with me in a way. I'm going to be dealing with that reality probably until the day I go. I keep trying to cut distance from it. And it just keeps coming back into my life. You know, I still do all of the other more rewarding creative work. The novel that I published, the play that I did, *Earl Long in Purgatory*, and the documentary on jazz funerals that I'm working on. Now, having said that, if you do a Google search and pull out some of the op-ed pieces I've done in the past four or five years, the language that I've used there and in some of the interviews I've given, you know, in the national media, it's rather spirited [*laughter*]. I think I called the Secretary of State of the Vatican a moral hypocrite or something like that. I said he should resign—Angelo Sodano—and I stand by my record of that. Everything I said was true.

AT: Spirited but warranted.

JB: The *Los Angeles Times* has been my most dependable outlet. I really went after Maciel, the head of the Legion of Christ. More recently, I did a pretty stinging rebuke of the cardinal from Chicago, Cardinal Francis George, who covered up one of these cases. I think a lot of journalists would say, hey, why haven't you moved on? You know, why aren't you doing something different? Well, the truth is, I do other things. I've written about a range of topics. I write a lot about music. Still do. Working now in the new edition of *Up From the Cradle of Jazz*. And I'm writing a lot for *Gambit*, the local journal on the music. All that said, I've got this body of expertise. The rest of the media has moved on. They're not interested in this. They figure it's an old story. Scandal. Yawn. And my attitude is about where it was in 1986, when I learned that the bishop had moved seven of these guys around. You know, you shouldn't get away with this. Somebody should call your hand. So, I do these pieces and there are plenty of people who still don't want them. I did an article a couple of months ago. I got a call from London from an editor at *The Tablet*, which is a very respectable and beautifully edited and elegantly written journal of Catholic opinion, published in the UK. And the editor asked if I would do a piece on the Pope's trip (Benedict XVI) and what it really meant, the fact that he apologized to the victims. Well, I did, and it did praise him. And I certainly think that he made an important step forward. And I salute him and hope he'll continue to stride in the right direction on this. But that said, the last or second to last day of his trip, Cardinal William Levada, who was formerly the Archbishop of San Francisco, at a luncheon at *Time* magazine, says, "Well, I don't believe that any bishops were. . . ." Words in effect saying that "bishops were not at fault. They were doing the best they could. And, if they made mistakes, they were getting advice from therapists who didn't. . . ." Open the window. Come on. You know, and of course, let's not give *Time* magazine, you know, any medals for bravery. They should've called that guy on the carpet and done the whole state job in the next issue. But they don't operate that way. They already put the Pope on the cover saying the Pope loves America. They're not going to come out and, you know, do an exposé of this cardinal.

Well, I had done a 7,000-word piece for *San Francisco Magazine* in 2005. I happened to be in San Francisco when John Paul the Second died and was watching all of this on television in between my interviews. I was doing a profile of Levada, having no idea that he was going to end up going to Rome a few weeks later. And, you know, maybe it's because I went to Jesuit High School and had this education and ethics and the idea that we're supposed to be morally responsible. I kept saying to myself, what gives you guys the right to think you can get away with this? So I just condensed a lot of what I had. Well, needless to say, his record in San Francisco is quite less than sterling. I will say to you, chapter and verse, you're more than welcome to make a copy of the article and take it with you. So I did this article for *The Tablet*. I mean, this is not, you know, big box journalism, but she wanted it in twenty-four hours. So I was sort of attracted to the idea of the quick turnaround. So I did it. I think I got paid $385 with the exchange rate. If we had a bullish dollar, it would have been more. Well, they haven't run it yet.

AT: And how long was . . .

JB: Oh, they paid me for it. You know this has happened before.

AT: Have you heard of any?

JB: Yeah, indirectly. I heard from the Vatican correspondent from this journal and he's a friend of mine and said that they're just very uneasy about attacking the hierarchy. Well, when you think about it, British Catholics are a minority to begin with. And the British historically have a rather reverential attitude toward hierarchy, you know, the monarchy.

AT: Oh, God save the Pope.

JB: Well, you know, I don't want to write another book about the church, but there's so much going on with the financial corruption now, and I've got a lot of material. I could probably do one. But I'm just trying to get my distance while I'm working on another thing.

AT: *Last of the Red Hot Poppas.* You were a yearning young novelist way back when. And that was an extraordinary work of fiction that had the ring of truth. I'm sure, like *All the King's Men* not being written about Huey Long, this one had nothing to do with some politicians we could name. Right?

JB: I was rather forthright in the little introduction saying that Edwin Edwards, now holding an endowed chair in a federal penitentiary, inspired the idea of Rex LaSalle, the governor who dies in the beginning of the book. But I also said that had there never been an Edwin Edwards, there would have been a Rex LaSalle. Some figure to embody the comedy of Louisiana politics. And at the same time, the way in which the comedian becomes the mask of the criminal. I mean, it's now commonplace in popular culture, but

I wanted to make Rex an appealing character. I never liked Edwin Edwards. I mean, the stories about him are legion, both about his sex life and his lines. I mean, he's one of the wealthiest men in America. Who else would say to an opponent in a governor's race, your problem is it takes you an hour and a half to watch *60 Minutes*. I mean, that's a pretty good line, you know? I could fill this interview with stories and quotes about Edwards, but I don't want to go there, because what I tried to do in that novel was take the idea of this comic political figure and explore the dark side of him in a love story. I began the novel in Paris in 1983, in time away from the rewriting of *Up From the Cradle of Jazz*. I didn't have to do too much journalism over there. I was getting a stipend of about $1,000 a month from the French government for the program I was on, and I had done a piece for *Reader's Digest European Edition*: "How airlines retrieve lost luggage" [*laughter*]. I went to four or five airports and hung around with the guys running the computer, the conveyor belt. Came back, wrote this piece. I got paid $2,500, which back then was pretty good. Money from the dollar at that time was trading ten to one.

AT: Oh, really?

JB: I got 25,000 francs for that piece. We lived, I think, almost four or five months on that one article. I did a few other articles, you know, and I had the money coming in for stipend and we had saved some. So we lived very well. But anyway, I had about ninety pages done when I got back in '83. Did a little more work in '84. But then when I began the research on the priest cases, I put the book away mainly because I felt out of kilter writing a comic novel at a time when I was venturing into. . . . I had done a fair amount of investigative work before, but never anything like this. So, the book really stayed on a shelf for, I don't know, almost eight years. I got back to it in the early nineties, worked on it gradually. And by then, I had changed. You know, when I started in '83, I wasn't quite sure where it was going. I don't think I realized at the time that it was going to become a comedy. I was quite exercised by the way that Edwards had allowed so many of these fly-by-night, toxic waste dealers, many from Texas, to come over here and just use the Cajun prairie as a dumping ground. And the *Times-Picayune* had yet to find Jesus on this issue at that time. Later, the *Picayune* became terrific. They hired Mark Schleifstein from the Jackson *Clarion-Ledger*. Mark is one of the best environmental reporters in the country and has since won a Pulitzer Prize. Mark had done a terrific series for the *Clarion Ledger* on BFI, Brown and Ferris Industries. And so with my own reporting, reading his, and stuff I'd dug up, I spent quite a lot of time working on a couple of articles on these little communities in Cajun country. My former wife grew up in Abbeville, and on a number of trips to visit her family, I got to know some of her childhood friends, one of whom is a guy named Lloyd Campisi. He is an insurance agent out in Abbeville. And he started telling me about all these barrels being dumped, cows dying in rice fields, food polluted, things like that. So, you know, the whole idea of violating nature like that really ate at me. I think I was about three quarters of the way through the first draft. By this time, it would have been '94, '95, maybe when I realized that this was not a novel about Edwin Edwards. This is a novel about Louisiana. By that time, I had written a lot about Edwards. I had attacked him in a number of articles. I'd written a lot about David Duke. And so I wanted to create a more timeless political landscape in the novel. I put it through a rewrite. It was maybe 2000, I kept working on the book and then putting it away because other things kept happening. I did the first big story on Maciel in 1997, the priest who founded the Legionaries of Christ and molested all of these people, and that led to what became the book Gerald Renner and I did, *Vows of Silence*, which we began in 2002 and published in 2004. So, every time I moved away from the novel, I developed more and more distance from the age of the young protagonist, Henry Hubbell, who is sort of a figment of me, you might say. But I also had greater distance from politics. And I began to develop a softer sense of these outrageous characters. I'm not so sympathetic as a journalist, but when you move into fiction, you can make these guys into more lovable crooks and rogues and things like that. So, by the time I finally finished the book, to my own satisfaction, it was 2003. For almost twenty years, I'd been around New York a couple of times in the interim, and I couldn't sell it, which was quite a disappointment, to say the least. But when I finally finished it in '03, I felt remarkably good about it. I had several people whose work I respected read it. Valerie Marton read it. You know, she won the Orange Prize. She's an old friend. Andy Greeley read it, and even though many people criticize his novels for not being, quote unquote highbrow, some of his novels, I think, were rather compelling moral fables. Moira Crone, the short story writer, and a couple other people read it. So, when this hurricane hit, I was going to submit it that fall. Anyway, then the hurricane hit, and I got back on day ten just to see if the house was okay, and it was. I gathered up a lot of things I was working on, the novel among them. I mean, if this house had flooded, the novel would have never been published, and I wouldn't have finished the film *Vows of Silence*. Anyway, I hooked up with a guy via the internet, Bruce Rutledge, [of Chin Music Press] who had sent out a sort of request to the world's writers. He wanted to do an anthology.

AT: Chin Music?

JB: Yes. *Do You Know What It Means to Miss New Orleans?* I had done an essay, a really on-the-quick reportage piece of just fleeing New Orleans. Tom Roberts, the editor of the *National Catholic Reporter*, called me and said, would you do something quickly? And he paid me a very generous amount for the article. It took two days. He loved it. It came out, and I gave Chin some names to help them with publicity and media things. And so I called Rutledge one day and I said, "I got a novel. Do you want to read it?" He said yes. Well, two months later, he made an offer. And so, I was delighted to get it out. Unfortunately, it did not get the press attention that I think it really deserved. And there were two reasons for that. The first is that Chin Music Press really did not have the kind of publicity or marketing apparatus that the trade hound big trade houses in New York have.

AT: Not the punch.

JB: Didn't have the punch. And the timing was really off. And I say this with great affection for Bruce. I mean, we've sold, I don't know, several thousand copies. But it came out when all of the hurricane books were coming out, or the second round of hurricane books. This would have been the fall of '06. The novel is set in the nineties and there is a huge flood at the end of the book in Baton Rouge. So in a sense, it was prescient. You know, I'd lived through smaller floods and, metaphorically, I guess the flood represents what I think about Louisiana politics. I must confess that I'm disappointed the book did not get more reviewer attention. Where it was reviewed, it was handled seamlessly.

AT: Well, again, as you well know, Katrina launched a fleet of books, which has not yet abated.

JB: Well, you know, well put. And in addition to that, I think people look at politics in Louisiana and ask themselves, is it really this over the top? I mean, Edwin Edwards once said he was safe with voters unless caught in bed with a dead woman or a live boy. He said that to Art Harris of *The Washington Post* in 1983, and Edwards beat the tar out of David Treen, who was a good governor, one of the better governors we've had. He beat him 63 to 37 [percent]. The novel, in a way, uses that just, outsized mentality of politics as a kind of cocoon, shrouding the characters as they move through this story about a group of people talking to God. The big man dies unexpectedly. What do all of these people do? It's the story of a cover up and everybody trying to figure out how they rationalize what they're doing to themselves. At one point or another, they're all asking, God, why am I doing this? So, in a sense, it's a religious comedy. You know, I've got this history as a writer of coming in and putting a finger on the button long before the explosion happens. I mean, the priest book in '92 . . . it's a third edition now. It's still out there after, what, sixteen years? So it's got legs. Then I came out in '04 with the book on the Vatican, *Vows of Silence*, right after the bishops met in Washington. The Archbishop now in Atlanta, Wilton Gregory, said the memorable line, the scandal is history. And at that point, everybody in the media wanted to go home. They were sick of it. *The Globe* had won their Pulitzer, and everybody thought, Okay, the church is corrupt. Let's move on. You know, John Kerry's running for president. That's more interesting. Against Bush. So here I come with a book unmasking John Paul. God bless him. He's covering up all these cases. You don't get on talk shows when the subtitle of your book is *The Abuse of Power and the Papacy of John Paul the Second* when that pope is in his last year of life and has Parkinson's. Everybody is saying he's a saint. So some of us have this problem.

AT: I'd like to conclude with, and certainly this is a topic that we could talk hours about, but I would like to talk to you a little bit. It's post-Katrina three years almost. And I can't think of anyone who is in a better position to offer some thoughts on what the storm has meant to the city of New Orleans in terms of its culture.

JB: I think there are two realities that have become numbingly apparent. One is that politically, the city is a horrendous failure. Nagin (Ray Nagin, mayor of New Orleans) is a narcissist beyond category who used the appeal of a demagogue in the Chocolate City speech to convey to Black voters that we need to keep city hall from the man. And he then got Al Sharpton and Jesse Jackson to bus people so that he could win. Let me just say parenthetically that Mitch Landrieu ran a horrendously boring campaign, not giving people a good reason to vote for him. Nevertheless, Nagin gets back in and proceeds to become invisible. No idea how to lead a genuine recovery, and has failed so badly, leaving so many people in these devastated neighborhoods with no place to go. He doesn't have the guts to hire a decent police chief. I could go on and on and on about how abominable a mayor he has been. Culturally, the city has seen a resurgence of the creative forces that in many ways endowed it with the better qualities that it had prior to the storm. In fact, I've done a piece for *Reader's Digest* that'll be out in September, probably late August on that very topic. Many of the musicians have returned. The literary community is quite intact. Quite a number of writers, as you've mentioned, have done books and more of them continue to. This is certainly one of the major literary cities of the United States. Small as it is, it's quite a flourishing colony of writers, our community of writers here.

AT: Let me interject this. A lot of people are armchair quarterbacks sitting back in Houston. People who have at least a deeper than passing knowledge of New Orleans say, you know, the culture of New Orleans was bottom up, rather than top down, and that it grew out of the African American community and the working class or poor communities. And that sounds like a sound argument. And they say these people are living in the exurbs of Houston and FEMA housing. They haven't come back.

JB: There is more than a grain of truth to that. But by the same token, Allan, it is important to remember that a lot of people from the second line culture have made it back and continue to come back. I went to a funeral maybe eight, ten months ago. And there's a woman standing there saying to a friend, "Well, baby, I've been living in San Antonio, and it costs me $750 every time I come back." And I made ten trips. I figure I'll be back by Christmas. You know, people, the people who were rooted here and have some degree of means, really have fought to come back against great odds. Now, let me just say, I certainly realize that a lot of criminals left and have wreaked havoc on other parts of the country, like Houston, like Atlanta. And we could digress and talk about, you know, why there was so much poverty and drug activity here. It is a smaller concentration of poverty, and the crime has returned almost with a vengeance. I guess what haunts me is how this sort of Social Darwinism is dictating the way the city moves. I mean, there's a huge reassembling of financial and real estate interests around the area of Tulane Avenue where they're going to build this VA hospital.

AT: This is where they want to wipe out a large area of Tremé, right?

JB: No, no, no, it's not Tremé. I'm sure this is going to be a big battle. They're probably going to try to wipe out a lot of this old working-class neighborhood, which is now composed of quite a number of homes that have been restored. It's an old German neighborhood. The plan to redevelop the riverfront is fine on paper, but ask yourself, for God's sake, why aren't we sinking money into Gentilly? Why aren't we sinking more money, more of the city's money, more of the state's money, into the Upper Ninth Ward? What are we going to do about the Lower Ninth Ward? No one has an answer for it. I mean, there are people living in scattershot areas surrounded by waist-high, tropical florabunda out there.

AT: Well, should some of these areas be green spaced?

JB: There's no leadership. No one has a plan. There is no viable plan for it. And you know, there are times, to be honest, where I feel embarrassed to be from this city. You see, I travel a lot in my work. I do a lot of lectures. I do a lot of research-driven projects. I'm on the road a fair amount. It used to be whenever I went to any place, you met people, you went to functions, you got invited to some dinner party. Where are you from? From New Orleans. Oh, I went to a wedding there. Oh, I went to Jazz Fest. What a great place. Now you say New Orleans. They look at you. They say, oh, I'm so sorry. And then people will say, well, what's it like and what they want you to say is well, we got hammered pretty bad but we're on the road to recovery. We're part of America. The truth is, we're the third world. This is a third-world city in the United States. And the political failures.

AT: They seem to have extended from every level. I mean, from local God knows to the White House, undeniably.

JB: Let's put both pieces in context here. When Katrina hit, government failed like a row of falling dominoes from George W. Bush to Kathleen Blanco to Ray Nagin. All three—national, state, local—were rife with failures. I mean, we proved that the country that put men on the moon could not rescue people in a flood. So once you stand back and pull the viewfinder back and get a wide angle shot on where we are today, there is a different reality that has set in. Congress, albeit belatedly, has been putting money into the Road Home program, which has had horrendous problems and bottled up funds. It's been a trickle rather than a rush of money coming to people who needed it in order to cover the uninsured losses. Slowly, I think it's gonna take another year for the resettlement of the urban fabric to become clear. The Ninth Ward is going to be a jungle for years to come. Nobody has the guts to go in and say to the people there, look, come to the other side of the Industrial Canal. Come live in a medium rise. Let us resettle you in a better neighborhood. We have no visionary plan to repair the exit housing stock that can be repaired. The school situation is surprisingly more promising. The Recovery School District was a bold, even radical move by the legislature, given how corrupt the Orleans Parish School Board was, or the management and administration of the school system, I should say, and some board members. Just to give you an idea, Congressman Jefferson, who's now indicted, his brother, Mose Jefferson, who's been his major factotum, made $900,000 persuading the Orleans Parish School Board to take a certain computer system. The president of the school board copped a plea, saying that she took a bribe from him of $140,000. So you've got the Jefferson machine, which is a really sleazy operation with many of its members now indicted. The remnants of the school board are still there, but it's a much smaller Orleans Parish School Board. The Recovery School District has taken over many of these schools. Some of them are doing better. This is a long road to reform. And then there are the KIPP and charter schools. So it's a sort of tripartite system with a lot of overlap or interlinking. It's tempting to say it's balkanized, but that has a pejorative meaning. My sense is a lot of people around the country are looking at it to see if it can work. The big problem with it is that you've got these educational consultants who come in at corporate rates and just make out like bandits with consulting fees that are off the charts. But even with that, we've got a better school system. What we don't have is a genuine social service net, to help the truly disadvantaged, to help those at risk. We've got a serious problem with gun violence and drugs, and obviously other cities do too, but when you have a city reduced by 40 percent of its population, everything becomes more up close and personal. How do you persuade young professionals to move into a city where there are not the kind of high functioning schools as easy to get into as in the suburbs of Philadelphia or certain parts of, I don't know, New York City or, places where there are decent public schools.

AT: How do the schools get that bad? I mean, even before the storms, we heard stories that were pretty alarming.

JB: The public school system was a horror show. There was a lot of corruption. I think some, like twenty-five or thirty people have been indicted. But it was a patronage hive.

AT: But I guess my question is, I mean, clearly you can't have a vibrant economy. You can't have a stable society if you have a rotten school system. And I'm wondering, how it got that way, how the public didn't rise up and say . . .

JB: You know, Allan, you're showing all of your journalistic and historian's smarts. The easy answer is for me to say, I have not done research on that, but I'll tell you what I think. This is a topic that is so explosive were it to be adequately investigated, I think for this reason. If you look at the history of urban political machines, you've got corruption that comes in waves. People go down, you got people with sweetheart deals. Somebody gets paid and you don't have to go to work okay. It happens. Nobody says it's good. But if a city is reasonably well functioning. . . . Look at Chicago. You go to Chicago, that is a very well-run city. Is there corruption in Chicago? You know, where does a bear go in the woods? Of course there is. But it is such a muscular economy that even with corruption at the fringes, it will roll on. What you had here was a city where Blacks assumed control or majority control of the political organism about 1978, and progressively so over the years it followed. And a couple of things happened during those years. There was a lot of corruption that sort of bubbled up from some of these ward groups that got greedy. I think the Jefferson family played a major role in this. And this is explosive because we're talking about African American politicians selling out their own people. I'm not saying it was only Blacks who did this, but sooner or later, I mean, you got to face it squarely. At the same time, the federal government slashed the available money that the city had relied on. And when the oil prices plunged, in the 1980s, there was a large out-migration of white-collar jobs. And then there was a third factor or fourth factor: Crack hit this city like a scriptural plague. So, you had the combination of loss of jobs, loss of productivity, money, and jobs, leaving the city, crime increasing on the streets, and this greedy, grubby political culture that was just spreading its tentacles. There is also a historic hostility among whites and middle-class Blacks to changing this regressive tax system so that you can put adequate money in schools and infrastructure and things like that. Well, when the hurricane hit, this was a failed city politically. Now having said all that, I think it is very important for the objective bystander to understand that this city was all but destroyed because of a federal agency, the Army Corps of Engineers, that did not do its job over many years. The Lower Ninth Ward would have flooded anyway, because of the Mississippi River Gulf Outlet, because of the erosion of the wetlands, because of oil companies. I mean, you know, there are a lot of reasons behind this, but that would have happened. The Lakeview area, my side yard, Broadmoor, and the areas that some of which took eight to ten feet, none of those areas would have been so damaged had the levees been properly built. They were poorly designed and badly built. And we're still struggling with that. What really burrows into my psyche is that we've got a governor now who ran as a conservative reformer. Bobby Jindal made his Faustian pact with the Christian right so that they're now pushing a closeted creationism bill, Intelligent Design. Restoring the coastline is not high on his list of priorities, nor is restoring the offshore areas that continue to erode. You know he wants more money from Congress. Great. Start doing something before you get it. I mean, why isn't that high on the list. I think what has happened is that New Orleans has become the bête noir of the legislature compared to other parts of the state. When I say the legislature, I don't mean the New Orleans delegation obviously. There's been a long resentment of the city as the Babylonian outpost at the bottom of America. The people from the Pentecostal woodlands look at us and just go, my God, you know. So where does a city like this go? How do we defend or protect ourselves against these future floods? Floods are in our history and in our future. I can take you out in the yard in a moment and show you the water line on the fence. I was so lucky it didn't get in the house. We're living on borrowed time.

AT: Your wetlands are eroding at an astounding pace.

JB: Sure, a football field I think every hour or something like that. I think what's going to happen is that we're going to end up here in the Gulf of Mexico, for all intents and realities, ten to twelve miles from the city. The only way to change it is by changing the course of the Mississippi River, so that [means] redirecting this levee system, rerouting the river south of Highway 90, so that much of that area can revert to wetlands, so we can reseed. Well, what do you do? How do you get communities to move? Everybody wants their piece of it. Nobody wants to say, yes, I understand. I need to take the buyout and move. Look at how they handled the Ninth Ward. Here you have a neighborhood. You have an area of poor people, many of whom have not come back. How do they go in and declare eminent domain when they can't find the titles to the land? I mean, it is a gigantic mess. And there's not a politician in this town with guts enough to tackle it. I think we'll have another flood. I hope it's not as bad as this one. I think it's inevitable. I also think, and I don't claim to be, Erasmus on the bayou, but I think it's inevitable that New York City will flood. I imagine Houston will. Floods are in our national future. That's just the nature of climate change and the fact that as a country, we are not engaging.

AT: We're in deep denial.

JB: We don't engage in disaster prevention, and we don't know how to handle postdisaster management. You know, when you think of the gigantic squandering of money that occurred here with FEMA coming in, I mean, they were putting up these blue tarps on people's roofs. The companies they subcontracted with to do that work were making out like bandits. They were companies like Halliburton, or like Shaw up in Baton Rouge. I mean, these companies specialize in postdisaster on-the-ground management, and they milk government. Where do we go? I don't know the answer. Culturally, the resilience of the city is a spectacle to behold. People are coming back. I was just putting together a list the other night of various CDs. There's a whole music of Katrina, as there has been, as you said, literature of Katrina. Not fiction for the most part. But all that said, I think people will be writing and singing and performing here until it sinks so deep that no one can live here. And if that does happen, then the place of the city and the memory of what remains will be exalted forevermore.

AT: You're the author of the piece in *The Boston Globe* about the new Pompeii. Well, let me put this bluntly. Do you think the United States is ready to see New Orleans go?

JB: Sure. Yeah. I think we're going to see this in years to come. And a lot of this, I think, stems from the selfishness of our generation, the baby boomers, people who had everything given to them and failed to. . . . I don't know how you change a mentality in which people want to blame the government and yet suck from the government and turn to the government when they need it. People don't want to pay taxes. They want all their vacations. And yet when something really bad happens, the first thing people want to do is make sure their yard is safe. I don't think the will is there nationally. Look, I'm sorry I'm being a little bit inchoate here. The biggest lesson of Katrina is that where the government failed and recoiled and withdrew, a surge of well-meaning Americans came to fill the gap. Tulane University is getting record numbers of people who want to come here because they want to be in New Orleans. They feel this is a place to be.

AT: To rebuild.

JB: Exactly. Yeah. It has become an outpost of hope. You know, there's so much bottled up, frustration mingled with optimism. How do we prove that we are the country that made such great strides historically, when we've been led by a president who's a selfish little fraternity boy who doesn't know how to lead. How do we regain some sense of national destiny in a time when, as we all know, there are huge problems, from climate change to terrorism in the Middle East? You can go right down the line. But to get back to your question, are people willing to let New Orleans go? I think politicians are. I think elected officials are. I think the legislature is in Baton Rouge. I think one of the things that happened is Congress looked to Louisiana and they saw Kathleen Blanco passing a pork bill, pork barrel budget, giving all this money to water parks or industrial parks in North Louisiana. Why the hell didn't they take $500 million and say, "Okay, New Orleans, we're going to give this to you. We're going to put it in a bank run by state and local banking officials. Rebuild your infrastructure. You need a billion. We're going to give you a billion and then make war with FEMA to get the money back." That's what a strong governor would have done. That's what a strong mayor would have done. Instead, you've got a governor who is in over her head, although an honest person and a decent person. Yes, she failed miserably on television. And you got a mayor of the city who is a chameleon, a narcissist. You could not ask for a worse political recipe. And look, I'm not somebody who believes in the great man theory of history. I think we have seen a diffused political topography here, a diffusion of failures spread over the political topography so that, if for argument's sake, let's say Mitch Landrieu runs again and wins. I think he's a bright guy. I think he's a capable guy. I think there's a decent chance that he could prove to be a forceful steward of the city's meager resources. The one chance that this city really has as the whole energy economy shifts is if we can genuinely repair the public schools. And I think it can happen if we can create a school system, we need to become a medical community, and we need an entertainment industry. Those are the two things that will make it work. We've got the rudiments of both. Farther along with the medical infrastructure, even though it hasn't been rebuilt yet. But I think that will come. You have a couple of high-powered medical researchers, physicians who do world-class research. You bring them here, they create departments here, and you're on the map. It can be done. You've got to have decent schools to do it. You have a clean city where the parks work, and you have to get crime under control. Crime fighting can be done. It's been proven in other cities. But the other piece, putting in entertainment, creating an entertainment industry is going to take foresight. It's going to take vision. I don't know if we have people here like that. The wild card is climate change. Will we flood again? If we flood again, can we manage the aftermath wisely? I mean, these are pretty big questions.

AT: Well, and the levee on the 17th Street Canal is still leaking, right? You have soggy ground.

JB: Yeah, the Army Corps desperately needs the equivalent of a GAO (Government Accountability Office). They need oversight. You also take the long view of history. Well, take this town, for example. I've been working on this long-term project. Everything I do is long term. It's a history of the city using burial traditions as the prism. And I've just finished a chapter about the colonial era. In 1788, almost 80 percent of the city burned to the ground. This was when the city was literally contained in the French Quarter. The governor, at the time, Esteban Miro, was a Spaniard. The city was under Spanish colonial authority from Havana at the time. Well, they did an extraordinary job of rebuilding the city—now, they had slave labor—so extraordinary that a visiting reporter from England wrote that New Orleans was one of the best managed cities in the country. In the spring of 1789, they got word that Carlos III of Spain, had died. The word comes by ship three or four months later. So what do they do? They put on a huge funeral procession. And the Cabildo scribes refer to the people we would consider the elite as the Illustrious Body. I love that phrase. The Illustrious Body congregates in the chapel of the hospital because the main church has burned [down] about eight months before. So it's a very hot day. And they've got this huge candelabra with these thick candles all lit. There is a canopy over the altar with more candles. The whole room is lit up by candle fire. And you've got the local establishment, all the important people, probably all a thousand of them, crowded into this tiny chapel. Everybody's burning up.

You can imagine people sweating under arms, getting drenched. And there they mourn the death of the king and tempt fate yet again. What happened? What would happen if that place caught fire? I mean, we are a bit like the Illustrious Body today. You know, what are we going to do? We're going to build medium rises along the river. Well, maybe it won't flood. I remember having dinner in Baton Rouge with Evan Cohen, editorial writer at *The New York Times*, in 2004. And he was talking to me about the perfect storm scenario. And the perfect storm scenario is that you get an epic Category 5 that comes in from the Gulf and comes up the river and you flood like a funnel with the water coming up the river. Well, that didn't happen. We know that Katrina came in slightly east, right. Hammered Slidell to the far east. But you know, even though the winds were huge here, we didn't get Katrina head on. And yet the water that came in was rolling sheets twenty feet high, higher than anything we've ever seen. Well, what are we doing three years later? We are one of the worst governed cities in the world. Not one of the best. True. We're not building water parks in the middle of a place that floods, but we're not getting money to the ground. And like those people in that chapel, with all of those candle fires aglow, we are tempting fate. We are tempting the gods, if you will, with the widespread political incompetence. That said, the resurgence of the musicians, of the writers, of the culture in general and the presence of so many of these idealistic young volunteers, is a story of humanity's better impulses and nobler aspirations. And I hope that side of it manages to carry the day.

Jason Berry: Church Whistleblower

Judy Ball / 2011

From *St. Anthony Messenger* 119, no. 5 (October 2011): 38–43.
Reprinted by permission of Sharon Lape.

Jason Berry doesn't mince words. It's not that he's impolite or rude. In fact, he's a soft-spoken Southern gentleman who is unfailingly gracious and considerate. But ask him a tough, direct question and you get a no-nonsense reply.

This is especially true when the topic at hand is the sins of the church—the church he belongs to and has written about for more than twenty-five years as an investigative reporter, primarily through books and newspaper and magazine articles.

Berry, sixty-two, was among the first US journalists to write about the incidence of clerical sex abuse in the Catholic Church. His groundbreaking and award-winning reporting, specifically about clergy sex abuse in his native Louisiana, was published in the *National Catholic Reporter* in 1985.

Seven years later, he published *Lead Us Not Into Temptation: Catholic Priests and the Sexual Abuse of Children*, the first major book on the subject. In 2004, he cowrote a book exposing the scandals surrounding Marcial Maciel Degollado, the late, now-disgraced founder of the Legionaries of Christ. Earlier this year, the Catholic Press Association of the United States and Canada honored Berry for updated newspaper articles on Degollado. Berry's reporting on the church has been years ahead of the rest.

Berry's new book, *Render unto Rome: The Secret Life of Money in the Catholic Church* (Crown Publishing Group), again finds him exposing the unsavory. This time, he shines the light on church financial practices, including how bishops manage money, as well as financial relations between Rome and the church in the United States. Berry leaves little untouched in his 400-page, extensively footnoted book.

The safety of the Sunday collection, the unprecedented numbers of parish closings and the selling of assets to help fund settlements of victims' abuse cases, the status of the Holy Father's special collection (Peter's Pence), the Vatican deficit: All come in for heavy scrutiny and review.

And then there are the men Berry names, including a retired cardinal who remains a higher-up in the Vatican. The US hierarchical figures he cites don't fare much better.

Berry isn't without hope, though. He offers constructive remedies and prescriptions in *Render unto Rome*. And he isn't single-minded. He has written about New Orleans jazz as well as its funeral traditions. He's produced documentaries and writes on culture for a variety of publications. His play, *Earl Long in Purgatory*, earned a Big Easy Best Original Work in Theatre.

But who is the Jason Berry who writes about the underside of the church? What impact have his years of research and writing had on his lifelong faith? How does he feel about the institutional church? Is he trying too hard to uncover its warts? By focusing so much of his professional energy on the Roman Catholic Church, is he saying or implying that churches of other denominations are without sin?

St. Anthony Messenger posed these questions and more a few months ago, when Berry was traveling the country to promote *Render unto Rome*. Berry's book tour brought him to Cincinnati, where he sat down with this reporter for a Q&A in the lobby of a downtown hotel. Later, he participated in a book-signing event and addressed a group at a nearby local bookstore. This article is based on his answers at both locations.

This magazine does not often print the views of such a strong critic of the church, but the editors feel that the fruits of his years of research and the important issues he confronts are worth putting before you, our readers, for your own consideration. And, as you will see, he's no "outside agitator." We make no claims about the accuracy of all of his book's assertions. But this journalist has been right before, on questions that were initially avoided by the Catholic media.

Question: Why don't we start with your relationship with the Catholic Church? Maybe you could begin with your religious upbringing and where you are today.

Answer: I grew up in New Orleans. My grandmother lived a short drive from my parents' house. Often I would go to her place on Friday nights and stay with her through the weekend. She was a Mexican Creole who had a very festive sense of faith. By the time I got to Jesuit High School in the mid-1960s, the Second Vatican Council had begun, and the civil rights movement was reaching high gear. I carried into my high school years a sense of rootedness about the faith but also a sense that the church was growing and changing, that the winds of modernity were blowing in. During and after my years at Georgetown [graduating in 1971], the church was the spiritual core of my life.

I don't think that changed until I stumbled onto the Gilbert Gauthe [clergy sex abuse] case in 1985. I was exposed to a range of information suggesting that this was not just going on in one diocese in Louisiana. I felt that this was a moral outrage that needed to be exposed and understood. I went through a period of mounting anger about what I learned.

Fast-forward to where I am now. Almost three years ago, my daughter Ariel died; she was seventeen. She had Down syndrome and was born with serious heart problems. [Berry is also the father of Simonette, aged twenty-six.] One of the things that keeps me anchored in the church is my parish, Mater Dolorosa in New Orleans. My pastor buried Ariel. Along the way I've also had help from a lot of priests who have gotten involved in the struggle of clergy sex abuse.

Q: What are the key points you are seeking to make in this book? What do you want readers to come away with?

A: We all need to question Peter's Pence, which is advertised as the collection for the Holy Father's charitable uses and determines where the money goes. The Vatican has released information about approximately 11 percent of the 2009 collection of $82 million; the rest is unaccounted for. What I learned during my research is that, for most of the last century, funds from Peter's Pence went to plug the Vatican's operating deficit. The Vatican Bank is not even listed as an asset on the financial records.

Secondly, we need to follow closely the wave of parish closings—an average of one church per week over the past fifteen years. The priest shortage is the primary reason. Demographic changes are relevant, too. So is the reality of costly abuse litigation.

A related issue is the use of suppression, the church-approved device by which a bishop literally seizes a parish and all of its assets for whatever uses he wants. In Ohio, for example, a bishop ordered a parish suppressed. When the parishioners raised $100,000 and hired an attorney [to keep it open], the bishop used almost $78,000 to pay his attorney to fight the parishioners. The court in that state ruled that the bishop owned the parish. When that decision was delivered, the bishop had the church torn down and used the parishioners' money to pay the legal fees. I see this as rank injustice and a moral outrage!

Another key theme in the book relates to embezzlements by priests and lay workers. Several years ago, the so-called Villanova Study was conducted by the university's graduate program for church management. Approximately 85 percent of respondents reported embezzlement of funds from the Sunday collection. In my book, I quote Michael W. Ryan, a retired US Postal Inspection Service manager and rock-ribbed Catholic who has studied this for more than twenty years. He estimates that, since 1965, the church has lost approximately $2 billion from the Sunday collection to embezzlement and theft.

Finally, a core theme of my book is that the Roman Catholic Church does not have an adequate justice system. Instead, we have these ancient tribunals at the Vatican that give bishops de facto immunity from prosecution. No matter what they do, the worst that can happen is they will "step down."

Q: How long did it take you to complete the book? Did it come easily?

A: It took about three years to complete. I had a lot of information and documents that had been revealed through litigation. By far, this is the most difficult thing I've ever done. Other books took longer, but they were written before the internet.

Q: Where did you travel to do your research? How difficult was it to get to the records you wanted to study and the people you wanted to contact?

A: I made trips [one or more] to Boston, Rome, St. Paul, Los Angeles, New York, and Cleveland. None of the US bishops would talk to me, but that came as no surprise. I did talk to one archbishop deeply off-the-record in Rome. Although my entire interview with him was on background, his interpretation of the Legionaries of Christ was instructive to me.

Q: Do you think the Catholic Church is being overly scrutinized by you and others in the media these days? Are other Churches/religious institutions getting a free pass?

A: I've done nine books, only three of them about the Church, and I have done other things in between them. It's not joyous; that's for sure. But with 1.2 billion members, the Catholic Church is the largest organization in the world, the largest faith in the world, and the largest church in the United States. Other churches do get scrutiny and coverage—Islam probably gets more coverage than any global faith—but when you have such blundering leadership as we have had, it's a wonder I haven't written more!

People say, "Why don't you get off it, do something else?" I would be happy to pack my bag on this tomorrow if I saw genuine change going on. I don't intend to make this topic my life's work, but at least for the moment, this is where I am.

Q: Did you learn anything new about the church in the writing of this book that stays with you?

A: It became clear to me in writing this book that, as Catholics, we really are shaped by a culture of passivity. It's not just "pray, pay, obey," as the old slogan goes. It's deeper than that. The biggest benefit the bishops have at this time is the apathy of the average Catholic. Most people go to church to hear the Gospel, to be comforted, to be part of the community. We are not disposed to think about the church as a political institution.

I think there is a parallel between the so-called Arab Spring and what's going on in the church. We are witnessing, I believe, the slow crumbling of the edifice of Catholic authority as we once knew it. We are living through the second Reformation. This one is coming from within—from Catholics who want justice from their own church.

Q: Could you cite a few key changes you see as important in light of your research? Are church leaders up to this kind of change?

A: First let me say that I'm not trying to turn the church into a democracy. The pope can maintain his sovereign powers and have a court system the way Great Britain does, something along the lines of a constitutional monarchy. That way, those bishops and cardinals who have disgraced the church so much would be subject to a basic code of legal reality. The pope has the power as the supreme pontiff to order an entire radical overhauling of the Vatican court system. It's not rocket science.

The bishops can easily adopt a nationwide policy to safeguard the collection plates. Just count the money after each collection on the weekend. Do a recount at the bank on Monday. It would involve a political battle internally, but the bishops could do it.

All dioceses should post transparent audited financial statements. Every parish should have an active financial council that shares financial decisions with the pastor. Already there are many great priests who function this way, who are collegial. But you have to have a system-wide approach. I would love nothing more than to see the church move in this direction.

These are problems that can be solved, but it takes men who are not afraid of the truth and of smart laypeople. So is there hope? Yes, if we heed the prophetic voices in our midst.

Q: What comes next? Another book?

A: I'm at a real crossroads. I may finish a book I started some time ago on the history of New Orleans burial traditions. Or I may turn to St. Catherine of Siena. I've been thinking about doing a biography of her.

"Tell Me About It"—Jason Berry at the Tennessee Williams Festival

Mark A. Folse / 2011

From *Toulouse Street—Odd Bits of Life in New Orleans*, March 24, 2011. Reprinted by permission.

Today I was working, but took a long lunch hour to see Jason Berry, a journalist who has also published a novel and a play on Earl K. Long and an excellent book on New Orleans music, *Up From the Cradle of Jazz*. One of the flaws of the "master classes" in the festival schedule is that they are not really master classes, but really featured lecturers, but Berry's "Finding the Nonfiction Narrative" was worth the price of admission just for the Earl K. Long anecdotes.

He spoke at length about the genesis of several of his works, including the play *Earl Long in Purgatory*, his book on New Orleans music and his forthcoming nonfiction book on Vatican finances. The cadences of speech have always been a large influence in his writing style, Berry said, a "primary lure" into writing.

He related an anecdote about a friend who worked in the Democratic cloakroom in the US Senate when Berry was at Georgetown University. His friend's job included answering the telephone and telling senators the agenda for that day on the Senate floor, and he would frequently do his best imitations of various Senators for Berry. The one that stuck in Berry's mind was Sen. Lloyd Bentson who, when the phone was answered would just say: "Tell me about it." The line stuck with him so long, he attributed that same line and manner on the phone to one of his characters in his novel about Louisiana politics, *Last of the Red Hot Poppas*.

Berry, who started out writing about politics, found inspiration for his fiction in reading Latin American magical realists, citing Gabriel García Márquez and Mario Vargas Llosa: "they were writing about where I live" was his immediate reaction, and he cited a *Paris Review* interview with

García Márquez in which that author spoke of his experience reading William Faulkner and finding techniques for describing a world at once as imaginary and real as Faulkner's Yoknapatawpha County.

He traced his interest in Louisiana's bizarre politics and Earl K. Long in particular to his introduction to politics as a young boy by his father, who called him in one night to see Long on television, "a man in a wheelchair flanked by two state troopers being dragged into a mental institution and (WDSU-TV) Channel Six was bleeping out the curse worlds. My father said, 'This is your governor.'"

Berry also spoke about the reissue of *Up From the Cradle of Jazz* by University of Louisiana Lafayette Press, and the 110 pages he added to the new edition focusing on musicians in the aftermath of Hurricane Katrina, starting from the lyrics of songs written in the aftermath. "What I tried to capture was the resilience of the musicians, and the writers and visual artists," Berry said. Calling out both the White House and city hall, he said, "Government failed and culture prevailed." The recovery of the city was closely tied to the determination of perhaps five thousand musicians and cultural workers, without whom the city would never have recovered, he explained.

He began the new chapter starting from lyrics to songs written after the storm, which he said were primary sources for the expanded edition, "as valid as the depositions and other legal documents that I used in the book about the [Catholic] Church." He did not limit himself just to musicians, such as his friend clarinetist and educator Dr. Michael White, but to other cultural contributors, including Mardi Gras Indian Chief Donald Harrison Sr.'s wife Herreast who was a fifth-generation quilter. It was the cultural leaders and their commitment to return to the city that made the recovery for everyone else, for "all the service industries that depend on them" possible.

Berry finished up by regaling the crowd with wonderful stories of the past misdeeds of bishops and others Catholic clergy that came up during his early research in his forthcoming book on the finances of the Catholic church, but the red meat in his lecture was, for Toulouse Street at least, in his discussion of Earl Long and the role of musicians in the city's recovery.

Rockburn Presents: Jason Berry

Ken Rockburn / 2012

From *Rockburn Presents*, a program of the Cable Public Affairs Channel (CPAC). A transcript from the program that originally aired on CPAC is printed by permission.

Ken Rockburn: Jason Berry single-handedly touched off the firestorm of controversy over sexual predators in the Catholic Church with his 1992 book *Lead Us Not Into Temptation*. The freelance investigative reporter has followed up with award-winning books on the massive cover-up by the church and two popes. He's also a jazz writer of distinction who watched music become a salvation of his hometown after the devastation of Hurricane Katrina. We met Jason Berry in New Orleans.

Jason, New Orleans is a polyglot place, and I was thinking as I was getting ready to talk to you that, in a way, your family background fits in perfectly with what New Orleans is. Your background is diverse to say the least isn't it?

Jason Berry: It is indeed. My great-grandmother came from Veracruz in the 1920s and then moved to Texas. My mother grew up in Texas and came here during the war. My dad was from Arkansas, and they met here. So I've got Irish and Mexican on one side, and I guess my dad was sort of an Arkansas Huguenot who came south. You know, growing up in a town like this, you appreciate diversity, as we now call it. As a very slow sort of process when you come of age in a place where the grown-ups wear masks and dance in the streets and you see Black men wearing grass skirts and blackface on top of floats giving out gilded coconuts at Carnival time, it sort of plants a certain optimism about the human experiment.

KR: [*Laughter*] Yeah, that's a nice way to put it, an optimism about the human spirit. Tell me a little bit about growing up in this town. I mean, as I've told you, I've been here a number of times and I think one of the reasons that I like it, probably many people do, is it seems, if I can quote Mark Noffler, it is the planet of New Orleans. I mean it does seem like its own place. Growing up, what was it like?

JB: It was a magical place frankly to be a kid in and not just because of Mardi Gras and the parades during the years, but it was a sort of place where one rubbed elbows with people of different colors and you didn't think that much of it until you got old enough to realize that segregation was the law. I can remember as a child riding the streetcar with my grandmother and the sign that said, "Colored Only," you know, sitting in the back, whites in the front, and gradually as a young person learn to wonder about that. And I suppose I was about ten or maybe a little bit older when the civil rights movement erupted and I can remember sitting in the living room with my parents watching on television as mobs at city hall were in a near riot stage saying "2, 4, 6, 8, we don't want to integrate!" Of course, we had had Black people who worked for our family, a woman from Honduras who came and lived with us, and it was such a jarring image of the city that seemed so kind and serene in its racial relations. Obviously, by the time I got older and got to know Black people, I realized that there was a whole hidden history that I was unaware of. But I think Mardi Gras had a lot to do with a kind of softening of the jagged edges between the races that you find in many other parts of the South during that period.

KR: Do you recall at all being shocked when you discovered that maybe the city you knew as you were growing up had another side to it that you were that you may not have been aware of?

JB: Yes, but it happened later. I got out of college, well I went to Jesuit High School in the 1960s, and there were probably seven or eight African American guys in my graduating class although we didn't use that term at that time. And you know the two overarching issues of that period in my life were the civil rights movement that was happening every night on television and the Second Vatican Council in Rome that was changing an institution nearly two thousand years old. By the time I got out of Georgetown in 1971, the civil rights movement had seen its crest. I went to Mississippi to work for a Black candidate for governor, Charles Evers. When I came back to New Orleans in 1972 and got to work on my first book, it was at that point that I really took a much harder, deeper look at where I had grown up and where I decided ultimately that I would come back and live. So these sorts of things creep gradually upon one's psyche, and I think the main thing that I sort of carried out of those years was the realization that Black people looked at us in a certain way, but didn't always articulate what they felt and white people, in contrast, once the law changed, wanted very much to feel innocent, and I was never particularly comfortable with the innocence.

KR: So tell me, the beginning of your work with Charles Evers led to a book that you wrote about him. Were you always inclined to go in that direction? Is that the career path you planned for yourself to start doing that sort of writing?

JB: Not exactly. I wanted to be a writer. My mother read to me a great deal. I lived in a house with books. I was a voracious reader. I wrote stories as a kid coming up. I would go see science fiction movies and get frightened by them, come home, and write out my version of them. Plagiarism at an early age. I actually won a short story award or came in second in high school, and I wrote for the campus newspaper in college. I wanted to go back to the South, but I wanted to make a difference. You know I had marched in demonstrations. I went through Georgetown in the middle of the revolution. I had one foot planted in the great books and the other was out marching at demonstrations. So, when I realized that Evers was going to run for governor, I knew someone in Mississippi who was close to someone who knew him, three degrees of separation, and so I just drove down there after college and presented myself as a volunteer. He and I had an immediate kind of spark. He liked me, I liked him, and so I got hired for $75 a week as the press secretary and it was a life-defining experience. I spent six months traveling through Mississippi looking at the world through the lenses of Black people and it changed me dramatically.

KR: That's astonishing that they would hire you as press secretary straight out of college in what would be ultimately a controversial milieu. I mean that's amazing.

JB: Well, he liked the idea that I was white, he loved the idea that I was from New Orleans, and he kept saying, "Well, you went to an Ivy League school." It's not an Ivy League school. It's a good school, but anyway, he and I just had a natural rapport, and you know I learned in that campaign so much about the difficulty in negotiating relationships with people of color. Today in society we take it as something for granted that you work in a diverse workplace for example, and people have to get along. But it was very much an experience that gave me a much broader viewfinder on life as it is actually lived. I moved back to New Orleans, and I spent about a year kicking around Europe on the advance money from the book *Amazing Grace*. The book came out. It was well reviewed, but certainly was not a bestseller, and then I decided to move back. I hadn't lived here in a number of years. I'd gone off to college, I'd spent the time in Mississippi, and I sort of discovered the city all over again in a very different way. I discovered the funeral parades, the second lines, the jazz clubs. I lived in a little apartment in the Irish Channel, and in a way, it was such a different existence than the rather ordinary middle-class upbringing I'd had. And it had its glue, it had its adhesive qualities, and I've gone off, come back, gone off, and I've been here for some time

KR: How were you making a living at the time?

JB: Oh I was a freelance writer from the time I started. There were two alternative weeklies here at the time competing—*Figaro* and the *Vieux Carre Courier*. I wrote for both of them. I wrote for *New Orleans Magazine*. I'm probably the oldest living person who has written for *New Orleans Magazine* I'm chagrined to say, and I started getting published in national outlets, *The Nation* magazine, *The Washington Star*, the *Village Voice*, *Southern Exposure*, places like that. I also was fortunate in getting grants from the Fund for Investigative Journalism in Washington, which helped me with the early work I did on the IRS harassing civil rights leaders and emerging Black politicians. That was in the 1970s, and then from there, I branched out and did a lot of environmental reporting about politicians in Louisiana who were making money on toxic waste pit deals and—

KR: What goes around comes around.

JB: What goes around comes around in an endless gyre, to borrow from Yeats. And in the middle of that, I realized how deeply the music was a part of my life. When I was growing up, Art and Aaron Neville sang together as a duo, Irma Thomas would play for the CYO proms and dances. Tommy Ridgely and the Untouchables, Deacon John and the Ivories-these are celebrities I would hear on the radio. There was such a human dimension to the music. It took me years to figure out that they were singing stories of the city. I used to go home from football practice, and you can imagine four guys densely packed in a little car, we're all sweaty, and we always caught the end of the Shelly Pope show on WBOK, the soul station. And he would always end by saying, "My darling the cocktail hour has come to an end," and you hear the tinkling of glass, and mind you we're sixteen-year-old guys in a car and you hear this just resonant Black voice saying, "The cocktail party has come to an end my dear, I am sad to see you go but I would do anything for your love. I would even swim the gasoline river with torches held high in both of my hands for your love," and then you get the drum roll and you're out and you get the evening news [*laughter*]. I mean when you grow up in a place like that, as I say, it plants a certain optimism about human relations.

KR: No kidding.

JB: So I started not knowing anything about music except that I loved it and grew up dancing to R&B. When I started writing articles about musicians, it just sort of came naturally, but what was so different now was that I was learning the back stories, the histories of these people. I would go often and spend three or four hours with a tape recorder jotting notes, not really sure where all this was going beyond a thousand-word profile. Gradually, as you know, I got that baseline of interviews, branched out into video work, and did my first film, *Up From the Cradle of Jazz.*

KR: Okay I want to come back to the music thing afterwards, but I want to talk now about the other side of this because there is this two-sided nature of the work that you do. At what point did you start applying your investigative journalistic techniques to looking at what was going on in the Catholic Church? I mean you did a story early on about a priest in Lafayette right, was that the first?

JB: Well, that came a little later. I was finishing *Up From the Cradle of Jazz*, the first edition of that book, and I was also at work on a novel and very much wanted to finish it. And then I got access to read the deposition of the bishop who had recycled this pedophile to a great many parishes. Mind you this was at the end of 1984, nothing remotely suggesting a scandal of this magnitude on the Catholic Church was on the national radar screen at that time. So I got an assignment, a joint assignment from the *Times of Acadiana*, a weekly paper in Lafayette, the hub of Cajun country, and the *National Catholic Reporter*, which is an independent weekly in Kansas City. I should add I had pitched *The New York Times Magazine.* I just did a piece for them. They said no. I tried everybody: *Mother Jones, Vanity Fair,* even the *Nation.* Everybody said no, we don't want it. And so I did this three-part series that got a lot of national attention, and soon along I started getting leads from other parts of the country. The story that drew me was not that one man could be pathologically ill and sexually focused on children and happened to be a priest. Priests are human beings as we all are. Remember this is ten years after Watergate. It was really what the bishop knew, when he knew it, and why he kept moving this man around. That story has now become a cliche in news coverage, but at that time no one else had done it. It took a long time to get all the facts. I had a lot of priests who interestingly gave me information and several nuns, so when the series came out, it hit hard and got a lot of ripple effects, and then I ended up working on a book, which took seven years to do.

KR: Yeah, now tell me a little bit about that because when you talk about getting information from other priests and nuns and so on, was this information that was offered up to you in a kind of clandestine surreptitious manner, or were people being forthright about it or was it something that was so upsetting to them that they didn't want to be on the record? I mean I'm assuming that it was difficult to dig out stuff.

JB: It was laborious. I spent hours every day on the phone, six, eight, ten hours a day on the phone. Most of the priests and nuns I interviewed only agreed to do it on a background basis; they didn't want their names used for fear of retribution. There was also a lot of information that had come out through the legal process through these civil lawsuits, so I was able to get certain names and then ask about the names in these documents, and you know, the deeper I got into it, the more I realized that there was this hidden world that I had no idea about. I'd had quite benevolent experiences with the nuns and priests who taught me coming up. I had friendships with several of them, and in fact, as I got into the reporting, I even went back to a couple of the Jesuits I knew, just to have sort of baseline conversations. I remember one guy very, very clearly saying to me, this has to come out, you've got to get it out.

KR: So a lot of these people didn't want to speak to you obviously for obvious reasons, but getting the material, well I guess what I really want to ask you is what did this do to you and your faith as you began to see the extent of some of this stuff?

JB: Well, it's a struggle that's still going on, to be candid. In the beginning, I was very angry and at some points almost furious. I remember spending an afternoon in Lafayette interviewing five women who were siblings who had all been systematically abused one right after the other chronologically by a priest, a guy named John Engbers, a Dutchman who had been an art teacher in this little Cajun community. And after spending the entire day with their attorney just taking down their stories, watching their body language, listening to the choked voices, sheets of cigarette smoke, people pacing, you know, I wrote the story. I guess it was one or two nights later, and I was just so enraged at this man, and so I went to see a therapist to talk about the anger. I managed to get through it. I had had an upbringing very much in harmony with the faith. My great-grandmother from Veracruz, who I guess I was fifteen when she died, and her daughter, my grandmother with whom I was very close, had such a festive idea of faith. Lighting the candles, the memory I had of bells and of just the serenity of sitting with those women during the services. My mother was often there, my dad joined the church much later on, but comparing that and the rigorous idea of faith I'd gotten from the Jesuit priests in high school who stressed this idea that faith and reason need not collide, that one could embrace science and have a healthy idea of your own spiritual life—all of that was just swimming around as I got deeper and deeper into this corrupt depth of the church. And it took a long time to work out and I think a lot of it in a way had to do with the birth of my second child. My younger daughter Ariel was born with Down syndrome in 1991, and I had to immediately embrace the idea that this precious little infant was going to be retarded and would need a lot of help and work and you know I just went back to church. I prayed a great deal for her health and for her survival.

KR: So your faith sustained you during this?

JB: Yeah it did. I didn't have any place else to go. I mean a situation like that, I guess one either becomes angry and disillusioned and embittered, or you embrace what comes your way and you know, put on your sunglasses and go through life. As Ariel got older, watching her consciousness slowly bud and the beautiful love that her sister, my older daughter Simonette, had for her little sister, all of that was part of a spiritual aura that I moved in. When I published the book in 1992, *Lead Us Not Into Temptation*, which was my third book, Ariel was just a year old, Simonette I guess was seven and a half by then, and as my little one got older, we got prognoses that were not good at all. By the time she was ten, we were told she had six months to two years, and when you have nowhere else to go metaphorically but on your knees, gradually the prayers get answered. I mean she lived past one hospitalization and another and another. And there were a lot of people praying for her. My wife and I had parted ways, I guess it was '94, '95 amicably. We coparented very closely. But that child was so deeply a part of—well both my kids were—that when you pray for someone to live and the child lives it's kind of hard to go storming out of the cathedral so to speak. I think the other thing that sustained me in a sense was the realization that a lot of people in the church were reaching out to me. I had a lot of priests and nuns who were giving me information, who were sending me emails and letters saying you're doing the right thing. Even though I came to feel that a lot of the bishops were sort of like gangsters, I didn't want those bishops to rob me of an essence of myself and to take something from me that had matured in other respects quite nicely.

KR: As you're describing that, I'm trying to imagine what it would be like or what it must have been like for you at that time. The book comes out, *Lead Us Not Into Temptation*, that's like the match lit to the end of the fuse that starts what we still see going on today. So you have the impact you have of your daughter going through this, your marriage falls apart, and you're the repository on a continual basis of more information that will become the source of other books that you will write. I can't imagine how you could.

I'm assuming, it had to have been the faith that got you through all of that because that seems like an overwhelming confluence of events and circumstances for most people.

JB: It was a tough period. In '92, I was on every television program in this country and made a few stops in Toronto and was nicely received by the CBC. You know looking back on it, I had no idea that the two years following that would be so difficult, but they were, and yeah faith was sustaining. I don't want to sound trite, but the music was also very important to me. I spent a lot of time going to Black churches listening to gospel music. In fact, one of the things that really kind of renewed my own faith back in 1971 in Mississippi, a lot of the campaign tours went to these small Black churches retracing the geography of the civil rights movement if you will, and listening to those choirs sing "Amazing Grace," "Oh What a Friend We Have in Jesus," "Jesus on the Main Line," there's such an intense personal connection with the savior in the Black tradition that is quite foreign to the Catholicism of my youth where we had the Latin mass. There's more of an austerity, or a serene kind of a nobility associated with it, but I was kind of moving between those two cultural spheres, and often I would end up doing a story spending an afternoon or a morning in a Gospel Church, and I just left feeling [like] there is a plan here. I don't know where I fit in, but I'm not being brought to my knees every night. and you just sort of get through. What I learned about the Catholic Church in those first seven years, on a certain level, I don't want to say it was frightening, but it was so deeply demoralizing, and I realized that it was very important for me to be living in this town where the flow of life percolated to streams of music, and every time someone died and there was a jazz funeral, I could go there and feel the tides of a resurrection sensibility and redemption that came in the form of music, not just prayer. All of that was very sustaining to me and it gave me a deeper sense of my own rootedness. And it was quite important to have that while writing about those other kinds of things.

KR: All right, you went on to write about one man in particular who became kind of a flashpoint for a lot of what you had written about before, Maciel. He was a bishop?

JB: No, he was the founder of the Legionaries—

KR: Legionaries of Christ right, the religious order, but fully integrated and ensconced within the Roman Catholic Church hierarchy.

JB: Within the Vatican Curia, yes.

KR: Tell me a little bit about how you got on to that story and where that ended up leading you.

JB: Sure. I got a call from Arturo Jurado, a Mexican national, who was teaching at the Defense Languages Institute in Monterey, California. When he introduced himself and told me where he worked, the first thing I thought was okay, he's got a defense clearance or National Security clearance in order to work, and it's the Defense Languages School that teaches people for the CIA, and the Defense Department. I've also learned they teach anchor people from TV stations in California but it's a place that largely historically has taught members of the American government who are going to go overseas. He told me this utterly baroque story about how he and these other young boys from Mexico had gone to Spain in this seminary and had been completely worked over sexually by this powerful priest, who at that time was very close to the pope. Frankly, at that point in time, I didn't want to write about this anymore. I had done my book and I felt like Cincinnatus looking for the plow. I said, "Okay, well send me documents, send me what you have." He did. There were nine long notarized statements, all but one of them in Spanish. I read Spanish reasonably well so I understood exactly what they were saying and on top of it was a letter in English by one of these men, Juan Vaca, who by this time was a psychology professor in Long Island who had long since left religious life, had written to Pope John Paul II saying I was abused repeatedly as a young man. In his 1989 letter, he was requesting to be released from his vows so he could marry. I'm reading this letter five years after he left religious life. I got on the phone and called him, and Juan was very uneasy about discussing it over the phone. I could hear the emotion and the tremors in his voice. We got through the interview.

JB: After more discussions with these guys, I started making pitches to different magazines, to several networks, and it was just like in 1984. I got nowhere. Well, in this case it literally led to John Paul II. And then one day, I got a call from Jerry Renner, who was the religion reporter for the *Hartford Courant* in Hartford, Connecticut. Jerry and I knew each other passingly, I'd met him at conferences, he'd written a very nice review of my book, so I was disposed to like him. He told me that he had done a couple of articles on this obscure religious order, the Legion of Christ, which had its American headquarters in Connecticut, and asked if I knew anything about it. I said, actually I do, I've got a lot of information on the founder. He's in fact an accused pedophile. And so, we embarked several months thereafter, he had to do some internal positioning, but he got us a joint assignment. I went to Mexico City. I interviewed six of the guys among others. He interviewed Vaca and another priest who was in the United States. So we had on-the-record statements, very long statements, from these men, and we couldn't get Maciel to talk to us. He claimed innocence but hired a law firm to try to get the newspaper to kill the story. The newspaper published the story. The Vatican refused to make any comment, and the rest of the press really sort of left it alone. It was one of those 7,500-word articles that just goes out there. Who knows why other people don't pick up on big stories? It does happen.

KR: Happens all the time.

JB: Yes, and the AP in New York did not put it on the international wire because they considered it a Connecticut story. Ah, the sophistries of wire services. The Mexican Press jumped on it: *La Jornada*, which is a daily. A cable station in Mexico City did a documentary. So it started bubbling up, but nothing really happened, and then a year later, Jose Barba, a college professor in Mexico City with a doctorate from Harvard, who was one of these nine men, went to Rome with Jurado, the man I had originally spoken with, and they filed a case with Cardinal Ratzinger, asking for canon law to excommunicate Father Maciel.

KR: Cardinal Ratzinger now being Benedict now, right?

JB: Yes, of course, Ratzinger later became Pope Benedict the XVI. It hung there for several years. Nothing was happening. I was shooting out these op-eds that were hitting like a tree in the forest that nobody hears. And then Boston broke. *The Boston Globe* started their big series. It was like a media chain reaction. Within two and a half months, Jerry and I had a book contract. *Vows of Silence*, the book, came out in 2004, and it goes into substantial depth, not just on the whole myth of Maciel's career. A lot of his career biography, we found out, was completely fabricated. It really came down pretty hard on Ratzinger and John Paul for not prosecuting the guy. Mind you, by this time in 2002, the American bishops adopted a Youth Protection Charter. The Vatican, to this day, has no Youth Protection Charter. Had Maciel been an American priest, by 2003, he would've been yanked. So here he is in the Vatican, basically being sheltered from prosecution. After the book came out, I kept waiting for the shoe to fall, for something to happen, and by the spring of 2004, I thought this is crazy, I'm gonna make a film, something's gotta happen. So I got a few people to grubstake me some money, and I started interviewing these guys. I hadn't done a film in almost fifteen years. Low and behold, five months before John Paul's death, Ratzinger breaks ranks with Cardinal Sodano, the Secretary of State who had kept a lid on this thing, and I got into this in both the film and *Render unto Rome* in great depth. Sodano is this Machiavellian figure who did everything he could, including accepting $15,000 cash, for saying Mass for the Legion of Christ, to prevent Maciel from being prosecuted. At this point, I felt like

I'm on the longest limb you could possibly be on. I do not hear *The New York Times* coming behind me. I do not hear anybody else raising a ruckus. But my lord, something is really wrong here. You've got nine guys who have gone on the record. Why isn't the Vatican doing something to this guy? Finally, Ratzinger orders an investigation. Sodano still tries to meddle with the investigation. And finally, Benedict succeeds John Paul as pope, and then in 2006, he banished Maciel from active ministry to a life of prayer and repentance, penitence. And I'm still struggling to finish my movie, which I did get out in 2008, but the Lord does write straight with crooked lines sometimes, because he leaves Rome, he goes to Mexico, a year and a half later, he dies. The Legion announces on his website that the founder has gone to Heaven. Now mind you, up until 2006, I was getting attacked on the Legion website. So was Jerry Renner, but more so, so were these men, the victims. There was quite a lineup of defenders of Maciel: Father Richard John Neuhaus, the publisher of *First Things* magazine, Bill Bennet, the CNN morals commentator, George Weigel, papal biographer, Mary Ann Glendon, who later became an ambassador to the Vatican. All these people have their own careers on the line. Well, after Maciel dies, a year later, the Order announces, somehow, they discover that he actually had a twenty-three-year-old daughter. And then it came out that he had two sons by another woman. Benedict then ordered an entire investigation of the Legion of Christ. The order is now in a kind of receivership. Maciel has been completely discredited. It took ten years. I was doing other things during those years—published a novel, did the film—but when you follow these things, I have learned, you don't expect immediate gratification. But now, I would say in modesty that a lot of the members of the national media recognize that the story Renner and I did, and the story I continued after Jerry's death, sadly in 2007, I dedicated the new book to him, saw justice in a rough sort of sense, prevail.

KR: Let me quote from the end of the new book, *Render unto Rome*, which is about money in the Catholic Church, so you're taking it even one step further. I just wanted to read this quote and get you to comment on this. You write, "the culture of passivity by which most Catholics receive the sacraments and give their dollars is a bedrock. As long as the people ask no questions about their money, the bishops can ban reformers from church grounds. The issue is not faith, but fear that people might see where the money goes." And you go on to talk about the beatification of John Paul, and you say, "Why beatify a Pope whose faith in Maciel and myopia on the abuse crisis left a trail of human carnage? The rush to spectacle can not airbrush facts from history." I have to assume that what you have written in this book and the others has resulted in. . . . I know there are attacks on you on the internet, it doesn't take much to find them, they're all over the place . . .

JB: Let me respond to that. Huey Long famously said that it's important to cultivate the right enemies.

KR: [*Laughs*]

JB: I don't actively seek enemies, but yeah, I get slammed a lot.

KR: Have you been threatened, during all of this?

JB: No. Only legally. [*Laughs*]

KR: And your response to the attacks? That doesn't bother you? I know people are questioning your faith.

JB: This is a tough topic. This is a game changer. This is a threshold issue, and I never thought it would take so long to get the works into print. The first book was rejected by thirty publishers. They were all afraid of it. Finally, it was the religion editor at Doubleday who accepted it. After Renner and I did the big investigative piece in the Hartford paper, we went all over New York trying to get a contract. We couldn't. Then when *The Boston Globe* did their series, suddenly we got a contract. I'm used to pushing uphill: Sisyphus with his shoulder to the stone. But I feel that I have found a plateau, and the bruise is lessening a bit. I'm standing upright, and I have information. Reasonable people have come to the conclusion that I was right, and that I'm not a barn burner, and that I want the church to reform so that the purity of faith can endure, as it should.

KR: Earlier in our conversation, you talked about how the music also sustained you during this. For the remainder of our conversation, I want to talk about music and this city. Also about the impact that Hurricane Katrina had on this city, and also the impact that the oil spill had on the city because that's the other big disaster that happened. And I'm thinking perhaps we can go out to a part of the city where the effect can be seen, where it might be more appropriate to talk about it. Are you up for that?

JB: If I can leave my coat here.

KR: You can. Alright let's do it—[*in front of Fats Domino's shuttered house*].

So Jason, this is the Lower Ninth Ward, and this is the area of New Orleans that really took the big hit from Hurricane Katrina. We were talking about the culture of this city and the music of this city being integral to the way the city has come back from that horrible disaster. I want you to tell me first about this neighborhood and how bad things were for the people here and what this neighborhood represented pre-Katrina as well.

JB: Well, the Lower Ninth Ward had a kind of mythical status within the city for years as heavily African American working class, thick with marching bands, jazz funerals, Mardi Gras Indians, the fabric of the city that is now being extolled in the *Tremé* TV series. It was also a place with a lot of crime, a lot of drugs . . . it was a rough and tumble outback to the city proper, and historically always had been. Back in the 1940s–'50s, parts of this area were open fields where people would go out and shoot squirrels, opossums, muskrats, things like that. So, it's the place where the blurring lines of a rural and urban culture slowly congealed, and it really had no national profile or status at all until the hurricane, when suddenly all over the world, people were watching these poor folks on top of their rooftops in New Orleans. And this is where the flooding was heaviest. There were many other neighborhoods that got hit just as bad, but they didn't get the media attention. We are standing just across from the house where Fats Domino lived for decades, where he and his wife Rosemary raised eight children. Adonica, Anatoly, Antoine III, every child's first name with an A . . . they were evacuated by local authorities with seven feet of water in the house. He went to the Superdome, spent two nights there, and then they were sent to Baton Rouge where some relatives took them in. It's been very sad because the neighborhood where he lived has a sort of lordly presence, but much beloved, has now taken an enormous beating, as you can see. Less than a fifth of the houses have come back.

KR: Where we are standing right now, which is in the parking lot of a now-shuttered supermarket across from Fats Domino's house. You're saying there was seven feet of water right here.

JB: At least seven feet. When people evacuated there was seven feet. In some parts of this area there was ten to twelve feet.

KR: Unbelievable.

JB: It really is. It flooded for two reasons. The first reason was the industrial canal, which bisects the Ninth Ward into the Upper and Lower sections, took a big hit when a barge became unmoored and literally smashed through the floodwall of the canal, and water just came pouring in. The other reason was the water coming in from the Gulf. The storm surges that Katrina pushed; [there were] waves as high as fifteen to twenty feet. There used to be a huge cypress water forest that lay between this area and the wetlands to the south, but in the 1960s, the federal government, with the leadership of Louisiana's political establishment, carved a long navigational canal from the river to the gulf, which later proved to be almost useless, but it destroyed a huge swath of wetlands which historically were buffers to the hurricanes. So now they are filling in the Mississippi River Gulf Outlet, as it is known. No one knows how long it will take for the wetlands to become renourished and replenished.

KR: You wrote a column once, I'm assuming it was in *New Orleans Magazine*, where you talked about being out on a book tour. Every author knows the horribleness of a book tour where you're going from hotel to hotel and doing interview after interview. You wrote how the music of this city followed you. Wherever you went, you were finding different versions of it, including Fats. That to me suggested the depth of the effect of the music that comes out of New Orleans on everywhere else, even in our country, even in Canada.

JB: I was in Boston, and I heard Johnny Adams singing a blues song in a hotel. One of the airports, I heard Fats, another I heard Louis Armstrong in a recording. The way the music has become a kind of soundtrack to our lives in this city has a great metaphysical pull, and it does follow us, because one can go almost anywhere, and invariably a New Orleans song will show up on a jukebox, if they still have them, or on the soundtrack at a bar or a restaurant. Especially since the flood, this city came back because of the musicians. The politics failed in the first year after Katrina. It was really the return of the musical culture that put the tourist economy back on its legs, that got the media interested and reporting a story other than the post-mortem of a disaster. When the Jazz and Heritage Festival was held in 2006, many of the artists still had not come back to houses. They were still trying to repair them and get back. It's not just the resilience, but that deep and rooted sense of place that drew so many of us musicians and ordinary folk alike back to the town.

KR: You said in that final chapter of the updated version of *Up From the Cradle of Jazz*, you have at the very beginning, "Politics failed. Culture prevailed." That's true, isn't it? That's what it all comes down to.

JB: I think so. I haven't had anybody throw a brick at me for saying it yet. Of course, in this town, anything's possible. When you live in a city that for much of its recent history has just been cursed by either incompetent or corrupt leadership, you sort of learn to shrug and move on with your life when you don't have the power to do much more. I tried for eight years to get a culvert in front of my house fixed so the front of the house wouldn't flood. This was before Katrina. You send letters to the city councilman, they don't even answer. It has changed. I think we have a rising civic ethos, and we have an excellent mayor now in Mitch Landrieu, who is far and away superior to Nagin, the mayor we had before and right after the flood, who was just a disaster on wheels. It's really the force of the music as a part of the cultural sensibility, not to mention the many artists and painters who live here. This is the third largest art market per capita in the US, after New

York and LA. It's a much smaller city, but we've got close to 150 galleries now and several prominent museums. It's become a writer's colony as well. New Orleans is here because the people who have returned or moved here are here by choice, and I think that's one of the best indicators of the overall health of the town.

KR: One of the things that I thought was the most interesting was the fact that because of Katrina, a lot of people just made the assumption that that was the end of New Orleans. And there were people who wanted it to be the end of New Orleans. That it was just as well that it was gone, and if it wasn't going to go away, that it was going to come back as a completely different incarnation.

JB: Congressman Richard Baker from Baton Rouge made the notorious statement that "God finally did what we could not," meaning that all of the poor people in the housing projects had left. There was a concerted effort to tear down the projects to keep the urban poor from returning. Many of these people are what we call tradition bearers: the people who are in the Mardi Gras Indian gangs, the people who make their costumes for the Social Aid and Pleasure clubs and parade through the city every weekend from September into June. There is a culture that people in poverty made here that is now extolled by the tourist industry, that is now part of the musical sensibility. You can't just drive people out because they don't have the same amount of money as folks who live on St. Charles Avenue, or where I live. And yet, there was an obscene political effort to do that. It caused tremendous racial divisions. The bottom line is that roughly 100,000 people of the population have yet to return, many are slowly returning, crime has returned, but as a city, we've got to negotiate and work out our differences. That includes, in my opinion, giving people the right to return who have not made it back yet. That's not a popular opinion in many of the parlors of this town.

KR: What do you think the implications of this are politically on a federal level for the United States? Because certainly there was a lot of criticism directed towards the Bush administration, but Obama has been in power now since 2008. You tell me, have things gotten any better under his administration?

JB: Oh yeah, they have. Obama has certainly delivered in a way that the Bush administration, at least in the beginning, did not do. A lot of the money was in the pipeline. Obama has certainly been fair to New Orleans. A lot of people criticize him for the BP crisis and forcing the oil companies to undergo certain regulatory measures before they can drill deep.

Personally, I think it's kind of the cognitive dissonance in this country. People want to "drill, baby, drill," but you have the worst spill on record and they don't want to put in the regulatory repairs that you need. Having said that, I cannot imagine an outlay of federal funds after a disaster such as we got after Katrina if another community were hit as hard because of the financial problems of this country right now. There was a lot of waste. The way I deal with it is this way: We were the country that put people on the moon, and we could not rescue people in a flooded city. That is an example of how the culture of governance decayed. I credit Ronald Reagan with bringing Gorbachev to the table, but look, he is the guy who told everybody the government is the problem. We will cut your taxes and we'll still give you services. Well, you got to pay for what you get. Right now, the Social Darwinists who control Congress want people to think that we can cut pensions and we can make teachers lead harder lives to pay off this debt. Well, the debt came about for a lot of reasons. But I think as a country, we have to learn to shoulder our responsibilities if we are going to deal with disasters like Katrina down the road.

KR: This could happen again. It could happen again here, couldn't it?

JB: We are talking here on a day in May when the Mississippi River is rising in Memphis. All of the indications are that they are going to have to open the Morganza and Bonnet Carre Spillways, which could well auger heavy flooding in other parts of Louisiana basically to save Baton Rouge and New Orleans. We live at the whim of the Mississippi. We know the power of the river. We also know that we are living through a period of such terrible political divisiveness in this country that the development and the maintenance of an infrastructure, which America did in ways that became the envy of the world in generations past, is now an open question. How do we move forward? How do we rebuild our roads and bridges and communities? I don't think we have a political consensus on that. It's sad to say.

KR: Are you optimistic about your city and its future?

JB: I would say this: This is a tough town. It's a resilient town. This is a holy city. This is where jazz began, and people here will not go down easily. I think there's a reason why we are here, and for that reason I have faith.

KR: Thanks a lot for doing this, Jason. I really appreciate you taking all this time.

JB: My pleasure.

Questions for Jason Berry

Zach Czaia / 2017

Interview conducted via email, May 26, 2017. Reprinted by permission.

Zach Czaia: Your writing on the Catholic Church spans a great deal of geography, but most of your other writing is regionally or locally focused, centering on the music, politics, and people of Louisiana. I know you've been a long-time resident. Can you talk about what it is about this particular place that has called you to render it in words?

Jason Berry: New Orleans was a magical place to be a kid. The Carnival parades and Catholic rituals gave me balanced joie de vivre. My maternal grandmother and great-grandmother lived close by and I saw them often; they had grown up in the same house in Mexico and shared a festive, Latin sense of faith. At Jesuit High, I got the Irish side. I went off for college at the end of the civil rights era. In 1973, two years out of Georgetown, I published my first book (*Amazing Grace: With Charles Evers in Mississippi*) and felt a deep pull to New Orleans. The music and politics furnished lots of raw material. New Orleans is an exotic, self-dramatizing town, comedy and tragedy at every turn.

ZC: From reading your journalism, fiction, and play, it's clear you have multifaceted gifts, talents, and interests as a writer. Why has the Catholic Church, specifically its shortcomings on the issue of clergy sex abuse, continued to demand your attention?

JB: People kept giving me leads. In 1992, I published *Lead Us Not Into Temptation*, and figured I was done with the abuse issue. I was doing research on jazz funerals when the Maciel survivors contacted me from Mexico; I ended up on a *Hartford Courant* joint assignment arranged by Gerald Renner, the religion editor, who had leads on the Legion of Christ. A terrific guy. In 1997, we reported that the Vatican and John Paul II had ignored accusations against Maciel. We ran 7,500 words: Most of the media ignored it. Jerry retired from the *Courant*; we did a long 2001 piece for *National*

Catholic Reporter on how the men filed canonical charges in Rome with Cardinal Ratzinger to oust Maciel. In 2004, we published *Vows of Silence,* which laid cover-up responsibility with John Paul II. At the end of that year, Ratzinger ordered an investigation, and as Benedict XVI in 2006, banished Maciel. By then, I was producing a documentary, based on the book, exploring the Vatican justice system. It came out in 2008, just after Maciel's death. A year later, the Legion announced he had children, which opened more leads that I tracked in *Render unto Rome* (2011). Over the next few years, I did a lot of reporting in Rome for *GlobalPost.* Eighteen months ago, I ran out of gas on church coverage and decided to refocus on New Orleans.

ZC: What writers, artists and teachers have shaped the ways you look at your own vocation—both as a journalist and writer? In what ways have they done this for you?

JB: Shakespeare and Dante, always. My mother Mary Frances Devine Berry was a primary influence, giving me books as a child; she did her master's thesis on Dryden at Tulane as I went through Jesuit. My grandmother, Beline Lamar Devine, acted in French Quarter plays when I was a kid. Imagine your Mia shambling as Mrs. McThing! At Georgetown, Professor John Glavin was inspiring; he made Yeats and Blake come alive. Writing that first book, I nearly overdosed on Faulkner. Still in my twenties, Clarence John Laughlin, a surrealist photographer, and Michael P. Smith, a photographer of Black culture, opened thematic pathways in New Orleans. Then came Camus, Hemingway, García Márquez, Orwell, Simone de Beauvoir, Walker Percy, Flannery O'Connor, Ernest Gaines, Albert Murray, and Wole Soyinka, each exerting influence as I stumbled into my thirties. When I discovered the abuse cover-up, I went deep into church history. I got to know Andrew Greeley, Eugene Kennedy, and later on, Garry Wills; I read many of their books, enjoyed their friendships. I miss Andy and Gene dearly and appreciate Garry's wisdom. Lately, I have been reading Robert Pinsky's poetry.

ZC: I couldn't put the *Last of the Red Hot Poppas* down. The vividness of each portrait in the novel, the intricacy of the backroom Louisiana politics, the outrageous and funny dialogue—all of them kept the best part of my attention as a reader for the entire book long. It made me wonder: How much are you conscious of the tools of the novelist—plot, character, pacing, dialogue—when you're crafting and assembling your nonfiction work—specifically your church-focused work?

JB: Thank you for not putting that book down. New Journalism was the emerging standard when I started out, authors like Mailer, Jimmy Breslin, and Tom Wolfe [wrote] using structural dynamics of the novel in magazine pieces and nonfiction. I wrote two unpublished novels before my second book, *Up From the Cradle of Jazz*, so I had a toolbox of sorts. In the three Catholic books, I found people thrown into a maelstrom tearing at their spirituality. The abuse survivors were like traumatized Vietnam vets; many lawyers representing victims lost their faith; the priests and nuns clamoring for justice added a powerful layer; Vatican officials I met on the second and third books were baroque figures. My goal was three-dimensional profiles, and a narrative line on people's lives in a clash with injustice and religious power.

ZC: In a play you wrote, *Earl Long in Purgatory* (which was staged locally), you have the Louisiana governor Earl K. Long speak from the afterlife. You wrote in your introduction to the text of the play that this was one of your most satisfying experiences as a writer. It occurs to me that you might be channeling a little Dante in a work like this. Can you talk about the ways this poet has influenced your work, both fiction and church-related journalism?

JB: I read *The Divine Comedy* at Georgetown and have been rereading for years. In the *Paradiso*, Dante meets St. Peter Damian, the medieval crusader against clergy sex abuse, some hope for sinful me. If Dante were alive, he would add a rung in the Inferno for the pedophiles and their sheltering bishops. Yes, as Catholics we believe in forgiveness and redemption, but St. Augustine hit the mark: "Justice is that virtue which gives everyone his due." The hierarchy sees crimes as sin. Earl Long invaded my life at age ten. Jason Sr. summoned me to the living room and pointed at the TV: "He's your governor. . . . Look out, now! Can you believe that? They're dragging him into a mental hospital and Channel Six is beeping out his curse words!" That was my first exposure to democracy. Earl Long had a breakdown in the legislature, battling pols who wanted to purge the 100,000 Black voters he had gotten registered. This was 1959. Most Southern politicians were at war over civil rights. His meltdown was on the right side of history. His wife Blanche tried to commit him three times; he got himself sprung each time. In spite, he began cavorting with a Bourbon Street stripper called Blaze Starr. Introduced her to reporters as the "future First Lady." In the play, I make him apologize to Blanche. That was much harder than writing about Vatican cardinals taking dirty money from Maciel. The next summer, 1960, Earl sent Blaze back to Baltimore, ran for Congress in the Pentecostal woodlands—and won. Nine days later, he died. In 2000, while swimming in Dante, I decided to put the self-styled "Uncle Earl" in a Louisiana version of *Purgatorio*. I spoke his lines out loud as I wrote on the computer screen, laughing as he realized he must argue his case for "the holy escalator." I hope to revive a production. No other work has given me such pleasure.

ZC: Readers tracking your church-themed work can notice you follow-ing up, in interesting ways, threads, commentaries, and even characters from earlier writing in more recently published pieces. In more than thirty years covering the clergy sex abuse issue, what have been some of the great-est surprises for you? What are things you couldn't have predicted?

JB: The impact of *The Boston Globe* series in 2002, ten years after I pub-lished *Lead Us Not Into Temptation*, stands out. I never imagined the book, the issue, or I would get so much new media attention. I gave scores of interviews, twice in one week on *Nightline*, and did a stretch as an ABC news consultant. One spring night in '02, I did a satellite interview from downtown New Orleans with Anderson Cooper, and walked into Southern Rep Theatre for the opening of *Earl Long in Purgatory*. The greater, continu-ing surprise is the hold of structural mendacity, institutionalized lying by bishops and cardinals. That is the root issue. John Paul defended Maciel for years, as if his victims didn't exist. How does one explain such hubris in the man who challenged Polish communism? The scandals don't surprise me much, but I do feel shock.

ZC: In your books and in interviews, you refuse to accept the title of "bad Catholic" (though some conservatives have doubtless given it to you anyway). How did your decision to publish articles and books critical of the hierarchy affect the way you've related to the church and to other Catholics?

JB: I have never attacked the faith. Bill Donohue of the Catholic League has been bashing me for years, which means I'm doing something right. Many of my best sources were orthodox Catholics, Republicans outraged over the cover-ups. The problem is the power structure; I worked like a political reporter, probing ecclesiastical governance. Walker Percy's *Love in the Ruins* has the subtitle, *The Adventures of a Bad Catholic at a Time Near the End of the World*. I love that novel for its satire of the post–Vatican II church. Percy has right-wingers sing "The Star-Spangled Banner" at com-munion. I identify with his protagonist, Tom More, the sinning doctor, fortified by bourbon, waiting for the apocalypse near a sand trap outside New Orleans. Tom More pines for old certitudes. I vote blue and miss Gre-gorian chants. New Orleans is a village wrapped in a city; quite a few people who knew my parents, and me in adolescence, were shocked when *Lead Us Not Into Temptation* came out. I don't know how many read it, but in the early wave of media coverage on abuse cases, I was interviewed a lot. Some people I knew avoided eye contact. Many more sent good vibrations. When Benedict banished Maciel in 2006, certain people became friendly again. After the 2009 news that Maciel had children, disaffected Legion and

Regnum Christi supporters began contacting me. Two Legion spokesmen apologized. Jerry Renner had died by then. We were hammered with Maciel victims on Legion websites for years, and by the Catholic League.

I had titanic struggles with the faith for many years; the birth of my younger daughter, Ariel, in 1991 sent me into a spiritual free fall; she had Down syndrome and struggled for years with heart disease. Ariel died in 2008. A lot of priests, nuns, and survivors reached out in consoling ways over those years. I visit her grave several times a month.

Ironically, in all the years I couldn't get a bishop on the phone, the Vatican press office gave me credentials and various officials spoke on background. Cardinal Achille Silvestrini avoided the hard questions, but was grand in discussing Fellini. I developed good sources in Rome because people in the Vatican were curious to know how much I knew.

ZC: I had the opportunity to speak with Jennifer Haselberger as I was in the process of publishing my own book of poetry in 2015, *Saint Paul Lives Here (In Minnesota)*. In part because of her witness, the Archdiocese of St. Paul and Minneapolis has become more transparent and the former archbishop, John Nienstedt, was replaced. Still, from Jennifer's perspective, the Catholic Church still isn't "getting it" on this issue, and in important ways. From your vantage point, is the Catholic Church a markedly safer and more transparent place than it was thirty years ago, when you began reporting on the cover-up of sexual abuse?

JB: There have been encouraging changes, yes; most bishops realize that they can't shelter sex abusers, or [they] risk huge scandal and heavy financial losses. The background checks and safe-touch teaching for kids in Catholic schools is a good step. But the culture of lying is incredibly deep, and I'm convinced a lot of it stems from the absence of women. Nienstedt and his inner circle behaved like Cardinal Law in the 1990s. How did they not learn? Jennifer spoke the truth and they tried to sandbag her—with Jeff Anderson's law firm down the street! Frankly, the bishops need oversight by police, prosecutors, judges, plaintiff lawyers, and the news media. Left to their own ways, too many bishops will revert to deceptive tactics.

ZC: [*Perhaps related to the above*] You've argued in *Lead Us Not Into Temptation* that there are systemic problems that help explain the problems the Church has had in responding to this issue. Has the church under Pope Francis done things to address the systemic nature of the problems?

JB: On the Vatican Bank, yes; on the abuse crisis, not much. The absence of a legal structure to remove bishops is his major failure. Canon law is malleable; too many cardinals close to the pope, like Pell and Errázuriz, concealed notorious pedophiles, but they kept their posts. Francis has met with a few survivors, and removed a few bishops, but there is no structure to secure justice. I admire Francis on many fronts, but absent a strong independent judicial mechanism for bishops, scandals are likely to stain his watch, just as they did with John Paul and Benedict. The world is too interconnected; information moves too fast, and reporters recognize critical mass when they see it.

ZC: Marie Collins and Peter Saunders, formerly members on the pope's commission to address issues surrounding clergy sex abuse, have recently resigned. In Collins's case, the issue seemed to revolve around the Congregation for the Defense of the Faith (CDF). In her view, it was resisting full transparency and was failing to acknowledge survivors of sexual abuse. How would you evaluate the role of the CDF? As a body, is it acting in substantively different ways than it was in previous eras since you've started reporting on the church?

JB: The CDF stonewalled on bishop accountability under Cardinal Müller, who has his own bad record in Germany. Vatican officials don't want oversight of bishops. Marie and Peter fought the good fight, without backing from Pope Francis. You wonder if he will reverse course.

ZC: Archbishop Diarmuid Martin has impressed many in the Church (and angered others) with his embrace of full transparency with Church files on clergy sex abuse in Ireland. Granted that the relationship between church and state is different in Ireland than in the United States and many other countries, what is the likelihood that the spirit of Martin's leadership will catch on in other parts of the church?

JB: Martin would make a great pope, but Francis did not make him a cardinal. The other cardinals would be afraid of electing someone so honest. Bishop Geoffrey Robinson of Australia is a visionary and [was] ostracized. The Curia is a medieval court system. Francis is bucking that tradition with his board of advisory cardinals, but how can he steer a path for justice with Pell of Australia and Errázuriz of Chile in that circle? He could appoint someone like a René Brülhart—who presides over the Financial Information Authority of Vatican City—as a prosecutor independent of the CDF in a judicial office that compels testimony from bishops and recommends punitive sanctions to the pope? I can hear canon lawyers sputtering. Look, the only way out of this long sick quagmire is an independent judicial mechanism that trumps the princely brotherhood. It's not a question of bishops showing new leadership skills. The power structure has no oversight. Democracies are flawed, but they do manage to prosecute corrupt politicians. The church needs that balance—or leverage if you will.

ZC: On a similar note, what can the church as a body learn from public inquiries like the Royal Commission's Investigation into institutional cover-up of clergy sex abuse in Australia? Is this model something the church could look to adopt on its own, as it tries to seek healing and provide justice to survivors of sexual abuse?

JB: I don't see how the pope can appoint an investigative body when he won't stand behind the survivors on his youth protection commission, people whom he personally gave assurances. Francis on this issue is passionate rhetoric, a few disciplinary moves of his own, but no structural follow-through.

ZC: Critics of your work sometimes point to the "accusational" tone of some of your church books. While I can see that there is a quality of judgment in your work, (that I find warranted), the more I read of you, the more I notice something else, the presence of so many human portraits of characters working for good—and often within the church itself. I'm thinking of people like Father Thomas Doyle, OP, Ray Mouton, Jeff Anderson, or Peter Borre, among many others. As you were writing about a topic that involved so much pain and grief, did you make a conscious choice to provide the efforts of those fighting for goodness, for the truth to emerge?

JB: What a wise question. I wonder if it was a conscious or unconscious decision on my part. My wife did her doctorate on Nabokov and almost became a Jungian therapist. I must consult her. The theme in all three of the Catholic books is monarchy vs. democracy, a church governed by a papal hierarchy colliding with a court system and free press. Tom Doyle is the most fascinating person I have written about. A priest who wants "to be close to God," becomes a canon lawyer at the Vatican Embassy, raises hell on pedophile priests, and gets sacked for doing so. Becomes an Air Force chaplain, starts giving expert witness testimony against the bishops he once served, and counsels scores of abuse survivors. That is a serious life arc. The raw facts of what the predator priests and complicit superiors have done make for tough reading. I tried to leaven that with textured portraits of people pushing for justice and reform, showing a better side of the church. The one who gave me the most hope is Sister Christine Schenk in Cleveland, a founder of Future Church. I'd love to see her in the College of Cardinals.

In a Long Career, Writer Jason Berry Turns Homeward Again in *City of a Million Dreams*

Susan Larson / 2018

From *The Advocate*, November 6, 2018. Reprinted by permission.

Jason Berry is one of the great journeyman writers of New Orleans, a virtuoso of genres. He has done it all—straightforward journalism (*Lead Us Not Into Temptation: Catholic Priests and the Sexual Abuse of Children*), cultural history (*Up From the Cradle of Jazz*), spiritual traditions (*The Spirit of Black Hawk: A Mystery of Africans and Indians*), and now, in time for this tricentennial year, he's published his long-awaited, character-driven history, *City of a Million Dreams: A History of New Orleans at Year 300*.

Reading and writing have shaped Berry's life from a young age. "My mother, Mary Frances Devine Berry, gave me books and prodded me to write," he said. She sent his first story, written at age four, to *The Times-Picayune*. "An editor sent her a nice letter saying that I showed talent; she used that on me for a while. I kept writing stories in grade school. We had a large library at home. My father was amused when I read *Lady Chatterley's Lover* at twelve; it was on the church's forbidden list—and my mother was a serious Catholic. . . . It took me years to appreciate how much her literary sensibility shaped mine."

His literary aspirations came early and stayed strong. "In my junior year at Georgetown, 1970, I edited a literary journal, wrote movie reviews in a student newspaper and marched against the Vietnam War, all the while anchored in the English department's great books curriculum—Dante, Shakespeare, Milton, Donne, Dickens, Austen, Yeats, Eliot, the usual suspects."

"After graduation in 1971, I went to Mississippi and landed a job as press secretary in Charles Evers campaign for governor. It was a life-dividing experience; the book I wrote in a white heat of ten months found a publisher, thanks to the kind help of Walker Percy, whom I'd met through a family friend," he said. *Amazing Grace: With Charles Evers in Mississippi* was published in 1973.

Now sixty-nine, Berry can look back on his long and distinguished career with an eye for the enduring threads, the steady struggle.

"*Lead Us Not Into Temptation* was an ordeal," he said. "I had just published *Up From the Cradle of Jazz* (1986) when the scope of the church cover-ups, beyond Louisiana, began materializing in my research. I spent years writing articles on a shoestring budget before the 1992 publication, when I got out of debt and into a starter house. At least thirty publishers rejected it; many were afraid of legal action by the church.

"I finally landed with the Doubleday religion editor, Tom Cahill, a former Jesuit seminarian. He saw immediately that it was amply documented. That book had quite an impact for its time. I did a lot of national TV. I still hear from people just discovering it. I never anticipated that abuse survivors would endure like the chorus of a Greek tragedy in my life. People kept contacting me, especially outraged nuns and priests. I went on to do two other books on the Vatican."

Other works brought pleasure. "I felt the most joy writing the play *Earl Long in Purgatory*, with the novel *Last of the Red Hot Poppas*, a close second," he recalled. "It's a comedy about the cover-up of a licentious Cajun governor found poisoned on page two. I sent it to Edwin Edwards when he was in prison. I got a form letter sent to all of his friends with a handwritten line, 'Thanks! Interesting!' I wonder if he ever read it."

While writing *City of a Million Dreams*, Berry also took time to work with former Mayor Mitch Landrieu on his memoir, *In the Shadow of Statues: A Southerner Looks at Race*. "We'd had a friendly if distant relationship for years, never once ate together before he asked me to help," Berry recalled. "He'd arrive at my house about 5:20 p.m. on a series of appointed days, drove himself, no driver. He was so scrupulous about not doing work on city time. He'd written several chapter drafts and had a lot on youth homicide when we came to terms. I took that material, along with interviews on a thirty-six-hour turnaround from a transcription service, [I'd] get a draft, he'd make changes and send it back. Mitch has a strong narrative sense; I was an editorial collaborator, not a ghost writer."

But of all of his works, *City of a Million Dreams* has a special place in his heart. "The city of my birth and the church in which I was raised furnished the major narratives of my career," Berry said. "They've intersected for years.

When I think of the agony I felt in six nomadic weeks after [Hurricane] Katrina, the city a muddy hellhole, I'd have to say *City of a Million Dreams* means the most to me as a resurrection story."

And for lagniappe, there's the upcoming documentary, a high point in his personal as well as professional life. "Losing Ariel, my younger daughter, to heart failure ten years ago was the hardest experience of my life. Now, to be finishing a film based on this new book with my older daughter, Simonette, as coproducer, is quite uplifting."

City of a Million Dreams is populated with great New Orleans characters. Three especially stand out for Berry. First among them is free man of color Pierre Cazenave, a French Quarter furniture dealer who went into the mortuary business and began hiring bands for funerals. Then there was Mother Catherine Seals, a faith healer in the Lower Ninth Ward who played the trumpet and had an orchestra. And last but not least, Sister Gertrude Morgan, the artist and mystic. That juxtaposition of the secular and the spiritual has always fascinated Berry.

Berry has created a portrait of "a city of spectacle in conflict with a city of laws," as he puts it. And what emerges is a beautifully told, exuberant history of his beloved hometown.

"I think we are a city apart from the rest of the country—a city that has been formed by so many cultures and strands of ethnic identities, and what makes it so remarkable is the way we all come together," he said. "To me, this city is a grand mystery, and with each passing year, I discover another layer that rivets me."

Catholic History of New Orleans Highlighted During Its Three-Hundredth Anniversary

Christopher White / 2018

From *Crux*, December 12, 2018. Reprinted by permission.

Thirty years ago, investigative reporter Jason Berry pioneered new territory by covering clerical sexual abuse in Louisiana. Since then, his name has become synonymous with the crisis that continues to loom over the Catholic Church today.

In his new book, *City of a Million Dreams: A History of New Orleans at Year 300*, Berry returns to his roots. In an interview with *Crux*, he details some of the city's rich Catholic history, its efforts to confront race relations, and why researching some of the city's saints proved far more fulfilling than his work in Rome.

Christopher White: You've spent decades uncovering and chronicling the Church's shameful history of clerical sex abuse and cover-up, yet this new book switches gears to tell the story of a city—your city—New Orleans. What prompted you to write this book?

Jason Berry: In 1985, when I began investigating clergy abuse cases in Lafayette, Louisiana, my second book was heading toward publication, *Up From the Cradle of Jazz: New Orleans Music Since World War II*. After six years on that topic, I had become intrigued with jazz funerals, how they arose, what they said about the city. As I gathered documents on clergy predators, the narrative taking shape for *Lead Us Not Into Temptation* (1992) became hugely consuming. I came back from reporting trips, numbed by clerical secrets and crimes, and invariably attended the funeral of a musician.

As the mourners danced in the streets, I felt strangely happy. My own church made me sad. The city of my birth was sending rhythms of spiritual hope.

This paradox went on for a quarter-century or so as I read about New Orleans alongside church history, while excavating rot in the ecclesiastical culture. Slowly, I found in the funerals' evolution a mirror on the history of the city. Over time, I got tired of the church reporting. What I'd concluded in the 1992 book is what I say in interviews today. How does one reform a hierarchy addicted to lying? I had to cut distance from the church reporting to give full time to the New Orleans book. I did my last leg in 2015 with Pope Francis's trip to Washington. I've done some op-eds since then, but shifted my focus to New Orleans.

CW: In many respects, this is more than just a history of New Orleans. It's a love letter to the city! Is it fair to say New Orleans enjoys some of the richest Catholic history of any city in the country?

JB: Well, Christopher, it's fair to say that the Catholic history of New Orleans is rich in its complexities (unbeknownst to most local Catholics), but please do not accuse me of being a mushy valentine scribe. It would disappoint some locals who loathe me for being a muckraker. Not to mention certain people in old-line Carnival clubs aghast over Mayor Mitch Landrieu's decision to dismantle four Confederate monuments who would gag over the idea of my book as a love letter.

Every book is a voyage of discovery. In this one I found that map-of-the-world neighborhoods give New Orleans its essence; it was a crossroads of humanity long before "melting pot" became a term. The culture of spectacle that arose from public dances of enslaved Africans at a park called Congo Square kept pushing against the official city after the Civil War with a force that fueled the popular culture. I followed that tension of culture vs. law as a thematic line throughout the narrative.

CW: How has the city, and in particularly the Jesuits, reckoned with their history of slave ownership?

JB: The city has had a Black voting majority since the 1970s and a string of African American mayors between the administration of Moon Landrieu [1970–78] and that of his son, Mitch, who recently finished an eight-year term. New Orleans is the city where jazz began and now markets that culture effectively. Nevertheless, as in much of the South, there is a contagion here of nostalgia-as-history; some prominent locals avoid the legacy of enslavement as if smiling at a garden party where nobody mentions the cadaver sprawled across the rose bushes.

Whitney Plantation is a museum of slavery in a town called Wallace about an hour or so by car upriver. It is a truly amazing place. The museums and universities explore slavery in conferences, courses, and symposia that widen our viewfinder on the past. The church is more complicated.

The Ursulines and Jesuits were major slaveholders in New Orleans during the French colonial era [1718–1767]. Emily Clark, a distinguished historian at Tulane, has done impressive work on the complexity of the Ursuline sisters' plantation and ownership of slaves, some of whom they educated. I have not found the same level of scholarship about the local Jesuits as slaveholders, though as I worked on this book, Georgetown University (where I earned my BA) embarked on a major project, confronting the 1838 sale of 272 slaves, whom the Society of Jesus sent to Louisiana, by seeking out their descendants in some rough calculus at moral atonement. The Georgetown Memory Project has had its twists and turns, yet strikes me as a model for higher education in a country where certain leading universities had serious involvement in the slave economy.

CW: Just last month the US bishops issued a new pastoral letter on race. How has the church in New Orleans historically dealt with race relations–and what's your assessment of the state of affairs today?

JB: The Church in French colonial Louisiana, despite the plantations of religious orders, welcomed slaves and free persons of color, a substantial presence in this society, at St. Louis Church on the main square. After the Spanish took control in 1767, African-blooded people who married, baptized their children, and buried their dead at the big church found a hero in Pere Antoine, a rebellious cleric who flaunted Church authority. He was a Spaniard who arrived as a secret agent of the Inquisition—imagine that, in sin city!—but clashed with the governor, who shipped him back to Spain. He returned from exile in 1795, after a triumphant appeal to the king; he then fostered a cult of personality. Pere Antoine went to war with two bishops over his control of St. Louis Church, forcing both to retreat. He's among the most fascinating figures to me in this character-driven history. A law unto himself, he died in 1829 with the equivalent of a state funeral.

The church soon swung around to supporting the Confederacy. Not until the late 1950s did the Church embrace racial reconciliation with desegregation of parochial schools under Archbishop Joseph Rummel. Given the historic role of African American Catholics here, and of the parochial schools in educating Black youngsters, the church in that respect is today an enlightened presence.

The greater story to me in writing this book was the nature of Black spirituality. Mother Catherine Seals, a faith healer of the 1920s, had a large compound in the Lower Ninth Ward, far from the city proper. She took in battered women and pregnant girls; she played trombone in a big tent where jazzmen like Harold "Duke" Dejan got his start; he went on to lead the Olympia Brass Band for forty years. The chapter I did on Mother Catherine draws on the unpublished family history of people who grew up in the manger—three siblings who got married there, one a noted trumpeter, Ernie Cagnolatti.

After Mother Catherine's death, an evangelist named Sister Gertrude Morgan moved into a house near the old Manger site, and in 1957, received a vision that she was a bride of Christ. That religious experience inspired her to paint. Her images of the New Jerusalem, a heavenly realm beckoning those in a fallen world, today hang in museums and command major prices when they come on the market.

She also wrote poetry and wrestled with her role as the bride of the Father and the Son. Sister Gertrude was a dynamic presence during the 1960s jazz revival at Preservation Hall. Her French Quarter art dealer could have come from central casting: Larry Borenstein was thrown in jail three times in Mexico for trying to steal antiquities; he adored her and found collectors and curators to buy her works, while falling in love with a woman half his age. I'm convinced that the proximity to her softened Larry. His daughter gave me access to the love letters he wrote her mother. Both parents are deceased. Sister Gertrude was a mystic whose dialogue with the Lord reminded me of the ecstasies of St. Catherine of Siena and the otherworldly verse of William Blake.

Researching Mother Catherine and Sister Gertrude was vastly more fulfilling to me than all of the reporting I did over the years in Rome.

The Triumph of New Orleans, the Tragedy of the Catholic Church: A Conversation with Jason Berry

Christiaan Mader / 2019

From *The Current*, April 24, 2019. Reprinted by permission.

By the mid-1990s, journalist Jason Berry wanted to move on from writing about the Catholic Church. His landmark book, *Lead Us Not Into Temptation*, published in 1992, was an incendiary act of reporting, breaking wide open a clergy sex abuse scandal that has embroiled the church ever since. In his bid to move on, he turned his attention to New Orleans, his hometown, and the other work-defining subject of his literary life, for a new focus in his career, beginning a history that would take him years to complete. When *The Boston Globe* published a landmark series in 2002, hanging the sex abuse scandal back on the national conscience, Berry was whisked once again into the throes of reporting that he began in and around Lafayette in 1985, writing on special assignment for *The Times of Acadiana*.

"I could have continued to write about the Catholic Church for the rest of my life," he tells me. After another decade exploring the secrecy and politics of Rome, Berry returned to chronicling New Orleans. In 2018, just in time for the city's tricentennial, he published *City of a Million Dreams: A History of New Orleans at Year 300*. A history teeming with life and detail, *City of a Million Dreams* contemplates the productive tension between extroverted African cultures and staid, orderly European society. New Orleans, in Berry's telling, is defined by that grappling—between hedonic pleasure and Old-World pieties, the Black spirit and the yoke of white supremacy. He's also working on a documentary of the same name, which will hit the film festival circuit in 2020, coincidentally the fifteenth anniversary of Hurricane Katrina.

Berry will make a pair of appearances discussing *City of a Million Dreams* in Lafayette this week. On Thursday, he'll speak at an event hosted by UL Lafayette's Center for Louisiana Studies at 3:30 p.m. On Friday, he'll deliver an address at a luncheon organized by Friends of the Humanities, at The Petroleum Club of Lafayette at 11:30 p.m.

We spoke by phone on Easter Sunday. The interview has been edited for brevity and clarity.

Christiaan Mader: The clergy scandal is still very much alive. Are you finding you have to keep fielding questions about it, even as you've tried to walk away?

Jason Berry: Well, I never walked away from it; I just decided to shift the focus of my work. There have been two major stories of my life as a writer: the city of my birth and the church in which I was raised. I've been going back and forth between the two for the better part of thirty years now. I still do write from time to time about the church. I did a three-part series for *National Catholic Reporter* that posted right before the [2019 Vatican Abuse Summit] in Rome. There's a lot about Lafayette in the first installment. I never imagined in the early nineties, after I published that first book, that the bishops would continue with the same mentality of deception and secrecy. I don't know if I'll do another book on the church, but I'll continue to do the occasional articles.

CM: Do you still identify as a Catholic?

JB: Well, I search for good liturgies, and sometimes, I find them. I haven't left, is a good way to put it. It is a titanic struggle I deal with every day. If the ship is going to go down, I want to be with it. [*Laughs*] Believe me that's a cynical joke. *City of a Million Dreams* bears a profound imprint of a spiritual sensibility. In some respects, [it's] the story of two interweaving or converging spiritualities, one African and one Catholic. And a lot of the book is about the way New Orleans became a crossroads of humanity and the role that music and cultural memory played in that long process.

CM: Do you have to be a New Orleanian to write about New Orleans or a Catholic to write about Catholicism in the way that you do? These are stories that seem to be intimate to you.

JB: Well, I guess they are. I sustain quite an inner struggle writing about the church, particularly in Lafayette. That first year and a half was very bruising. The experience at *The Times of Acadiana* was quite good on most levels. Steve and Cherry Fisher May [then-publishers of *The Times*] backed me to the hilt. Linda Matys, the original editor when I began the work, was a superb editor. And then Richard Baudouin during the second half of my year and a half there. I got hit pretty hard by *The Daily Advertiser*. They went after me and *The Times*. I realize it was under previous ownership . . . but when you attack the messenger rather than looking at the message . . . that was a sobering lesson for me.

New Orleans is a city of migrants, and the story of the city is one of different peoples converging and learning to adapt . . .

The New Orleans history was one of the most rewarding tasks I've ever taken on. I had no idea when I was getting into the final stretch of the writing in 2016 and 2017 that the story of a city triumphant, emerging as a robust metropolis after the terrible flooding after Katrina, would stand as a statement of hope at a time when America was covered in such political darkness. New Orleans is a city of migrants, and the story of the city is one of different peoples converging and learning to adapt and enriching themselves in partaking of the different folkways and traditions of the various home cultures, from Africa to Sicily to France and Spain.

CM: There is no shortage of books on New Orleans, yet it still seems somehow so exotic to me in your writing.

JB: The argument of the book is that the city's beguiling personality is the product of a long tension historically between a culture of spectacle rooted in the slave dances of Congo Square and a city of laws that was long anchored in white supremacy. So chapter by chapter, the book follows the manic thread of culture pushing against the law, and you certainly see that in the Sister Gertrude chapter [excerpted by *The Daily Beast* in 2018]. When all of the political and social forces of the day are converging in the French Quarter, segregation is still the law. And yet as Sister Gertrude is there, the mystic who is bearing witness and painting these otherworldly pictures, the freedom riders are coming through and gay culture is slowly coming out of the margins. . . . The pressure was building. How do you maintain a tourist economy when Black people and white people cannot sit together in the same music club, or for that matter in the same restaurants? How the city changed in a sense reflects a political accommodation to the popular culture. You find that moving forward through the various phases of the three hundred years.

CM: But wasn't it more accurate to say that New Orleans was bucking against the American cultural mainstream?

JB: Well, certainly in the South it was. But New Orleans in a way was a New York before New York. The first opera house was in New Orleans not New York. [Then] New York became the great metropolis, really the city of cities, where people from across the globe went to find their way. And we now see it, sadly . . . that most people of ordinary means cannot afford to live in Manhattan anymore. Contrast that with New Orleans, which is human scale, but it is a place where the social mosaic holds a mirror to the Caribbean, in many of its mores and at the same time, has that long touch of French and Spanish sensibility; it's certainly there in the food and some of the mannered ways that people interact. You could say that's Old South, but it's also European. I think the city has an allure to people from other places, and ever since Katrina it has become a kind of recovery narrative that keeps drawing greater numbers of visitors and tourists.

The sad thing to me is, here we are a generation later, and the current bishop just continues to practice not being forthcoming.

CM: You argued once that the lesson of the abuse scandal in Lafayette was why a strong press matters. Hearing you recount your experience, I don't know if as a local journalist I would have been afforded the ability to do that same reporting today. And I mean that financially. Local press is under an economic assault in a way that's really troubling.

JB: I understand what you mean. There are a couple of ways of looking at that. What was striking to me about the experience I had in Lafayette was not that *The Times of Acadiana*, or Steve May particularly, had the gumption to go ahead and let me do it. Plenty of alternative weeklies back in the 1970s and '80s were doing really fine investigative work. What jumped out at me the most was getting attacked by the daily newspaper for doing my job as a journalist. The people who wrote those things are gone now, or at least no longer writing. I think the idea was so hard for people in Cajun country to really wrap their minds around that the church could be an institution so layered in secrecy and covering up such a range of sexual behavior patterns. The sad thing to me is, here we are a generation later, and the current bishop just continues to practice not being forthcoming. You know the television station [KATC] really did the work the diocese itself should have done. They've done extraordinary work. . . . But now it's kind of pathetic, in a way, that this bishop acts like nothing has changed, that the world is the way it was, and took his time, dragged his feet with all these questions lingering.

CM: *City of a Million Dreams* seems hopeful. Why is there hopefulness, given all the slings and arrows pointed at New Orleans and Louisiana at large?

JB: I think the city's resilience is an American success story. I am not a triumphalist by temperament. Quite the opposite. One of the things I say in the book is that policy fails, and culture prevails. The first several years after the hurricane, the state didn't come to our rescue. There was no massive line of funding that came from Baton Rouge. FEMA was certainly actively present. It took quite a while before Congress authorized the Road Home program, and there were bureaucratic problems with that, getting the money into the accounts of people who needed the funds. In the end, it did work. But many of the musicians came back even when they didn't have homes. And they kept playing, and had the music not returned, I don't think tourism would have rebounded as quickly. Before the hurricane, I would periodically get a call from a reporter . . . and he or she would say, "Look I've been walking around the French Quarter. What's it really like to live here?" I would always say the same thing. Politically nothing important happens here. This place is a backwater; it's at the edge of America, and people yawn at corruption. But culturally, this city is rich as gold.

The Jazz Writer: Jason Berry's Quest to Understand the Place Where He's From

Tom Roberts / 2019

From the *National Catholic Reporter*, November 20, 2019. Reprinted by permission of NCR Publishing Company, www.NCROnline.org.

Jason Berry loves character-driven narrative. He's good at writing it, sending wonderfully drawn figures, whether wretches of the clerical sort or zany, colorful Louisianans, on journeys along a tight weave of data and history.

And himself? Berry, who recently turned seventy, is a character who's bounced between those poles, the weave supporting him a mix of his intense examination of the ugliest side of Catholic reality and the soul-restoring gumbo of Louisiana life, particularly his hometown of New Orleans.

NCR has run tens of thousands of Berry's words on our pages in the past three-plus decades, but we've never spoken *to* him or *about* him much in these spaces. This is a stab at doing that, a gathering up of conversations that have gone on for years and, more recently, during the months since the release of his latest work, *City of a Million Dreams: A History of New Orleans at Year 300.*

Full disclosure is warranted: Berry and I count each other as friends, meeting first as deliverer and recipient, respectively, of pitches for stories about the Catholic clergy sexual abuse scandal; then as writer and editor going round for round over the words, the data, the characters, the numbers; and spending hours on conference calls with lawyers vetting stories that delivered the details of ecclesial corruption—sexual and financial.

And beyond, as husbands, fathers, and Catholics who by dint of profession had read more transcripts, communiques, and depositions detailing ecclesial depravity and mendacity than most. We've spent more time than perhaps anyone should trying to figure out how such outspoken public moralists as the Catholic bishops had become symbols of the utterly immoral: How so many of the loudest, publicly self-proclaimed devout refused to believe any of it until the evidence overwhelmed.

I recall a conversation during the late 1990s or early 2000s—likely a discussion over yet another possible assignment having to do with the sex abuse crisis—when Berry announced in rather strident terms that his first love was not writing about the church's failures. "I'm a jazz writer!" he said.

Whether that was more unfulfilled wish than entirely true, I can't be sure. But in an appearance earlier this year at Politics and Prose, a landmark Washington, DC, bookstore, he described toggling back and forth between church scandal stories and the jazz funerals that began to captivate him nearly thirty years ago. "What explains the ritual of jazz funerals was the question that started the research that resulted in" *City of a Million Dreams*, he told a crowd jammed into the back of the store.

He explained that historically, the bands played dirge-like pieces heading into the cemetery, but once "unto dust you return" was pronounced, the tunes went up tempo, into music that would give the impression of anything but sadness and death.

In the mid-1990s, the music and the movement of the second line, the troop of dancers that spontaneously gathers to follow the band, turned to something wilder and edgier. The performances began to reflect, Berry said, the mood surrounding the funerals of increasing numbers of young drug overdose victims. "Different cities tell their stories in different ways," he explained. He found the funerals for the victims "arresting" to witness, and he began interviewing older musicians who were upset "about the spirituality of the event being ripped out by the wildness of these funerals. That's what set me on the road that culminated in the book," he said.

"The story of my life since then has been a series of long intervals where I went off writing about the Catholic Church and the crisis which I chronicled for about thirty years," work that resulted in scores of articles and three books. Because of the years during which Berry was the principal—and often sole—chronicler of that crisis, he became its expert by default. But the New Orleans project kept pulling him back. When Berry cleared the decks for the final push on his latest book, he realized that after all of the interviewing and reading and research, he had come to the conclusion that "the story of the funerals began with the story of the city." The two stories were inseparable.

These twin forces, the cultures of Catholicism and New Orleans, have driven the main character in the Jason Berry narrative for the past few decades.

Early Years

The seeds of fascination with the city in which he was born and the church in which he was raised were planted and nourished long before his own work—countless articles and a pile of books including a history, a novel, and several resulting from deep investigative reporting—began to pile up on his shelves.

His mother, Mary Frances, half Irish, traced her matrilineal heritage to Jalapa, Mexico. His father, Jason Sr., was raised in Arkansas. His parents, now deceased, met in New Orleans after World War II, during which his father had served in the military. His father was a businessman, head of a cafeteria chain. His mother, who later in life was but a dissertation away from a doctorate in literature, was "really a radiant lady," and "probably the reason I became a writer." His childhood, he said, was "wonderful."

"When you are raised in a place where the adults wear masks and dance in the streets, it does promote a certain optimism for the human experiment. And I carried certain joie de vivre, even through Jesuit High School, where I got the Irish church in full measure."

Berry also got a good dose of Jesuit social justice indoctrination, enough to eventually put him on the sympathetic side of those who marched for civil rights and protested the Vietnam war.

"I came out of what was almost a nineteenth-century background, and it was framed by faith, family, and the extravagant public rituals of New Orleans."

His college career began at Loyola University New Orleans in 1967. With his transfer his sophomore year to Georgetown University, his emergence into the twentieth century was complete. "Georgetown was a new world. Reading the [*Washington*] *Post* every morning was an education in itself. The civil rights movement had a greater urgency in Washington."

The English department at Georgetown worked on the great books approach. "It was the grand tour of Western literature. I don't think I read Hemingway until I got out of college; I know I didn't read Faulkner there."

During an entire semester on Milton, he "fell in love with Satan, what a great character. I speak in a literary sense."

With Georgetown degree in hand in 1971, the young man who would work ungodly hours over a lifetime while never holding a conventional full-time job, headed directly for Mississippi and spent the summer after graduation in the longshot gubernatorial campaign of Charles Evers. "I wanted to be part of the movement for changing the South. And it was an eye-opening and almost life-dividing experience."

Evers, whose brother Medgar was assassinated by the Ku Klux Klan in 1963, lost by a large margin, "but we managed to elect fifty-two African Americans to local office, which was a real breakthrough for Mississippi," said Berry. "It was the first major test of the Black vote following the 1965 Voting Rights Act."

Berry then spent "ten months writing in a white heat after the campaign" and had his first book contract within a year of graduation.

Southern novelist Walker Percy, whose works were often set in New Orleans, had seen a piece Berry had done on the politics of the South for the *Vieux Carré Courier*, a French Quarter alternative weekly. "I was sitting there working away one day in August when the telephone rang and it was Walker Percy. I almost had heart failure that he would call me." Percy put him in touch with an editor at Saturday Review Press.

Amazing Grace: With Charles Evers in Mississippi was published in the fall of 1973.

Berry took the advance money from that book and in December 1972 went to Europe for several months, spending some of that time in Paris, where he became fascinated in a new way with his home city of New Orleans, the one he felt compelled to leave just a few years earlier.

It became apparent that the dream of the freelance correspondent life in Paris was beyond reach. "I had no tools; I couldn't get hired." But he kept noticing eyes lighting up in fellow American wanderlusts when he would answer endless rounds of "Where you from?" with "New Orleans."

"I realized that there was a lot about New Orleans—a whole side of it—that I didn't know. And that, in large measure, is what prompted me to go back."

From people who had never lived in New Orleans, Berry began to understand what he never saw growing up there, that "it was a place of mystery and intrigue . . . it had a certain mystique."

Back in New Orleans and scraping by on freelance wages, he was beginning to get work placed in national publications, book reviews for *The New Republic* and articles for *The Nation*.

He did a major piece with backing from the Fund for Investigative Journalism, revealing that the IRS had audited twenty-seven Black leaders in Mississippi. It was published in 1975 in the *Delta Democrat-Times*, a progressive paper run by Hodding Carter III, best known for his later role as undersecretary of state for public affairs for President Jimmy Carter.

During that period, Berry was also writing a lot of fiction, "the brilliance of which eluded New York publishers," and pulling all-nighters "writing novels that never saw the light of day." He was also moving into videotape work, which led to production of a documentary and book of the same name, *Up From the Cradle of Jazz*. The documentary aired in 1980 on Louisiana Public Broadcasting. The book, done with coauthors Jonathan Foose and Tad Jones, was published in 1986.

In hindsight, the dual track of his life is obvious: an instinct for the journalistic deep dig and an ear attuned to the soul of New Orleans.

In 1982, newlywed Berry and his first wife, Lisa LeBlanc, put all of their possessions in storage and headed to Europe.

When the couple arrived in Paris following travel in Italy and elsewhere, they found out that Berry had been accepted into a program called Journalists in Paris, a ten-month language school and travel program. On the side, he did pieces for *Readers' Digest* (on how airline luggage retrieval systems worked) and for the *International Herald Tribune*. "We managed to make a go of it for about fifteen months, and then came back."

That marriage ended in divorce in 1996. They had two daughters, Simonette, a graduate of Tulane University in studio art, and Ariel, who died at age seventeen in 2008 of heart failure and complications from Down syndrome.

The couple moved back to New Orleans from Paris just in time for him to finish work on *Up From the Cradle of Jazz* and, in the fall of 1984, see the first news about Father Gilbert Gauthe, a serial pedophile and a priest of the Diocese of Lafayette, Louisiana. That news would change the course of Berry's life.

Exposing the Abuse Crisis

Lead Us Not Into Temptation: Catholic Priests and the Sexual Abuse of Children, was published by Doubleday in 1992, seven years after Berry's original work about Gauthe appeared in 1985 in the *Times of Acadiana* and the *National Catholic Reporter*, and fully ten years before *The Boston Globe*'s spotlight reports documented the abuse in the Archdiocese of Boston.

Those earliest accounts from the mid-1980s are journalistically cautious and measured, though detailed and precise. The pieces make for deeply disturbing reading, breath-catching in their preposterous newness. Most Catholics of the time couldn't imagine priests doing what Gauthe, a serial pedophile, had done to children with whom he came in contact.

By the early 1990s, Berry had done enough of the type of reporting required to construct the distinguished narrative that elevates his work above many others. The opening scenes of *Lead Us Not Into Temptation* are darkly riveting, understatedly infused with the pain and rage of parents becoming aware that a favorite parish priest, someone who sat at their table and who had taken three of their sons, all altar boys, on camping trips, had been repeatedly molesting those youngsters for years.

It was shoe-leather journalism of an era that preceded databases and email and the nervous flutter of social media. Berry conveys anguish understood by way of hours of interviews and conversation and firsthand observation, wrenching as it was. He describes, conversation by conversation, what would later become recognized as the Catholic institutional preference for protecting the perpetrator over concern for child victims.

His work on that 1984 case in Louisiana broke open what the sociologist priest Andrew M. Greeley described in the intro to the 2000 paperback edition of *Lead Us Not Into Temptation* as "the greatest scandal in the history of religion in America."

It is easy to speculate that were Greeley alive today he would amend that comment to reflect that the scandal has gone global and is yet bedeviling church leaders.

"He was the Woodward and Bernstein altogether," said David Gibson, an award-winning journalist and author who now heads the Center on Religion and Culture at Fordham University, referring to the legendary investigative reporting duo of the Watergate era. "He was the shoe leather that doggedly constructed the narrative of the scandal piece by piece."

Berry represented, said Gibson in a phone interview, "what real investigative reporting involves. Everyone wants to go for the brass ring, the big expose, but that's not the way it normally works. Classic investigative reporting involves reporting this one thing. And then the next, and the next."

Said David Clohessy, cofounder of SNAP, the abuse victim advocacy group, "No single reporter anywhere has done more to expose—and thus help to remove—this horror from the church. For years, it felt like he was practically the only journalist who took victims seriously and listened to us compassionately. And he was perhaps the first reporter to recognize that we were more than isolated victims, but in fact a potential collective force for good, as we started in the 1980s and 1990s to organize ourselves first into support groups and then into advocacy work."

"He was the first to look at the crisis in a broader way, as more than a handful of 'bad apple' priests and to look at bishops' self-serving claims with a careful eye," Clohessy said.

Being the first wasn't easy. Berry was watching the story develop bit by bit in minimal accounts in local media and felt there was need for a deeper dig suitable to a national outlet. He knew lawsuits were piling up in Lafayette. "How many other kids were out there?" he asked. He tried a number of national publications: *The New York Times, The Washington Post, Vanity Fair, The Nation, Mother Jones.* No takers.

He did three months of investigation on his own in early 1985 before calling Linda Matys, then-editor of Lafayette's weekly, *The Times of Acadiana.* She was interested, offered a month's salary and expenses, as well as permission to publish reports in national outlets after they appeared in the local paper. Before heading off to Lafayette to continue his research, he called Thomas C. Fox, then-editor of *National Catholic Reporter.* Berry had been told of *NCR* by someone at the Fund for Investigative Journalism, which had also rejected his proposal seeking funds.

Fox, who since has served as publisher and is currently CEO/President of *NCR*, said the publication had begun gathering similar information from other parts of the country "though not in any systematic way."

In *Lead Us Not Into Temptation*, Berry wrote that Fox cautioned the church "was not subject to the same checks and balances as a government." But that "if child abuse had crept into that tradition and could be proven, NCR would report it."

"This is an important story," he quoted Fox in the book, "but as a loving critic of the church, I want it done in a way that will spur the hierarchy to act responsibly. We don't have to pull punches, but there has to be a motive beyond sheer exposé."

By the time Berry began work in earnest for *The Times of Acadiana,* he knew that reports of priests molesting youngsters, and of possible cover-up, had surfaced in at least several states. This was different from a run-of-the-mill corruption story. "The violation of children by men in the church was something I couldn't walk away from. And I kept getting more and more leads," he told me.

What followed is a saga that, thirty-four years later, is nowhere near running its course. The original exposé that appeared in the Acadiana paper was the basis for a four-page spread in June 1985 in NCR. Berry continued to dig, and to write and report, and long before it became a story widely believed, he knew that its tentacles spread globally and to the highest echelons of church governance.

Exposing the Maciel Scandal

One of the most notorious figures of the abuse scandal in the Catholic Church was Marcial Maciel Degollado, a Mexican cleric, founder of the highly regimented Legionaries of Christ, and an enormously successful fundraiser. Maciel was a caricature of overweening piety with breathtaking amounts of cash to throw around the Vatican. He also enjoyed a certain insulation against investigation of numerous substantial accusations of horrific sexual abuse of minors because he was a favorite of Pope John Paul II. Consequently, he was also the favorite of John Paul's highest profile acolytes in the United States, who ridiculed and dismissed the reporting of Berry and his friend and colleague, the late Gerald Renner, when, in articles published in 1997 in the *Hartford Courant*, they began to expose Maciel and the practices of the Legion.

Eventually, the truth caught up to Maciel, a predatory abuser who also fathered several children by different women. Under Pope Benedict XVI, an investigation went forward, and he was confined in 2006 to a life of private prayer and penance. He died in 2008.

The world came to know about the hypocrisy and crimes of Maciel through the reporting of Berry and Renner, who was then a religion writer at the *Hartford Courant*. That paper carried the Berry/Renner initial reporting about the Legion in the United States. Berry wrote extensive pieces for *NCR*, published in 2010, about Maciel and the influence his money was able to leverage at the Vatican.

In March 2002, Father Richard John Neuhaus, one of the principal intellectual authors of the religious right in the United States, wrote a scathing and quite personal condemnation of Berry and Renner's initial reporting on Maciel.

Neuhaus, who died in 2009, had already thoroughly disparaged and largely dismissed Berry's early reporting on the crisis in a lengthy review of *Lead Us Not Into Temptation*, his first book about the scandal. The review appeared in the January 1992 issue of *First Things*, a magazine Neuhaus founded. He gave only grudging concession to the factual accuracy of Berry's accounts. The scandal did not fit the narrative preferred by Neuhaus and his followers, and he insisted on blaming most of it on the influence of homo-sexuality in the priesthood, an assertion debunked by most professionals and eventually in an extensive 2011 study of the situation by investigators at the John Jay College of Criminal Justice.

In the 2002 review, Neuhaus slammed the work of Berry and Renner, as well as NCR, which ran an account of the *Courant* reporting, as trading in rumor and slander. He called the reporting "an attack" on Maciel, "the much-revered founder of the Legionaries of Christ, one of the more vibrant and successful renewal movements in contemporary Catholicism."

In thousands of words, Neuhaus continued his blistering personal attack on the journalists, demeaning their work, condemning them as motivated by hatred of the church and working every angle to erode their credibility. Neuhaus concluded: "I have arrived at *moral certainty* that the charges are false and malicious [emphasis in the original]," he wrote. For emphasis, he added that the charges "should be given no credence whatsoever."

At the time, Neuhaus's reputation was yet untainted by the facts that eventually showed him to be as wholly incorrect as he was morally certain. At the time, his moral bluster created quite a headwind against which Berry and others had to fight to keep reporting honestly about Maciel and the Legion.

In the long haul of the story, the insistent denial by Neuhaus and others sank beneath the enormity of the evidence, which continues to accumulate to this day, of what Berry repeatedly referred to in our conversations as institutional mendacity. More simply, bishops lied and covered up, and he knew it. Today, he "shrugs," he says, at the displays of breathless ongoing "discovery" of old evidence that continues to demonstrate the degree to which the hierarchical structure is corrupt and incapable of confessing its own sin.

It took him six and a half years to research and write *Lead Us Not Into Temptation.* The book was rejected by thirty publishers. It had been to different editors twice at Doubleday, but finally found a home there when Greeley, who had been reading chapters for Berry and giving him reactions, paved the way to yet another editor at Doubleday, and he took it on. Berry said his agent at the time "told me on several occasions that he sensed that editors were skittish on reading it. That they feared their publishing company would be sued by the church."

But "things were starting to shift" in 1991 as the public was slowly coming to terms with the scandal, and the book, finally published, caused quite a stir and landed Berry on a lot of national TV news shows to talk about it. "I guess in a sense the long struggle with the reporting and to get it published was vindicated."

Back to New Orleans

As the marketplace took root, Africans used the land to dramatize their past, resurrecting burial choreographies of the mother culture. The living danced their tributes to the dead in sinuous rings, moving to the rhythms of strings and hide-covered drums. As time passed and crowds grew, the dancers formed concentric circles, rings within rings. Several hundred people at a time flow to spirit tides that surged out of the past.
—City of a Million Dreams

Berry's CV runs to twenty and a half pages, starting with ten books—including one quite nicely done novel that did make it beyond his study, *Last of the Red Hot Pappas*—a one-man play, *Earl Long in Purgatory,* five documentaries, a full page plus of awards and honors, pages listing his major work published in scholarly journals as well as mainstream outlets. (Between the CV list, which runs to 2012, and what's appeared on the *NCR* website since, I counted at least forty-seven pieces that have run in this publication.) He also lists two pages of grants and fellowships from an array of foundations and funds. Berry's prolific output is matched only by the amount of time and energy he's had to spend hustling for the money to make the projects possible.

Asked if he's ever held an actual job, he paused long, lips moving slightly as he silently ticked through the catalogue of accomplishments. "No," he answered.

In 2004, Berry married Melanie McKay, who recently retired as vice provost for academic affairs at Loyola University New Orleans, where she also taught English for many years. She once suggested he return to school and acquire an additional degree so that teaching might be a fallback position. But, he said, "I had no interest in teaching at all." So he kept scrambling and writing.

The demands of investigative reporting—as Gibson put it, first one thing, then the next, and the next, fact linked to fact—leave little room, beyond raising the next logical question, for moving beyond the evidence. It is a meticulous enterprise.

History, at least of New Orleans, and even in describing above the activity of slaves in transforming a patch of land, provides space for Berry's more lyrical side, and he deploys it with an accomplished hand. There is an accompanying documentary, which bears the book's title, coproduced with his daughter, Simonette. An explanation by Berry and a trailer introducing the documentary can be found here.

Forward Reviews termed the book "a hypnotic biography of a unique American city."

Wrote *NCR*'s reviewer: "Drawing upon the best scholarship in military and political history, culture, music, food, and urban geography, Berry's resources offer delightful insight into the vast mosaic that is this global city."

It was formidable enough work to earn a review by Garry Wills in *The New York Review of Books*, an examination that validated Berry's ambition. Wills moves from one fascinating character to the next in what he describes as Berry's technique of "overlapping narrative."

Starting with the city's flamboyant founder, Jean-Baptiste Le Moyne, Sieur de Bienville, then traveling through eighteenth-century monks and church disputes that preshadow the current era, through musicians and politicians and spiritualists of every imaginable stripe, and through the devastation and resurrection out of Hurricane Katrina, this is, indeed, a breathtaking guided tour through an American city that can't begin to be captured in travel brochures. It's just too quirky, too out of the mainstream narrative of settlers and rugged individualism.

"I wanted to understand the place where I'm from," said Berry during his presentation at the bookstore in Washington. "I figured the best way to do that is to understand the daily life of people across the first three centuries."

As so many times before in the course of his own character-driven journey, he figured correctly.

Grace Under Pressure

John Baldoni / 2021

Interview conducted on October 12, 2021 via LinkedIn Live. Reprinted by permission.

John Baldoni: Welcome to another edition of *Grace Under Pressure* where my guest today is Jason Berry. *Grace Under Pressure* is a show that focuses on the good stuff in life, which is too often dismissed: the caring, the commitment, and compassion we show toward others. And as you'll discover from Jason's life, he has been one who has sought to bring people together by telling the truth, sometimes the unpleasant truth. And with that, I want to introduce you. Welcome Jason Berry.

Jason Berry: Thank you, John. It's great to see you again and to be with you

Baldoni: Jason and I go back, way, way back to our college years. And Jason was a few years ahead of me and graduated, and he went onto the big bold world, and he was the first person I know ever to have published a book. So he has been something of a hero to me, and I truly mean that because he's an exceptional reporter and writer and gifted storyteller. He's also the author of a book called *City of a Million Dreams: A History of New Orleans at Year 300*, and there's a documentary film that he directed, and we're going to show a clip of that later on in the show. Jason has been an extraordinary reporter, and [he was] one of the first reporters to uncover the priest abuse of children in the Catholic Church. He wrote a book called *Lead us Not Into Temptation*, I believe it was 1992, and he's been covered in the media from *Nightline, The New York Times* . . . you name it, Jason has been there. He's an exceptional and caring person, and it's such an honor to have you on the show. Welcome Jason.

Berry: John. It is a great pleasure and thank you for those kind comments.

Baldoni: You have been doing this a long time since our days at the *Georgetown Voice* where I was a photographer and you were an editor with our dear departed friend and editor, Steve Pisinski . . . so a shout out to Steve there. You were among the first, if not the first, to investigate the priestly abuse of children, and you wrote a book about it. What led you to investigate, Jason? And it cannot have been easy.

Berry: It was not. Toward the end of 1984, I had become a parent for the first time. My older daughter had been born that December, and I got a lead from a lawyer I knew about a priest who had just recently been indicted for abusing altar boys out in Cajun country. As it happened, I went to high school at Jesuit in New Orleans with one of the attorneys who had filed lawsuits against the diocese of Lafayette. He let me read the depositions of the bishop and other church officials. I could believe, I could understand that a priest like anyone could have some pathological illness, but when I read the cold printed words on paper, the bishop trying to explain why he had sent this priest on assignment after assignment, I realized, this is the story of a coverup. This is outrageous. They never should have put this guy back in commission. So that's how it began. It was a series of articles. I had a joint assignment for the *Times of Acadiana* in Lafayette, Louisiana, and *National Catholic Reporter*, an independent weekly in Kansas City. And the series stretched out over the spring and into the summer and got a lot of national attention. And soon thereafter, I began working on the book that came out six years, seven years later.

Baldoni: Well, recently you came back into my horizon more vividly with a video or documentary that *The New York Times* did. And I thought, *The New York Times* doing a documentary on a reporter, that's special. That's like the new Nobel Prize Committee talking about its members. So that's really cool. And they titled it "Almost Famous." Where did that title come from?

Berry: I don't know. I wish they dropped the almost, but I'll take anything in *The New York Times* when it comes. Actually, the way it happened was a young woman called me. She worked for the production studio in Los Angeles and she said, "We're doing this series of people, 'Almost Famous.'" She said, "I see you did a lot of reporting on the Catholic Church crisis before *The Boston Globe* series in 2002." And I said, "Yes, indeed. I did." So she asked me what I felt about that. And I said, "Well, I thought it was a very good series." She asked what I thought about the film. It was a great film, deserved the Academy Award. And that's kind of how the preliminary conversation began. And eventually Ben Proudfoot, the producer-director, decided to do a piece on me. We did a nine-hour interview, which I can assure you was quite daunting. And you know, the piece they edited I thought was, if I may, quite eloquent, and how he handled my story.

Baldoni: Well, truly it should be shown in every journalism program because it gets to the real Jason Berry, and from my perspective, your heart, your compassion, but also your doggedness and the resilience that sets you and reporters such as you, especially independent reporters like you, [apart]. And I think it's interesting, because I do remember vividly watching *Spotlight* and seeing your book shown right on there. That was pretty darn cool. So what was the backstory [behind] your book being in the actual movie?

Berry: That story is that one day I was sitting at my desk, and I was working, and Mike Rezendes of *The Boston Globe* called me. I knew everyone in the *Spotlight* team. In fact, I did a good deal of writing for the *Globe* in their commentary pages that year. And Rezendes called and said, "Oh, I need a favor." I said, "Yeah, sure. What do you need?" And he said, "Well, we're on the set right now." And I didn't know what set he meant, I said, "Great! What are you doing?" And he said, "They're making a movie out of *Spotlight*." And I said, "Oh, terrific." And I guess I vaguely knew that. Anyway, they had called Doubleday to get permission to put the book cover in the movie. And one of the lawyers for Doubleday said, no, no, you can't do that. Well, lawyers are trained to say no. He said, "Well, look, can you help us?" And I said, "Yeah, don't listen to that lawyer. The rights reverted to me several years ago, of course you can use the cover of the book." Would you send us an email? Sure. I'll send you an email. So I sent the email, they thanked me profusely. I hung up assuming, you know, I'll be on the cutting room floor. And then months later I was at a reception at the New Orleans Museum of Art. A woman came up to me and said, "I saw the film." And I said, "Wonderful. What did you think?" I didn't know what she was talking about. So what did you think? And she said, "Oh, I thought it was very well done. And they showed your cover in that movie." And then she said, "I was at Telluride for the festival," kind of showing that you have a little stroke in life. And so I realized that I had made the final cut, and when I saw, of course I was delighted.

Baldoni: Oh, that's great. Now I want to segue into your project of the moment. You wrote a book a few years ago called *City of a Million Dreams*. So what led you to that? And the next step is the movie. And we're going to tease our audience. We will show a clip in just a moment. So, tell us the backstory of that, Jason, please.

Berry: The backstory John, is that there have been two stories that really defined my life as a writer, the city of my birth, where I was born and raised and grew up and where I live today,

Baldoni: Which is New Orleans.

Berry: Yes, indeed. And the church in which I was raised and still struggle to remain a member of. So, I started following jazz funerals. One of my earlier books is a history of New Orleans rhythm and blues. And I began following jazz funerals in the late nineties. I wondered where they came from, and the more I studied the story of burial traditions of the city, I realized that they held a mirror to the story of the city itself. So the book and the footage that I kept shooting was an overlapping project, trying to convey the history of New Orleans through these caravans of memory, the funerals that the musicians played, and tracing their origins back through a public park, known as Congo Square, where enslaved Africans danced burial choreographies to the mother culture. So that's kind of how it began and took shape.

Baldoni: [*On the film*] What a wonderful tribute, and it just opens with a bang, and I'm watching it and I haven't seen the whole film yet, but I see a sense of spirituality, but the operative thing for me is hope, am I correct in this Jason?

Berry: Absolutely. Actually, the film is streaming over the next week at the Heartland International Festival in Indianapolis, your viewers can link on and see it there. It will also be streaming in New Orleans, November 5 to 21 at the New Orleans Film Festival. And it's also screening right now, I believe, at the Martha's Vineyard African American Film Festival, virtually is the way a lot of festivals are doing it now. I had the great advantage of working with a brilliant editor, Tim Watson, whose fingerprints are on every frame in that film. And he lived it, he breathed it, and he worked closely with my other coproducer, Simonette Berry, my daughter, who played a major role in orchestrating the Congo Square sequences that you saw. We also had a terrific executive producer, Bernard Pettingill, who was two years ahead of me at Jesuit High School and came in when we really needed financing in the home stretch and has been great, shoulder to shoulder with us. It's a story of redemption and a belief that even when we die, we go to a better place.

Baldoni: Well, if there's any, if there's any city which exemplifies a redemption, it has to be New Orleans. I mean, so many catastrophes just recently a hurricane there, and of course Katrina, but the city doesn't die, and it doesn't mean that it just doesn't die. It has a vibrancy and a life to it. And by you shining a light on a tradition that most people, well, certainly me, didn't know existed. I knew about jazz funerals, but not Congo Square. So what a powerful story.

Berry: Well, thank you. Uh, I think the city does have a life force, and you know, many people the world over come here spend a few days or a week or so, and they take away memories, but you have to live here over quite a period of time to really appreciate the resilience. And also, the social mosaic. I mean, this city is a crossroads of humanity. It was a melting pot long before the academic term was coined. And I think it stands today, honestly, as a tribute to the best impulses of America, of people. You know, jazz is a metaphor of democracy, improvisational voices, finding a common melody, and I think the city exemplifies that.

Baldoni: When you've been writing about jazz for a long time, if I'm not mistaken, you were involved in some projects, what, forty years ago or something?

Berry: No, you date me, but I forgive you [*laughter*]. Well, the book I did in 1986, *Up From the Cradle of Jazz*, grew out of my first film, in fact, and it's a story of neighborhoods that created the postwar rhythm and blues sound, which includes the masking Indians, the Mardi Gras Indians. You know, I've been collecting the stories of people in this city for years. And I'm always fascinated by the ways in which character is fate, as the Greeks held. For so many people, there is a drive, not just to survive these days with the elements seemingly against us, but to celebrate and to be thankful for what we have. In a city like this, there's great food, good architecture, and the tradition of parading, which I think is a unifying factor across the racial spectrum.

Baldoni: That's powerful. And then getting back to the jazz, and you had noted improvisation. In my world of leadership and management, jazz is often referred to as an insight into collaboration because it's the, you have a set theme and then one goes off and different instruments play there and different musicians, play different things, but they all come back together and it's, and the best musicians are those who are generative, you know, and they talk about whoever it was, you know, Miles Davis or John Coltrane or Charlie Parker, you know, they like to share things. And so that's germane to us. And I think, and in just the little clip I've seen of this . . . the humanity of this comes through, and we're different, but we're all united. Are we not?

Berry: Oh, listen, this is music to my ears. The protagonist of this film, Dr. Michael White, is a professor at Xavier University. He's done something like two dozen CDs and albums, and he lost his home in Hurricane Katrina. It's a very powerful sequence in the film. I followed him the day he got home and went through with all of his intellectual capital as mush underfoot. I mean, his compositions, his books, his CDs, and to follow someone like that as he recovered, not just recovered, but rebuilt his career. He is, to my way of thinking, a kind of everyman of New Orleans. So working with him was a great privilege. And I think the film reflects his role as a mirror of the larger mosaic of the city.

Baldoni: Well, one of the themes of this show is "grace under pressure," which is the idea of keeping it calm and collected and being there for others.

And the work that you've done, Jason, is akin to that in the sense that you've tackled tough stories to two things: the jazz stuff, which is powerful in your city that you have love for, but also the Catholic church, which I sense you have a degree of love for, but yet, sometimes the best form of love is you have to speak truth to power. And you've certainly been doing that for a long time. And a lot of people I'm sure wish you would just go away. So how do you steel yourself for that, Jason?

Berry: Oh, well, I listened to a lot of music. I try to find good Bordeaux, red, for the sullen moments. Yeah, you know, there was a period, oh, in the mid-nineties when I was not exactly the most popular person in the Catholic Church, but after *The Boston Globe* series, as my book started to get wider circulation, a lot of people realized I was kind of the canary in the coal mine, if you will. And I do think Pope Francis has a reform agenda and he's following it—

Baldoni: He's a Jesuit, of course,

Berry: I went to Jesuit High School. I cannot speak ill of a Jesuit. But we haven't finished the interview yet, so we hold out hope. There's hope, it's always eternal. No, but I think his agenda of radical mercy is prophetic. You know, the idea that we cannot let migrants simply fall off the face of the earth. We have to think about a way of welcoming them as Angela Merkel did as the Chancellor of Germany. And there's a dimension of that in this film, because one of the characters in this film is a woman named Deb Cotton who was shot at a parade, and what she manifested toward the young men who were arrested. . . . It was a very moving sequence in this film. And, you know, parading is a metaphor of life in my view. And parading with music as we have done historically in this city is a way of telling the story of the city, and I hope that that form of grace has a certain arc and transcendence that viewers of this film and the people who read the book will embrace.

Baldoni: Well, I mean, certainly when you see the concept of parades and the verb you made there, a gerund you made it, parading, that's a form of community, is it not? And it's an open manifestation of "I'm here together with my brotherhood and our sisterhood," and all of that. So that's very much in the concept of grace, which is that commonality that binds us together.

Berry: I think you've put it quite beautifully.

Baldoni: Of course, it's my show.

Berry: That's right. And I'm the guest, and you're not paying. But you know, parading is a tradition in New Orleans that spans the many peoples who have come here. Rex, the king of Mardi Gras, typically a civic leader, follows on Carnival day the crew of Zulu, which is the African American parade. And there are parades in many of the neighborhoods. And I think what draws people to the streets, to the music, to the cadences, and certainly the costumes, is a celebration of the better angels of our nature.

Baldoni: To bring in President Lincoln, one of my favorites, so that's good. But anyway, and as you go forward in this, I mean, when people come to New Orleans, they like it for its charm, its food, and stuff like that. But you know, you said it takes a long time to understand the city. And so, I'm going to ask a dumb question, but I mean, people from the outside . . . given the rising levels of sea level, does New Orleans have a future? So, what are the people of New Orleans thinking about climate change?

Berry: When they're not parading, we think a lot about it. Well, the levees held this time with Hurricane Ida. The Army Corps of Engineers did a $15 billion rebuilding of the levees after Hurricane Katrina. You know, these are issues that many communities face today, and I think we're at the beginning of a long road. We need restoration of the coastal wetlands offshore to the south of the city. And by the same token, many of the communities that lie between New Orleans and the Gulf of Mexico—Houma, Thibodaux, and many of the smaller towns along those roads—are facing a kind of existential crisis. And it is a moment that begs for principal leadership. And I think we all keep our shoulder to the wheel and hope that we can push to get the right solutions.

Baldoni: Well, I think your film is going to shine a very positive light on the traditions of New Orleans and its environments. And that can only be a good thing. You know, let's save this for what it is. It's such a unique city and it's so different. So anyway, we're coming kind of coming to the end of our show, Jason, and viewers know that I always ask someone a story of grace, and I know you have one to share with us, Jason.

Berry: Well, I guess the story of grace I would share has to do with my younger daughter, Ariel, who had Down syndrome and had heart and lung issues and was with us for seventeen years and manifested a joy of living that touched her mother, her sister, both of her grandmothers, her aunts and uncles, and yesterday was her birthday. She would have been thirty. Although we miss her, her spirit lives with us.

Baldoni: Oh, that's great. And what a wonderful story of that and grace, and I would say the work that you do is . . . grace is that ability to come together as a catalyst for the greater good, as you probably know, from our good judgment that taught us. And maybe it went over my head, but probably not yours. Jason.

Berry: Men for others. Men and women for others, I think is now the phrase.

Baldoni: I am an admirer of all the great work that you have done. And because you were an ancillary to grace that is often not known and its courage, and I know in your work, it's not easy, what you have done, and to keep doing it year after year, decade after decade. And it's wonderful now that you have such as celebratory story to tell. That's great. So Jason, it's been such a treat to have you on the show and how can people find you?

Berry: My website is jasonberryauthor.com and the film website is cityofamilliondreams.com. Please pay us a visit.

Baldoni: Great, well, we will put those in the notes and Jason, it has been an honor to have you on the show and with that, I'm going to close out.

Berry: Thank you.

City of a Million Dreams Fulfills Twenty-Five-Year Documentary Quest for Jason Berry

David Johnson / 2021

From *OffBeat Magazine*, October 27, 2021. Courtesy of New Orleans' *OffBeat Magazine*. Used with permission.

Among the many films to be screened at the 2021 New Orleans Film Festival is *City of a Million Dreams*, a documentary that examines the evolution of the jazz funeral tradition in New Orleans. Through vintage photos and archival films, historical recreations and filming of modern-day jazz funerals, the film traces the evolution of the tradition—and New Orleans itself—from the late eighteenth century to today. From the African rhythms and ring dances of Congo Square to the influence of European marching bands and Sicilian brass bands—along with early twentieth-century jazz musicians—to the present day's rollicking processions, this epic documentary shows the cultural memory of Black New Orleans and rituals of resilience as never before.

The project, which includes a companion book published under the same title in 2018, was the culmination of twenty-five years of extensive research and tenacity by investigative reporter, author and filmmaker Jason Berry. He spoke with *OffBeat* about the circuitous journey from initial concept to the big-screen premiere for a film that took many unexpected turns, including the upheaval of Hurricane Katrina, coverage of the Catholic Church abuse crisis, the unexpected death of a protagonist in the documentary, and, most recently, the pandemic.

David Johnson: You are a native New Orleanian? When did you attend your first jazz funeral?

Jason Berry: The first jazz funeral I went to was in 1973. It was for De De Pierce, the grand old man of Preservation Hall, a pianist. It was at Corpus Christi Church. I remember I had seen him before, but I didn't really know him other than as a spectator. I remember standing outside on the sidewalk watching the coffin come out and the musicians put their instruments up, almost like a military unit putting up swords. The sun was coming down and dancing off the saxophones and the trumpets and the clarinets. It was one of the most beautiful spectacles I'd ever seen. I was mesmerized by it. Then I followed the procession as they put the coffin into the limousine. Then the band moved out. I was walking with the crowd and then they turned on the up tempo music and people danced the soul away.

When it was over, I was walking back to my car and I was just thinking, this is so beautiful. I've never seen anything like this. As the years passed, I kept going to funerals. And I did articles about them. I did a long piece when Chief Pete of the White Eagles died. Often I went to funerals, not even with an assignment. I just went and I took notes. I went as part of a community. I went to pay condolences, often for someone I had known, or even if I didn't know them. Sometimes I went because I thought these are important events to attend. And I began slowly to form the view that these funerals were stories about the city at a given point in time, like moments of history unfolding.

Then when I really started doing the serious research, late nineties, early two thousands, I kept wondering, how did the tradition begin? I knew that Congo Square was a key piece because Sterling Stuckey, in his book *Slave Culture*, says that everywhere the ring dance is performed, it is an homage to the ancestors. And I realized, okay, these are burial choreographies that have been transplanted after the Middle Passage on the New World soil. So there is this element of life after death in the eyewitness accounts of Congo Square. Of course the people who were writing those accounts weren't really aware of that. Probably the best example is—I have a chapter on him in the book—the architect Benjamin Latrobe. He has one of the most detailed personal accounts of a visit to Congo Square. What struck me about that was the attention to detail.

There's a kind of veneer of racial insensitivity—racism would certainly be an accurate term—referring to people as savages and heathens and things like that. But once you peel away the editorializing of the Western eye, you realize that this guy is writing about the transplanting of a profound ritual. Later on, scholars like Ned Sublette and Freddi Williams Evans, in their books, draw the linkages to Kongo—Kongo with a K—as the region where the dance traditions Latrobe was documenting came from.

As all of this material came out, I realized that there was another side to it—namely the brass bands, which are a European tradition. And the metaphor slowly came to me that the ring dances of Africa and the linear processions of the European bands signaled the coming together of the ring and the line. And to me that image, the fusion of the ring and the line of Africa and Europe, defines the cultural essence of New Orleans. It took me many years to understand that: Not only years of going to second lines and funerals, particularly, but also the heavy reading I did over many years to understand the depths of historical memory and the spiritual underpinnings of these traditions.

I had published *Up From the Cradle of Jazz* in 1986 and I was writing a lot of pieces about New Orleans music for different outlets. I had also been going to jazz funerals for quite a number of years, and I was getting more and more curious about the origins of the tradition. At the same time, through interviews with Dr. Michael White, Gregg Stafford, Milton Batiste, and Harold Dejan, I awakened to the realization that this beautiful tradition was being threatened by the drug culture, by the crack epidemic. So many young people—young boys not old enough to vote—were going to early deaths. The second line parades for them, those funeral parades, were quite different from the others.

DJ: How was the jazz funeral tradition changing?

JB: The musicians worried about a spirituality being removed from the whole procession with just hard-edge, fiery dancing as a way for people to get their sorrow out. And so I pitched a proposal to the Ford Foundation saying that I was doing research on a book and that I was focused on this conflict between continuity and change. And the grant officer who got back to me was fascinated with the topic. And she told me they weren't giving research grants for books anymore, but this would be the perfect topic for an oral history, a video oral history.

So I spoke to Bruce Raeburn, then the director at the Hogan Jazz Archive, and I contacted the Payson Center at Tulane. A friend of mine, Bill Bertrand, who had just retired as a chair in public health, he was very interested in it. And so between those two offices at Tulane, I got the institutional support. So for two years there were consecutive grants.

I was interviewing musicians and filming funerals and wakes. The long and short of it was that after all that work was done, I spent a good deal of time working on a treatment and a proposal for a full production at Congo Square. The dramatization of the dances of the enslaved Africans was a center piece of that proposal and treatment.

A guy at the Ford Foundation came back to me and said, look, you've got great footage, this is a fascinating story, but reenactments have a bad odor at PBS. Back then, before Netflix, before streaming outlets, PBS was pretty much where you went. The NEH [National Endowment for the Humanities] basically said the same thing to my proposal, but then a NEH grant officer said, look, you've got all this great research and you want to do a book. And you want to do a film. Why don't you apply for a Guggenheim Fellowship and write your book? Get the book out and then come back to us. Well at that point, I really had nothing to lose. So I applied for the Guggenheim and, to my shock, I actually got it. So I spent almost a year doing a great deal of research. Not only at the Hogan Jazz Archive, but in other libraries and outlets.

I was moving well along with the book. And then in 2002, it was at the end of that year of work when *The Boston Globe* began its big series on the Catholic clergy crisis, which I had written about in my 1992 book [*Lead Us Not Into Temptation*]. And within a couple months, I had a contract to do a sequel. So the next couple of years, I was going back and forth to Rome working on what became the book *Vows of Silence*. And then I did a documentary on that. Well, in the middle of all that work, I was still attending jazz funerals. And occasionally, when I had enough money, filming one. Then Hurricane Katrina hit. I called Dr. Michael White. I was in Plano, Texas, at my sister-in-law's home. And he was in Houston when we finally connected by cellphone. He told me that he had been on Google Maps, and he was pretty certain everything in his house had flooded.

So I asked and he agreed to let me film him going into his house, which I did with Philip Braun, a great cameraman who was with me for many of those shoots. So the film grew episodically as I filmed events. And I had a long stretch after that actually doing another book on the Catholic Church. And then finally in 2015, Dr. White had regrouped. He had gotten back in a new home, and I just decided to put the Catholic Church reporting behind me because I really wanted to finish both the book of New Orleans and the film. And so I began fundraising in earnest toward the end of 2015. The last five and a half years have been a path of production work, halting to raise money, and then more production. And you know, that's the way documentaries are often made. The big turning point came in 2016 when we did a Kickstarter.

One of the people I had on the Kickstarter list was Bernard Pettingill, a guy I had gone to Jesuit High School with who became a forensic economist in West Palm Beach. He's done well. And he said, "I don't do Kickstarters, I don't do charity." And I said, "No, this is not charity really." I was trying to explain it and he said, "Look, how much you need to finish your movie?" So

I swallowed and gave him a healthy six figure amount. He said, "Oh, I can do that." So all of a sudden I had an investor, an executive producer, and he has been extremely helpful in many ways. He really has supported the film through all of the tribulations that came with the COVID, cessation of work as everybody else experienced.

DJ: Deb Cotton, another journalist who documented second line parade culture, is prominently featured in *City of a Million Dreams.* How did you meet her?

JB: I was actually doing a piece for *Global Post,* a foreign-affairs website, which sadly has since gone under. I was doing a piece on the Dalai Lama's visit to New Orleans, which coincided with that terrible shooting on Mother's Day at a second line parade in 2013. I started reading about Deb Cotton, who had been shot, and the fact that she had issued a statement from the hospital offering a—how can I put it?—she issued a statement saying that, as a society, we need to look at these young people on the edge and why they were doing things like this. And I was just struck by the compassion.

I made some calls and learned that Deb was in a severe state at the ICU at the university hospital. And then shortly after that, Linda Usdin, a close friend of hers, made a statement on her behalf to the city council echoing that sentiment of not wanting to be retaliatory toward these men. Not forgiving them, but asking that we see what they had done in a larger social context. It was really profound, too. After Deb stabilized, many surgeries later, I was introduced to her through Mark Hertsgaard, the journalist in the film who speaks about her. Mark and I have been friends for many years. He's now the head of Covering Climate Now.

He had been coming to New Orleans on assignments dealing with the wetlands and environmental issues. And he was shot in that parade, too. I saw it on TV that night and I sent him an email saying maybe you've left town. Thirty seconds later, I get a response. He says, "I'm at the airport. I did get shot, but I'm okay. I'm going back to San Francisco. I'll call you tomorrow." And we had a long talk. He was hit in the calf, I guess that would be correct. So he as a journalist had a deepening interest in what this was all about. And he got to know Deb and he then introduced me to her. And I originally wanted to film her after she had made that profound statement to the judge at the sentencing hearing of those four young men.

I wanted to film her going into the prison and having a conversation with the guy who shot her. This is beyond what we typically see in films and documentaries. The idea of forgiveness. It's Shakespearean. It's like Portia, *The*

Merchant of Venice. The quality of mercy is twice blessed. But that did not pan out. Getting access to the prison posed substantial problems. In the meantime, I was really getting to know Deb and it was a slow process. We hired her as an advisory producer. And as part of that, she gave us access to a lot of the video that she had done for her blog about second line parades. We had a good many conversations. I was taking notes. But I wanted to figure out the best way to film a textured interview with her. And at this point, we didn't really know how the film would end. That's fairly typical for documentaries. Nonfiction films often plunge into a set of events, and you follow them through to however they end.

So the dialogue continued until one day I went over to her house for a meeting. It was basically a long pre-interview before we decided where to set up the camera. Where to have her and what she would talk about. She didn't show up, which is most unlike Deb. She was a very professional person and a good writer. So several days later she called me and apologized. She had an emergency visit to the hospital. Then I began to realize that her condition was more dire than I thought. We continued having our conversations, but I was a little concerned about pressing her to sit down and do an interview on camera when she was dealing with a lot of health issues. And then very suddenly, she died.

When she died, we, all of us who knew her, were numb and devastated. And then we realized, okay, we have to film her funeral. We have to do justice to who she was. We did film the funeral and the second line. And then we had to figure out how to end the film. And we knew in some way it had to end with Deb or Lolis Elie, a prominent elder within the Black community who had also died.

For purposes of the film, we went back and forth for almost a year trying to figure out the sequence of events. And we had focus groups. And the clear consensus in the focus groups was you need to end the film with Deb's death. That posed a whole host of other considerations. When you have this. . . . I mean, there are two protagonists. Dr. Michael White searching for his ancestral past after the flood is one theme. And his beautiful music of course surrounds that.

At some of the focus groups, people were crying. Yes. I think some people have wept seeing the end of this film today. We worked very hard to create a final passage or coda to her funeral. I never remotely imagined that the film would end with a person whose life becomes such a dynamic presence to the viewer, so you really do have the experience of going to a funeral of someone you know. This was never anything I imagined we would do. But we did. We had to. We needed to find a tone at the end. And when COVID hit, nobody could go out.

So we got footage of the city in the pandemic. And at that point, we began to realize how important murals were. All the murals. One with the phrase "we won't bow down" with nurses having the masks across their face. That said so much.

Then finally I went to Dr. White and I said, "Look man, we really need a song at the end. Something to bring people up." So he wrote the song that John Boutté then sang in studio, which I think does provide a certain uplift at the end, in keeping with the celebratory response of the second line. But the film is only just out. And I guess in that sense, the jury is still out too. Although thus far, the reviews have been quite favorable.

Filmmaker 5 with Jason Berry: *City of A Million Dreams*

Kami Spangenberg / 2022

From *Classic Couple Academy*, December 2022. Reprinted by permission.

Celebrating the music, pageantry, and historical legacy of New Orleans through the observance of honoring the dead, *City of a Million Dreams*, the documentary film, is making its way to film festivals and public screenings around the globe. Based on the 2018 book of the same name, *City of a Million Dreams* traces the evolution of the jazz funeral tradition in New Orleans from its earliest days in the late eighteenth century to today's modern memory pageants.

Author of the book and director of the documentary film *City of a Million Dreams*, Jason Berry shares his love of the city of New Orleans in our *Classic Couple Academy* interview here.

Kami Spangenberg: To tell this story on film, you present the jazz funeral tradition using vintage photos, archival footage, historical recreations, current interviews, and filming of modern-day jazz funerals. How did this combination of material influence how you structured the film?

Jason Berry: I began meeting in 2016 with Tim Watson at his studio Ariel Montage; we'd worked on several projects over the years. Tim is a superb artist of visual narratives. Owing to the range of materials you cite, I also turned to my daughter Simonette Berry, a painter-sculptor who had been working for several years as a film set artist; she'd also written for a local magazine years before. That's a good skill set for any documentary. Sim joined us and began a massive inventory of photographs and historical images. The three of us spent much of the next four years planning the production shoots, working on how to meld the range of materials, and shaping the script through more changes than I can count.

Tim and Simonette are coproducers; though the film is based on my book, I felt they deserved to share script credit because of the collaborative effort. Simonette had done a storyboard for the Congo Square sequences when I cast lines to find a choreographer, someone with the historical knowledge of African dances in the antebellum era. Monique Moss is a dancer with deep knowledge of the African diaspora. Within an hour of our first meeting, I knew she was right for this. Monique insisted that I bring in Titos Sompa, a master percussionist from Kongo, who was living in Detroit, and his brother, Jean Claude Biza Sompa, who teaches in the music program at University of Michigan. Among the fifteen or so musicians we also had several drummers from Ivory Coast living in New York, and Seguenon Kone, an Ivorian multi-instrumentalist who performs and teaches in New Orleans. I must also give great credit to Harris Done, our DP, who made several trips from Los Angeles for key shoots and didn't mind sleeping in my guest bedroom, and George Ingmire, the sound engineer who wove through the funeral parades with a brilliant ear for balancing the instrumental voices.

You make a film like this with people who believe in what you're doing. Everyone gave me the in-law rate. I had tremendous artistic allies. When Tim saw the Congo Square footage, he told me, "We've got the heartbeat."

KS: You have a couple of central characters in the film—Deb "Big Red" Cotton and Michael White. What drew you to their two stories and how did you collaborate with each of them on this project?

JB: Michael was a primary interview from the start; the film follows him from the late nineties through the traumatic losses of the Hurricane Katrina flooding, as he becomes a New Orleans everyman. As a scholar, his search for information on an ancestor, Papa John Joseph, who played in the early 1960s at Preservation Hall, guides the storyline as a quest for roots, how Papa John emerged in the dawn of jazz. Funerals emerge as memory caravans.

Tim discovered footage of Papa John's jazz funeral in the remarkable Jules Cahn Archive at the Historic New Orleans Collection; Jules filmed in the 1960s before TV stations discovered Black culture. Michael is a college professor with a courtly persona on film as in life. In contrast, Deb Cotton exudes a radiance, wit, and charm; I knew her work as a blogger and videographer covering the parading culture. She was wounded in a crossfire at a Mother's Day parade in 2013 and put out a statement forgiving her shooters, calling on the city to do more for youth on the jagged edge. That statement, so profound, echoes what Pope Francis calls "radical mercy." It took a while to set up a meeting, as she had surgeries and a long recovery haul, but she was back on her feet, a force of nature when we met, and she agreed to join our production team.

KS: This is certainly a film rooted in place as it depicts a distinctly New Orleans tradition. What experience do you want audiences, especially those who have never visited the city, to take away from the viewing experience?

JB: I have been fortunate to travel extensively on assignments in Europe, the Caribbean, and Latin America; I've been to cities that share a certain essence of New Orleans—Havana comes closest. New Orleans is the American city with the deepest African identity; music more than literature shapes the popular memory, a force you see in the funerals, weekly parades of social clubs, and the rich density of jazz, R&B, hip-hop, and gospel. This town has been a crossroads of humanity since at least 1809, when the population doubled, to nearly twenty thousand, with the arrival of migrants from Haiti. We are still a city of migrants. The foodways, tender courtesies of daily life, the rocking artistry of costumes and float-making in Carnival season—don't try to sell me New York or London. This is a town that people either fanatically embrace, or scheme to leave because of subsidence, sea rise, cracked streets, recurrent flooding, a dismal performance of democracy, yadda yadda. For me, it's the most human place on earth.

KS: How is *City of a Million Dreams* a community film?

JB: We built this documentary on the stories of brass band musicians and the second line culture, the parading tradition rooted in funeral processions and celebrational dances for the dead. As we orchestrated their stories into the script, we decided on an assembly narration, advancing the action of the film and historical sequences through the voices and reflections of people in the film.

A celebrity voice-of-God narrator might have generated more publicity but the approach we took made for a film with many more grace notes. We did focus groups with community members, particularly with Black Men of Labor and the Social Aid and Pleasure Club, whose processions weave through the film; they gave us candid insights we drew upon in editing. We made donations to bereaved families in filming wakes and second lines for their loved ones. For the Congo Square filming, artistic director Monique Moss selected some two dozen dancers with whom she had worked over the years, New Orleans artists steeped in danced memory rituals of Mali, Senegal, and the bamboula burial dances of Kongo. Titos Sompa, the pivotal interviewee on Kongo culture, ended up moving to New Orleans after participating in the film. With a few notable exceptions [DP Harris Done, editorial adviser Doug Blush, special effects artist Alexey Terenoff], everyone else involved in the production is part of the growing film industry in New Orleans. The Louisiana film tax credits we received were extremely helpful. But we could not have made this film without the support of executive producer Bernard F. Pettingill Jr., a forensic economist who grew up here, saw the potential, and believed in what we were doing.

Questions for Research

Halley Jepson / 2022

Interview conducted via email, November 10, 2022. Reprinted by permission.

Halley Jepson: While you were at Jesuit High, was there ever a time that you noticed or heard of misconduct of the priests?

Jason Berry: No. The priests who taught me in the 1960s were for the most part sensitive men and serious intellects, a few of them with quirks, but overall, men most of my classmates and I admired. Many years later—in 2018—the church released the names of predators from that era which included Father Donald Pearce who had been the prefect of discipline when I graduated in 1967. His name came as quite a shock to guys I knew, and to me.

HJ: Did that have any influence on why you were interested in looking into the church?

JB: One reason I was drawn to that early reporting on the clergy abuse case in Lafayette, LA in 1985 stemmed from my sense of priests and nuns as benevolent figures. The issue of a single priest abusing altar boys was jolting, but I thought any man, even a priest could have some kind of criminal pathology. It was learning about the bishop's coverup of Father Gilbert Gauthe, and other priests, that got me going—a political story, the abuse of power and the coverup. In fact, a Jesuit priest encouraged me in the reporting, Father George Lundy.

HJ: You recently finished the film *City of a Million Dreams* with your daughter. Do you still find time to help and advocate for victims with your focus on culture and music?

JB: Not a great deal. I haven't actively reported on the church crisis since 2015. I've written some commentaries and get interviewed periodically, but the New Orleans project, book and companion film, has taken up most of my time.

HJ: Do you believe that it is more difficult to be recognized as a sexual assault victim when the assailant was a priest versus a sexual assault victim that is not victimized by the church?

JB: That's a hard question. Beyond reading news coverage of #MeToo and the many cases of adult women accusing coaches, I haven't read any study of how clergy abuse survivors compare. One sign is clear, though. After thirty-plus years of investigations, lawsuits, criminal trials, grand jury reports, and deepening Vatican response, most bishops and religious order superiors now seem averse to castigate survivors as enemies of the church. Many dioceses have victim response programs, and while the record on how they have done is unclear, those moves and "safe touch" programs in Catholic schools to give children greater awareness, along with employee background checks by dioceses and schools, are important moves. Still, I think as a society we are awakening to the realization of the widespread patterns.

HJ: In the 2001 *Chicago Tribune* article, you discussed your reconnection with Barbara Blaine. You mentioned people that went from "victim to survivor." What does that process look like? What are the criteria to be considered a survivor?

JB: Good question. I hesitate to say that my take is *the* answer, as interviewing a survivor would give you more nuance and detail. I think the decision that any victim makes to become publicly identified is a major step away from feeling trapped in shame and isolation; many people don't want the notoriety. You can become a survivor without "going public," by working with a therapist or support group to rebuild an inner confidence and strength, to achieve wholeness. To file a lawsuit or seek prosecution of a sexual predator with your name made public is a bold move; most media do not identify victims by name unless they request it. To become an activist, dealing with the press, meeting with prosecutors and legislators, goes well beyond support groups with private disclosure. But you don't have to give news interviews to be a survivor on the road to happiness.

HJ: The 2001 *Chicago Tribune* article also mentions that 6 percent of priests had abused men and women. What do you suspect that percentage is today?

JB: I haven't done research, but based on the continuing cases reported daily in The Abuse Tracker, an email digest of links to news reports sponsored by BishopAccountability.org, the online archive and news source, I would say the 6 percent estimate is low. Given the upsurge of numbers being reported and conversations I have occasionally had with people in the field, my guess is that it's closer to 8 to 10 percent. That is awfully high.

HJ: There are multiple interviews, as well as your own writing, where you have questioned your faith based on your findings, as well as personal struggles. As of today, where are you in your faith journey?

JB: Mass gives me a sense of closeness to my younger daughter, Ariel [1991–2008], a Down syndrome child who died of heart failure at age seventeen. Ariel enjoyed mass; so did my mother and grandmother, with whom I was quite close. I have walked out of services because of idiotic sermons, though not in loud protest. [Guys routinely go to the restroom. I just keep walking.] I don't go every Sunday. I haven't found another church might be the better answer. God is a search.

HJ: Do you believe that the age of the victims of sexual assault contribute to whether they are believed or listened to about their abuse?

JB: Yes, but most of the children who were abused do not report it until many years later. They don't know how to process that kind of trauma, which causes lots of them to act out.

HJ: In the interview with David Clohessy, he stated that for years you were practically the only journalist who took victims seriously and listened to them compassionately. Why do you think that was?

JB: I know several journalists who did early reports at roughly the time I did but moved on to other topics. I was trying to see the extent of the cover-up; as I got to know survivors, their stories triggered all kinds of questions, a trail I kept following. I came to see them like the chorus of a Greek tragedy, warning that a moral order has been broken. What they shared of their lives moved me then and still today.

HJ: Was it hard to stay objective with your investigations because of your background in the Catholic Church (growing up in the church, going to Catholic school)?

JB: I was acutely aware of how much the church and particularly the Jesuits had shaped my thinking about faith and life. I turned out pretty well. That realization disposed me to see the church in a broader context, as a force for good in many parts of life, despite patterns of corruption in church history. I knew intuitively that for my reporting to be taken seriously, I needed a voice of dispassion in reporting on the institutional dynamics. The survivors' stories were a powerful counterweight.

HJ: In recent years, with the #MeToo movement and openness about sexual assault, do you believe that it is easier for victims to be taken seriously and believed than it was in the nineties?

JB: Yes, the media landscape has changed dramatically.

HJ: Do you believe that the #MeToo movement affected the number of survivors of pedophilia to come forward? Why or why not?

JB: I don't know, but I suspect it did.

HJ: As a supporter and an advocate for these victims, did you ever find yourself in a position of potential victimization because of your outspokenness of the church's misconduct?

JB: I took heat from the appropriately named *Daily Advertiser* in Lafayette during the 1985 reporting; one columnist called me a "vulture of yellow journalism." From time to time, I was criticized for things I wrote, but if you're an investigative journalist, you expect things like that, as part of the territory. I did face legal challenges in some of the reporting, which I write about in the 1992 book, notably the events in Cleveland where the church threatened to sue the *Plain Dealer* newspaper over an article I did. [Too long to go into here.] Many of the articles I did and all three of the books were closely vetted by attorneys before publication. On a personal level, I've experienced a cold shoulder now and then from Catholics or priests who see me as some kind of menace, but not much in recent years.

HJ: In your findings/investigations, was a race or ethnicity victimized more than others? If so, which race/ethnicity?

JB: No.

HJ: Out of all your works about the Catholic Church, which one are you most proud of? Why?

JB: I guess the 1992 book, *Lead Us Not Into Temptation*, because it put the issue on the map. It took nearly seven years to report and write, which I did as a freelance.

HJ: When breaking the story about Rev. Gilbert Gauthe, were you ever afraid that it would negatively affect your career?

JB: No. I thought it would boost my standing; I had no idea it would take so long or confront so many challenges.

HJ: Do you believe the birth of your first daughter, Simonette, pushed you to continue the investigation of the horrible things that were happening to children by Rev. Gauthe?

JB: Becoming a father was very much on my mind when I learned about the Gauthe indictment and began reading documents. In my daughter's early years, I was learning some awful stuff through the reporting from which I had to detach at the end of the workday; perhaps it made me more determined to see that her mom and I gave her a happy childhood. I think we did well.

HJ: In terms of sexual assault/molestation, do you believe it is more difficult for those survivors to be taken seriously and acknowledged for their victimization than say other crimes such as robbery or physical assault? Why?

JB: I have not done any comparative research in this realm. But sexual abuse is so deeply personal compared to robbery. The media coverage today is widespread, society more sympathetic and willing to believe victims than when my articles began in 1985. I suspect the attitudinal shift also has to do with families; roughly one-fourth of young women have been abused in adolescence, according to studies. That's a huge number! Imagine the impact on a mom or dad learning much later. Therapists on college campuses increasingly deal with sexual assault. But this is a broad area beyond my expertise, such as it is.

HJ: In the field you researched, and in general, why do you believe that a lot of victims do not come forward with their abuse?

JB: It takes years to break through the shame and confusion. Children raised with love and expectations of innocence, and gradual awareness of the greater world, are ill-equipped to fend off a seductive adult or understand what it means when sexual awareness comes prematurely. When innocence is plundered, the child's path toward a healthy identity is thrown off track; for many it takes years to find a road toward self-definition, and healing.

HJ: Does receiving awards such as the Sean P. McIlmail Hero Award encourage you to continue your investigations into the church?

JB: No. I'm grateful for the recognition, but I published that book thirty years ago, and since 2016, have put the church research behind me in moving on with my career.

HJ: Do you suspect other branches within Christianity, such as Protestant and Orthodox, have the same severity of pedophilia as the Catholic Church?

JB: I don't think so, but I haven't kept up with the research.

Jason Berry Oral History

Mark Cave / 2023

Interview for the Williams Research Center at the Historic New Orleans Collection. February 13, 2023. Printed by permission.

Mark Cave: Last time we talked, you had mentioned an investigation of David Duke that was going along at the same time as your investigation into the Catholic Church. Talk a little bit about your work on David Duke.

Jason Berry: Sure. Let's see, in 1989, when he was running for the legislature, I knew that he had been a Klan leader. I was aware of him, and I started doing research, and I did an op-ed for *The New York Times* basically saying, "The chickens are coming home to roost for the Republican Party." I made the point that after years of the Southern Strategy, Nixon and then Reagan particularly had courted white Southerners to join the Republican Party, often using coded racial language. Reagan started his 1980 campaign in Philadelphia, Mississippi, where three civil rights workers were brutally murdered saying, "The South will rise again." I mean that's strong stuff. Anyway, based on that article, Beth Rickey contacted me. Elizabeth Rickey was a young Republican, and she was about thirty-two. She was on the state central committee, and her father had marched with General Patton in World War II. She was working in political science as a graduate student at Tulane and was appalled by Duke. And soon along, there was a small group of us who were trading information and talking every day. I did a couple more articles for other outlets, and the more I dug, I realized that this guy had been selling hate literature for a long time, Nazi books and things like that, and he was much more than just a long-ago Klan leader who had become a newborn Republican. So, I was midway through writing the book, *Lead Us Not Into Temptation*, when all this happened, and over the next couple of years, I did a lot of reporting and writing about Duke. I gave some speeches for the Louisiana Committee Against Racism and Nazism.

For years, I thought only Louisiana would need a committee against Nazism, but now, the Nazi movement, call it what you will, far right, extremist, is quite pronounced in different parts of America. So, we all worked very hard in different ways to try to get a lot of the information out. The *Times-Picayune* did a very poor job in covering the primary in 1989 that Duke won. Local TV was just awful; you could see them treating Duke as a kind of celebrity without really digging into what he had really done, who he really was. So, he won the election by 226 votes. I could give you a long, verbal accounting of David Duke, but he, of course, eventually sank after the 1991 governor's race. I mean he still makes news now and then, but he's a marginal figure. And, yeah, I was working on that sort of conterminously with the last stage of reporting and writing on the book about the Catholic priests.

MC: Was Jimmy Swaggart, your investigation into that, around that same time too?

JB: Yeah, 1988, I did that at the same time.

MC: Well, you mentioned that you had the interviews with one of the prostitutes that he was with, but you didn't really talk about it.

JB: I got a call from a guy named Bob Vernon. He was a rock and roll pitchman, was from Alexandria, Louisiana, and was a booking agent for Fats Domino among other musicians. And he called me the night of the "I Have Sinned" sermon. It was 1988 in February, and he said, "How would you like to have an interview with the young woman who was with Reverend Swaggart?" and just sleaze dripping off his vowels. He's dead now. Anyway, that's unrelated, but I don't want the lawyers for the collection thinking that I'm trafficking in defamation. Anyhow, he picked me up the next morning, we went out to this law office at the end of Metairie Road, and it was a shotgun building that been turned into a law office. And these lawyers were representing Debra Murphree, the woman who had been with Swaggart about whom he apologized. I don't think he mentioned her name. And there was a prostitution arrest warrant out in her name by the Jefferson Parish Sheriff's Office. And so, these guys were trying to cash in on the story and the notoriety, and they kind of grilled me and made me sign this non-disclosure agreement. They were scared to death that I would—if I learned anything, I would go write about it, and I said, "Look, if you let me do the interview, I'll have to find an outlet first, and I'm not going to double-cross you." So, I signed some sort of agreement to that effect, and then she came in. It was the end of February and a warm day, and she was wearing a kind of—I don't know what you would call it—a top and matching shorts with a halter top underneath. I mean nothing lewd about it. She took off the jacket, and I noticed that she had a tattoo in one arm that said *Debbie* in a crooked scroll, and the other was a Maltese cross, which I found interesting. And the first thing I thought was Jimmy Swaggart's been doing it with a woman on Airline Highway who has tattoos. This is not like a glamorous vixen in some distant hotel tower with secrecy and all that; I mean he was driving along Airline Highway. I think one could safely say that, in some sense psychologically, he wanted to get caught, but I don't have that social science pedigree to state it for a fact. So anyway, I did the interview with her and the most interesting thing to me, toward the end, she spoke pretty bluntly about what they did, and a lot of it was almost adolescent voyeurism. Anyway, I said, "Well, what would you do after the interlude, in the thirty-five-an-hour, no-tell motel?" and she said, "Well, I'd go back to Chef Menteur Highway," where she had an apartment with her boyfriend, and they would stay up snorting cocaine and watching Jimmy Swaggart sermons—

MC: Oh, no.

JB: On cable TV, which I thought was a wonderfully ironic, kind of, sewing it all up. Anyway, through a long process that went on over a couple of days, my literary agent secured a deal. I was hoping he would get *Esquire* or some outlet like that, but it ended up being *Penthouse* magazine. And the editor with whom I spoke was just thrilled with the idea that Swaggart's girlfriend had tattoos. This was before tattoos were common among young people and models in *Vogue* magazine. And so, there was a reporter, Art Harris for *The Washington Post*, who had been tracking these events, and he had been reporting on the Swaggart broadcast ministry, and as part of the deal with *Penthouse*, Art flew down. And I'll never forget, he came into the law office, and the two of us went into a room alone, and he said, "Well, I've been following your stuff on the priests, it's great reporting." And I said, "Well, thank you very much," and I was certainly aware of his political coverage, as he was terrific journalist. And he was wearing this handsome blue blazer and yellow aviator glasses, and he was completely bald. We're about the same age, I mean he just looked like he'd stepped out of *GQ* magazine. And he said, "Jason, you've done the interview with the girl, I've got the stuff on the ministry, let's split the assignment. And I've done something previously for *Penthouse*, I'll see if I can get them to boost the money, and we'll just split it." Well, I really had no choice at that point; we were about to go into the room with these guys. The team around Debra by then had spread to about five or six men, and some of them I think were probably paying her hotel fees. They kept moving her every night afraid that

Harry Lee's deputies might find her. I mean, it was really a comedy. And so, we went in, and Art had a satchel, and one of the lawyers in this booming voice said [*mimics voice*], "We want a deal, and we want it now," and hit the table authoritatively. Art nodded, and said, "Gentlemen, I am here as Mr. Guccione's eyes," referring to Bob Guccione, the publisher. And then he opened his satchel, and he passed out five or six copies of the magazine, and these guys started looking at the centerfolds. I mean it was almost a scene out of a comic movie of some kind. And so, all of a sudden, they believed him because he had the magazines, and so finally, they agreed to let him do a second interview with the understanding that they wanted a bunch of money for her to pose in the magazine. And what I had said from the beginning with these guys was, "Look, I am doing an article, I want to get paid for the article, I don't want anything to do with whatever agreement or negotiations you have representing her." And so, Art did a second interview with her, and we turned the article around very quickly. It's actually a pretty good article—rather graphic, more so than most of the things I've written about sex abuse, but I will say this. The reason *Penthouse* was so interested was because Swaggart had been giving sermons condemning convenience stores for carrying *Playboy*, *Penthouse*, and magazines like that. And so, we did the story, and Bob Vernon, the guy who got me into the thing, orchestrated the day when they shot the photographs. I think they did it at the Columns Hotel, and I kept far away from all that stuff. But we split a $15,000 fee, which in 1988, [was] $7,500 each, minus the agent's 10 percent, [which] was pretty good money back then. The *Times-Picayune* did an article on the magazine and what it had said without mentioning the two people who wrote it. My mother chuckled after reading it, and she said, "Well, honey, even though you didn't get your name in the newspaper at this time, that might not be so bad." So that was my adventure with *Penthouse*.

MC: Did Miss Murphree get paid quite a bit for her photos?

JB: Yes, I believe the fee was $188,000, but Bob Vernon and the lawyers and the other people immediately contested it. The lawyers I think took a bunch of money claiming that they had out of pocket expenses for hotels. I never got into that except that there was a lawsuit with Vernon suing them trying to get his money. This all happened a long time ago, and I don't know where the lawyers are today. Bob died about a year ago, but I remember Peter Bloch, the editor of *Penthouse*, telling me at one point, "You know, we see a lot of sleazeballs who come in here wanting us to get their women in the magazine, but these guys dealing with her, they're real sleaze buckets," and I said, "Welcome to Louisiana."

MC: So, the book (*Lead Us Not Into Temptation*) had come out when you were doing this?

JB: No, no, four years before that book was published *Up From the Cradle of Jazz* had come out, and at this point it had been out about two years. I was struggling financially working on the book about the priests because I could not get very few major outlets to take articles of length on that topic. And by this time, I had moved on from the early reporting in Lafayette, and I was doing mainly opinion pieces, in the *Baltimore Sun*, and *Cleveland Plain Dealer*. I did have a much longer article with the Cleveland newspaper, which is covered in the book in some depth, but the money from *Penthouse* certainly helped.

MC: And so, after *Lead Us Not Into Temptation* was published, you were kind of making the media circuits and doing some things.

JB: Yes. When the book was published and I would go off, to appear on all these different talk shows like *Oprah*, and I was on the *Today* show when the book was published with Father Andrew Greeley, and an abuse survivor. And by now, civil cases across the country were mushrooming with some criminal cases, so I was quite in demand. Most of the newspapers covering it used the figures from my book and cited it. Four hundred priests and $400 million in payouts, which had taken me forever to calculate, and that data held for a couple of years until it became obvious that there were more and more settlements. I can't remember when the church first released its own. Maybe it was 2002, after *The Boston Globe* series, but they eventually released figures showing that they had spent well in excess of a billion dollars. I think now it's at $3.5 billion or something like that. But, yeah, I would go off on airplanes, or I would sit in my home office and do radio or press interviews, and I was meanwhile searching for my own spiritual rudder. It was a very difficult period, and it went on several years.

MC: I think to jump back to the—how do you say the name, "Ma-ki-yel?"

JB: "Ma-si-yel."

MC: Maciel?

JB: Yeah.

MC: Well, talk about how you got involved in that?

JB: Sure. I believe it was the end of 1994. *Lead Us Not Into Temptation* had been out for a couple of years. I had gotten a lot of press and done a lot of media interviews and written a number of articles subsequent to the book. And I was contacted by a guy named Arturo Jurado, a Mexican who lived in Monterey, California. He was teaching at the Defense Languages School where the CIA and military send people for language instruction, and diplomats go there. I mean if you're going to be posted somewhere, you spend a year learning the language, that kind of thing. And he wanted to talk about this priest who had abused him as a boy. And the first thing that registered on me was that this guy must have a security clearance to teach at the defense languages school. And I just listened, and he told me this, just baroque story of how this powerful priest in Mexico took these boys to Spain and then on to Rome and just mowed them down. So, I said, "Well, look. . . ." And I was trying to get away from the topic by then. I figured I put in eight years on this, Cincinnatus must go back to the plow. And I said, "Well, send me notarized statements by the victims and by your fellow victims, and I can't make any promises, but let me see what I can do," and then Jose Barba called me from Mexico City. Jose Barba is now retired. He was a distinguished professor at ITAM, Instituto Tecnológico Autónomo de México, and quite a polymath. He spoke excellent English, [was] fluent in Italian. And I remember when he called me, the first thing he said, "How is your family, Jason?" and it was a very Latin way of opening the conversation, as if we had known one another for a while. And so, he told me a lot more about this powerful priest, and he was the one, I think, who arranged for the other men—there were six of them in Mexico City if I'm not mistaken—to send their documents, and most of them were in Spanish. I was able to read the Spanish fairly readily, although I needed a little help on a couple of the translations. But it was obvious that each had been molested and while the others did not know it. They had all left the Legion of Christ, the religious order, and now had moved on—they were all accomplished men. There was an engineer, a college professor, I think maybe two professors. Alejandro Espinosa was a rancher who actually wrote the first book on it, called *El Legionario*. It was published in Mexico City. But I was going through quite a lot at the time. I was trying to raise money with the Ford Foundation, which took about a year to get the grant to film jazz funerals. I was doing consulting work at Tulane for the office that reported to Eamon Kelly (president of Tulane), and I wrote some things for Eamon Kelly, and admired him greatly. Meanwhile I sent proposals to several places. I think it was *The New York Times* where I experienced the same thing in '85, almost, ten years earlier, "Well, this is something that happened in Mexico—why would Americans be interested?" And, of course to me, the story was that one member of this group had written twice to Pope John Paul II laying out all the allegations and had never heard back. So finally, I kept saying, "Look, if you guys can find someone else to do this, by all means do." "No, we want you, we want you," which was flattering but also a bit disconcerting. And then I got a call one day from Gerald Renner. I think it was maybe either in the spring or summer of '96, and I had published *The Spirit of Black Hawk* in '95, which was my fourth book, and I was really working hard to get support for this jazz funeral project. More and more, I was looking at funerals as a kind of storytelling tradition that held a mirror to the larger story of the city as time passed. Anyway, Renner called, and I liked Jerry, I'd met him once or twice at a bishops' conference and he wrote a very favorable review of *Lead Us Not Into Temptation*. And he said, "I'm wondering if you know anything about the Legion of Christ? I've been doing some reporting on that group up here, their headquarters, they seem to be a strange lot" or words to that effect. And I said, "Yes, in fact, I have quite a bit of information about the founder," and I insisted that we go off the record. So, I told him what I had, and he said he had found out a lot about the Legion in the United States, and I knew very little about where they had chapters and schools. I mean this was a religious order that after Vatican II did everything possible to, if you will, to steal away market share from the Jesuits in establishing schools with high academic standards. Well, it's a very long story, but Maciel was an extraordinary fundraiser, I mean he had gilded fingertips. And he went to some of the wealthiest men in Mexico and Latin America and presented himself as a vigilant anti-communist, and his vision of the Legion was to restore a church that had lost its way with the liberal reforms of Vatican II. His mission was to rebuild the church along the lines of militant orthodoxy. And the Legionaries, as they were called, were considered a spiritual army. So, he was arguably the greatest fundraiser of the postwar Catholic Church, and he impressed Pope John Paul II, who admired the Legionaries, and he saw this guy bringing in young recruits. And so, when our big article came out based on interviews with these eight men in the *Hartford Courant*, we couldn't get the Vatican to even respond, there was just silence. And that was an important signal to Jerry and me because Maciel hired a big law firm in Washington, Kirkland & Ellis. Kenneth Starr was a partner at the time who was investigating and later prosecuted Bill Clinton. Well, let's see, it was fall of '96 when we were preparing the story and it came out in February 23, 1997. I mean Starr had nothing to do with this, it was just a big law firm, but, of course, they were saying that these were slanderous statements by men who were disaffected, former followers and so forth. But all of the information that they gave us came from people who were closely involved with the Legion of Christ, and we did a big sidebar quoting them all. I had no idea that it would be nine years before Pope Benedict finally removed Maciel, and even then—even today, information keeps coming out. The Legion of Christ is, in my view, a cult.

The rest of the media, the big media, ignored the story for years. In fact, when it came out in the *Courant*—*Hartford Courant* is the major newspaper of Connecticut, it was a huge piece, I think about 7,500 or 8,000 words. And Renner called the AP international desk in New York because he was following the wire very closely. This is just when the internet was starting to circulate, and articles moving, attached files, things like that, and we were both kind of dumbstruck that this thing did not create a splash. *New York Times* didn't touch it, *Washington Post* didn't do anything, *The Boston Globe* didn't do anything, none of the networks. Well, of course, the story led straight to Pope John Paul because one of these eight men, Juan Vaca, had had written the Pope and told him everything. I mean it's an astonishing document: In fact, we open the book with Vaca and his letter. So, by this time, I'm filming jazz funerals and thinking, okay, I've done my piece, I've put together a book proposal, it bounced off all the walls in Manhattan Island that would publish books. And I remember one guy wrote to the agent, I think he was with Simon & Schuster, and he said, "If what Mr. Berry and Mr. Renner have is true, then I prefer to step aside on this one." And I was thinking to myself, if what we have is true, why would he doubt our credibility? Well, it's a nice way of saying, no thanks, not for me. So, Jerry retired from the *Courant* in 2000, and he died in 2007. I think he was about sixteen, eighteen years older than me, a wonderful guy. We did a big piece in 2001 for *National Catholic Reporter,* but it was held up for months for publication because of the 9/11 attacks. I went back to Mexico, and I interviewed these guys again because by this time, they had gone to Rome and filed a formal canon law request with Cardinal Ratzinger to have Maciel banished from the priesthood. They wanted justice, and it was as striking a quest for justice as anything I've ever seen. So that piece came out toward the end of 2001, and then just a month or two later, *The Boston Globe* series began, and I started getting thirty phone calls a day from producers, from journalists, from survivors. I mean this went on for a month. I was on *Nightline* twice within about a week, and by the beginning of March—mid-March, I had a contract with Renner to do the book. So thereby I started the first in a series of trips to Rome that stretched over the next ten or twelve years. Anyway, that's how I got into the Legion of Christ.

MC: Talk about Richard Neuhaus and his criticism of the book.

JB: Well, Neuhaus had been attacking me for a long time in *First Things*. He disparaged *Lead Us Not Into Temptation* and said that I specialized in scandals. You know the irony of that kind of criticism from the Catholic right is that many of the leads I got and many the most outraged people

I interviewed, especially the chapter on San Diego, were orthodox Catholics who were appalled at what was going on in their diocese. It took me a long time, Mark, to come to the realization that this national pattern I was piecing together in initially a kind of patchwork fashion was all part of a criminal sexual underground that stretched across the entire domestic church, and I now believe is an international phenomenon based on everything happening in other countries. And I don't say that to be melodramatic or give one of these booming soundbites or something; I think it's borne out by the facts. Huey Long said it's important to cultivate the right enemies. I never set out to make an enemy of Richard Neuhaus or the guy at the Catholic League, William Donohue. But you assume when you do this kind of reporting—and I'm not trying to posture myself as some sort of bold, daring muckraker—that some guy in a trench coat with a law degree was following, and sooner or later, we'd sit down at a table, and I'd have to cough up the evidence, it was a reality in my life. There were many times I spent hours and hours in a given day with lawyers for newspapers, for magazines, for books, and it was always—"Okay, what's your source on this?" So, when these guys started attacking me, my thought was, okay, take your shot, but you can't change the facts. And surprisingly in recent years, I have not been attacked very much. In fact, what's happening now is that there is an extreme right-wing presence in blogs, online publications, and magazines. A lot of these people are homophobic and are determined to prove that the abuse crisis is a homosexual crisis. That's the position of William Donohue. So, I eventually wrote Neuhaus and told him that he owed an apology to the men in Mexico, and I took him to task as well for disparaging a book by Leon Podles (*Sacrilege: Sexual Abuse in the Catholic Church*), a colleague and friend. I said, "Look, you owe an apology to Podles and you owe an apology to these men from Mexico." And he wrote an email about a month later apologizing, saying that it had gone into the wrong folder or something, and I wrote a letter to be published by *First Things*, which they did not do. But he said that he recognized that I'd made a contribution, and he would, in due course, make reference to that, and of course, he didn't even address the substance of the letter, which was you owe these guys an apology, which never happened. I never met Neuhaus. I read several of his books, but I never met him.

MC: Did you ever meet Maciel?

JB: No.

MC: No?

JB: Tried to, the lawyers got in the way.

MC: I wanted to dive into your work on New Orleans' culture.

JB: Thank you. A little uplift for this day.

MC: Okay, as you were doing all your research on the scandal in the church, you were also doing a lot of work on New Orleans' culture, and so you noted two projects, *The Spirit of Black Hawk*, your book on Spiritual churches, and your work on jazz funerals. Was this your true love, and was the church scandal more of an obligation you felt and how did you balance the two avenues of your work?

JB: Well, first of all, let me credit you for a very wise question, and I'll try to see if I can answer it with some degree of reflection. I kept writing about the church. I guess it was partly obligation, but I was just genuinely curious about how deep it goes, how high does it go, and people kept contacting me and sending me things. And then as more people began writing about it and I continued reading church history, I gained a wider lens on it, you might say. And when you know a great deal about a given subject and it becomes a continuing narrative in the news media, at what point do you step aside? So as a freelance, I had always worked on a couple of things at once, over-lapping projects sometimes; the *Black Hawk* book came about because the chapter in *Up From the Cradle of Jazz* on the Lastie family dealt with Spiritual churches, and I was curious about the whole Black Hawk connection. I suppose that book, in some way, was kind of a recovery project for me after *Lead Us Not*. It's a book about the faith lives of certain African Americans and the ritual way they speak to God. And in a sense, as exotic as it was, and as marginal as those churches may seem, it gave me a certain hope to write about it. I ended up being much more intrigued by Mother Catherine Seals and her role in Spiritual churches. Oh, let's see, the book came out in '95, I guess I started the Ford Foundation project shooting funerals in '96, so I was gaining a wider lens on the culture. I had written about a great many musicians at that point, both in *Up From the Cradle* and in continu-ing articles. In '94, for example, I began writing a music column for a New Orleans magazine. I came to see funerals as a storytelling tradition, almost like a short story on a given neighborhood or a community, with the pas-tor, the family who had died, and the musicians. And the variations on the rituals, the music, and particularly the sermons, all of that, yet how do you explain what curiosity such as mine for expressions of religious belief? I was searching for my own kind of spiritual anchor you might say. I felt often in the funerals that these people singing and dancing, sometimes in cathar-tic ways, were expressing a closeness to God that I did not feel at Sunday mass. Sometimes, I'd come back from a long trip to Rome or somewhere in the United States, and I'd read a death notice in the *Picayune* or someone would call me, or I'd hear it on WWOZ. And I would go out the next day to a funeral, not with the camera, but with a notebook, sometimes with a tape recorder, and I went to so many of those funerals, and I was just moved as a writer by the narrative power of those events. Some of the sermons were almost spellbinding, stem winding you might say. And then watching the sorrow of the bereaved, of the family members, these were expressions of grief and agony. And I can only imagine what the funerals are like right now with so many of these young, Black men who go down as gunshot victims. It's like a plague, it's a scourge, it's to me like the yellow fever epidemics, which could've been put to rest if they'd only believed in public sanitation in poor neighborhoods, but they didn't, because they didn't want to spend the money. Today, they don't want to—either they don't believe in gun control, or they don't find it politically possible, and so I don't have to go off on a tangent about the madness of American political stances on guns. The proof is in the blood spilled every day. So, I guess there was a long stretch of time when I was going back and forth. I would go to Rome and sit in these great Renaissance churches overwhelmed by the beauty the art—particularly in the church off of the Piazza del Popolo in Rome with the Caravaggio paintings of St. Paul struck from his horse, I would sit there sometimes, and I would think of Ariel. I kept asking myself—not so much asking myself, but telling myself, this child is in my life for a reason, and I need to understand that reason. I mean I've written about a lot of subjects as a freelance. The book reviews, I've done hundreds of them on a range of topics, including novels, histories, and such. But there are two core themes to my work, the city of my birth and the church in which I was raised. Even the novel I did, *Last of the Red Hot Poppas*, in a certain sense, is a spiritual comedy. It's about a cover-up, a licentious governor has died, the first lady wants to bury him with dignity and figure out who did it and why.

MC: Mm-hmm, we didn't talk about *Earl Long in Purgatory*. Do you want to talk a little bit about that?

JB: Sure. I had long been fascinated with Earl Long; I had read the available histories. The idea of this barnstorming populist having a breakdown on the floor of the legislature, fighting all these racists who wanted to purge Blacks from the polling records and he had registered 100,000 Black people to vote in the 1950s when all of these other Southern governors were doing everything they could to remake Jim Crow, that paradox really struck me, and so I just started writing the play. I guess I started in 2000 because I'd finished first draft by the fall of '01. It didn't take long; I think I wrote it in three or four months. I just sat down at the computer, and I started talking it out. I mean I'd said it all out loud, it was almost like I dictated it to myself. And then I called Perry Martin because I knew of the work he had done with *The Kingfish* and John McConnell. I figured these guys have done it once before, they got it all the way to New York, I should get to know them. So, we had a reading in Perry's backyard. He lived on Crete Street near Grand Route Saint John, and as John (Spud) McConnell was reading through the play script, I was sitting there imagining changes. Now, Perry is legally blind, he can see, but he needs enhanced vision glasses. He's a hell of a director, and he kept making comments about how a plot would turn at this point or that. So, I put it through a couple of revisions after that, and then I said to Perry, "Well, I think we're ready to go," and he said, "All right, you got a budget?" And I said, "Well, I don't know, I mean can't you just open the play?" and he said, "No, you got to have publicity, it's going to cost, and you got to be able to pay Spud for the rehearsals and guarantee him a certain base." So, we went back and forth, and I said, "Well, how much do you think I need?" and he said, "You need at least $25,000 to start." I had no idea where to go, so I called Rob Couhig. He and I had been friends since high school. We went to Jesuit together and went to Georgetown together and. . . . So, I went down to his office. I told him on the phone, and he said, "Well come on down, let's talk about it." And [*laughs*] he sat there, and I said, "Look, I got this play." He said, "Tell me about it." So, I told him, and he said, "That sounds pretty good, that could work." I said, "Look, you want to read the script?" He said, "No, I don't want to read the script." [*Laughter*] And he said, "Jason, what is the most I can lose on this?" and I said, "Well, Rob, I don't think you're going to lose money, I think you'll make it back." And he said, "Well, what do you need?" "$25,000." "Well, how much of that do you think I might lose?" and I said, "Well, I don't know." "What's the most I can lose if I put in twenty-five?" and I said, "I don't know, you might lose ten," and he said, "I'll do it." [*Laughter*] And so I said, "Well, look—" and at the time, I was doing these talks for Elderhostel. Do you know?

MC: Hmm.

JB: Yeah. And so, I called Barbara McCurdy a wonderful woman, a former nun, and I said, "Look, I'm working on this thing, would you mind letting me do one?" I was giving talks on literature and politics, and people liked them, and I'd sell books. And I said, "I've got this play, would you let me do a reading? It lasts about ninety minutes," and she said, "Yeah, yeah, that sounds good." So she booked a room upstairs in Ralph & Kacoo's restaurant. I guess it was a banquet room or something or a little bit bigger. So, there were about fifty people there, and I called Rob, and I said, "Look, I'm going to be doing a stage reading, and John McConnell is coming, and Perry Martin is coming. If you could come, then the four of us could talk afterwards and then I think we can move forward on this." He said, "Great, I'll be there." So, I did the reading, and everybody loved it, people were clapping and laughing, and I realized I had the audience. Perry and John were sitting in the back, and Perry, as I said, is blind and so he's kind of got his hand over his forehead, and he's looking, and he can see people. And Spud was looking down most of time, and I know what he was doing, he listening. He was letting the rhythms of the monologue roll in his thought field, and Couhig didn't show up. So, we finished the thing, everybody's clapping, everybody's leaving, and I go up to the two guys who are going to do the play, and at that moment Rob Couhig walks in, and he's wearing a downtown lawyer suit, and he's got his tie on. And he said, "I'm sorry, I'm running late," and he turns to Perry, and he says, "It's a hell of script, don't you think?" [*Laughter*] Perry said, "Yeah," he said, "All right, let's sit down." Of course, he hadn't read the script.

MC: Yeah.

JB: And hadn't seen the play. So, we go downstairs, we order oysters and beer, and we sit there and talk about it, and Rob says, "I'm in." The play opened in March of '02, at Southern Rep, which at that time was in the Canal Place complex. And *The Boston Globe* story was just taking off like a rocket. There was a chain reaction all over the country, and I went downtown, and I did a satellite interview with Anderson Cooper and a lawyer from Boston and a survivor from Boston. And I stood on Canal Street and gave this brief summary of how terrible Father Maciel was, and I think it went over their heads, because they didn't know who he was, and they're talking about Boston, Boston. And when the interview was done, I walked into the theater and watched the opening night of my play.

Jason Berry with G. Howard Hunter

G. Howard Hunter and Adele Layrisson / 2023

Interview conducted by G. Howard Hunter and Adele Layrisson for University Press of Mississippi on July 27, 2023.

G. Howard Hunter: I did my math. It's been thirty years since *Lead Us Not Into Temptation* was published. What's changed since then?

Jason Berry: Well, there's been a legal battle on many levels going on, much of it really since 2002. When *The Boston Globe* series began, many of these survivors began to give public statements, and eventually after a lot of hard slogging by trial lawyers representing these people, the various dioceses and religious orders were just hammered year after year, month after month, with lawsuits. When I did *Render under Rome*, which came out in 2011, the church was hemorrhaging billions. According to Jack Rule, a CPA/professor of accountancy who was a very good source of mine, he estimates the figure to be 10 billion dollars, and money alone does not capture what has happened. I think the decline in people going to mass—the Pew Research Center and Georgetown's CARA (Center for Applied Research in the Apostolate) indicates that the number of Catholics in the country has declined by about 6 or 8 percent, which is substantial over a thirty-year period, and the number of nones, people without any religious affiliation are now second to that of Catholics. If I'm not mistaken, the second largest number is ex-Catholics, people who have left church.

GHH: I think it would be helpful if you could just lay out the linear connection between the pedophile scandals and the closing of parishes.

JB: It's a good question Howard. I spent the better part of three years trying to answer it in the book that came out in 2011 (*Render unto Rome*). As many of these dioceses began dealing with high stakes litigation, there were two factors that explain the wave of church closing. One is demographic: old ethnic neighborhoods where you had Polish, Irish, and Italians and so forth moving out to the suburbs or to better neighborhoods socioeconomically, leaving these large urban churches that were expensive to upkeep. So in some cases it does make sense to close the church and sell it. Well, you look at places like New York and California; the urban dioceses there have had staggering settlements. Los Angeles alone was up to I think $700 million when I last did that work, and there were churches being sold all over the country, so there's a definite cause and effect as to impact. I don't know any economist who has yet been able to say the X number of church closings are the result of these large settlements.

GHH: But we know there's a correlation.

JB: There's an absolute correlation. And I think it was most outrageously shown with the case of Raffaello Follieri, the Italian sort of flimflam man who was in business with Cardinal Sodano's nephew, and they were going around lining up churches to buy, and he did buy and sell in some cases before he ended up going to federal prison.

GHH: He's probably out by now.

JB: He is, and I understand anecdotally that he's trying to sell churches in England. I guess he's got the skill set.

GHH: Well apparently. I was reading about him in *Render Under Rome*.

JB: He's quite an extravagant personality.

GHH: I know any guess is as good as any in this situation, but you've done so much work on this. What do you see as the future of the church?

JB: Well, I think it is going to be smaller numerically.

GHH: But you make the case that some of the cardinals want that.

JB: Well you know, Ratzinger, before he became Pope even, seemed to endorse a smaller, leaner church.

GHH: A more militant church?

JB: I don't know if militant was his exact word, but he's the one who railed against the dictatorship of relativism, all the while cardinals and bishops were hiding child molesters, which is kind of a state of relativism—I would say moral relativism. I think the church at least in the United States is going to be numerically smaller, darker as more Latinos come to this country and carry their faith tradition with them, and not nearly as wealthy or powerful as we saw from the rise of the immigrant church roughly speaking before the Civil War to the early twenty-first century. The lawsuits and attendant media coverage that happened in the early nineties when my book came out was part of it, but I think those cases would have happened anyway. The fact that there was a book with data and an analysis gave the press something to really hang analytical pieces on. By the time of *The Globe* reporting in the Spotlight series starting in 2002, the landscape was really changing as more and more victims came forward. The media for a period of two years had a scandal narrative building momentum, and it finally ended in 2004 when the bishops released the study by the National Review Board, which I think wasn't nearly as strong as it might have been. Wilton Gregory, who was then the Archbishop of Atlanta, now a cardinal in Washington, gave the memorable line "the scandal is history," and I can tell you a lot of journalists who had been covering this were tired of it . . . especially the religion reporters. There are fewer today sadly because of the shrinking number of people working in newsrooms, but a lot of the religion reporters were having to write about the abuse of Catholic children and what the survivors were saying, and it didn't help them maintain . . .

GHH: Their own faith.

JB: . . . That, but more so it made dealing with the local chancery more difficult, and yes I think with their own faith as well.

GHH: Reading your books, I was amazed that when you look at the archbishops—some are cardinals, some not—of Los Angeles, Chicago, New York, Boston, Pittsburg . . . they were all of Irish descent. The ones who were not of Irish descent were anomalies.

JB: We are an Irish Church. Really the Irish American presence in this country shaped the church that we know. It's changing to some degree with more and more ethnic people coming, not just Latinos and Vietnamese. You go to St. Augustine church here in New Orleans—it's closed right now because of the recent hurricane—but those liturgies are quite different from what you have at Holy Name, which is on St. Charles Avenue with a rather affluent parish base of people in the neighborhood. When the Irish church itself in Ireland started to crash with all of those government reports and the relentless media coverage and television coverage, you could almost hear the sonic booms. I think for better or worse, the Irish church is, at least in this country, passing. I don't mean it's dying, but you don't have the same number of young Irish American men going into seminaries as you did thirty or forty years ago. They're really struggling just to get men to go to seminaries.

GHH: The bishops in New Orleans in the nineteenth century tended to come from France, Alsace, Netherlands. It was a little different.

JB: Well, Louisiana was an extension of the French church, and you know when the original diocese was headquartered in St. Louis in the early nineteenth century, it was pretty much a given that there would be French or Francophone bishops to minister to New Orleans. Père Antoine, who was actually a Spaniard, but he was an anomaly in many ways—he just sort of established himself as this cult figure and power base, and from all the historical information I could gather while working on the book *City of a Million Dreams*, he really opened the church to people of color. That very much so changed by the time he died, and then when the Civil War began, the church changed dramatically, supporting the Confederates.

GHH: From what I gather, the segregated Catholic churches started about ten years before World War I. I have to wonder if some of the Black people thought that was okay because they could have their own church.

JB: I really don't know the answer to that. One could speculate the strength of the African American Catholic rootedness; I guess you'd say this city stands apart from so many other parts in the South where you don't have a great many Blacks who are Catholic. They're members of the Black Baptist or Protestant congregations, African AME (African Methodist Episcopal) but I think the tradition of free people of color in New Orleans who were rooted in the church had a long influence in the generations after slavery. When Archbishop Hughes announced that he was going to close St. Augustine church in 2006 not long after the hurricane, it created an absolute furor. I remember I interviewed Jacques Morial both for an article and later for the section of the book *Render unto Rome* that deals with New Orleans, and he said something that really struck me. In effect he said, if you want to raise money, because Saint Augustine was behind on its arrears, what it owed the diocese—well it wasn't, in terms of revenue coming in and revenue going out, it wasn't like say St. Pius X by the lake or Holy Name uptown. So with all this money owed, Father LeDoux, the pastor who was an absolute heroic figure in that community, was doing everything that he could while maintaining his pledge of obedience to the bishop. Anyway, Morial said look, you've got a priest who is a folk hero, everybody wants to help New Orleans, get Oprah, get Danny Glover, do a big fundraiser, raise the money that you need. In the meantime, Mike Valentino, a member of that congregation, offered a million dollars to help shore up the funds that they needed—they needed a lot of work on the church—the only condition he said was let us keep our pastor, and so they turned him down. They turned down a million dollars so the bishop could maintain his position. This is part of the myopia and the foolhardiness, to use mild terms, of the hierarchy.

Adele Layrisson: I am a teacher at the Academy of the Sacred Heart here in New Orleans, and I was wondering if you had any insight for the upcoming generation of Catholics and Catholic educators who may feel disillusioned from the church because of the scandals.

JB: That's a hard question Adele, and the first caveat is I'm not an educator, so give me a pass on that one, but I think the same problem exists in the realm of what we used to call civics. How do you give young people a sense of history when so much of history has been covered up, and the sort of underside is now surfacing? True historical writing, investigative reporting, lawsuits. You know on the one hand, you have the MAGA people who don't want children taught the truth about how the country treated Blacks for so long, and on the other hand to your question, how do you teach kids about the church in an era of such relentless scandal? All I can think of is to spotlight certain people in the history of the church who stand out for their manifest virtues: Dorothy Day and the Catholic Worker Movement would be one, the eleventh-century cardinal St. Peter Damien who made an issue of clergy abuse. The pope thanked him and then did nothing. So I look at someone like Catherine of Siena; the mystics hold so much history in their lives and teaching children elevates them to a higher level might be one way of doing it. That's not my area. . . . I wish I had a better answer for you.

GHH: I'm wondering if when you wrote about the Black Spiritual churches, if that kind of spirituality was similar to your mother and grandmother's notion of spirituality from Mexico?

JB: Well, let me put it this way: The Day of the Dead represents in Mexico an exaltation of the beloved dead. The skeletons are the satirical image of that, but I went to a Day of the Dead ceremony in a suburb of Mexico City, I guess this was 1996, and I was really struck by the way these families came and set up tables, chairs, dinner cloths, and so forth as children were scampering around the little narrow walking beds between the graves, and there would be a picture of the grandfather or the mother or whoever had died, and they would toast that person. There is a parallel of sorts with the Spiritual churches, the ones I wrote about in '95 were I think much more animated, much more dramatic of people caught up in the spirit. I guess I've been fascinated with the way in which spirituality manifests itself in different people and traditions. I don't know if it was a conscious realization on my part when I did that work. I will say that it was a wonderful way to decompress from all the cover-ups.

GHH: But you get that sense of a transcendent power that's very real for these people, and I'm not being condescending.

JB: Yeah, I understand. I would say that the trance-like possessions that you find in many of the African American and certain of the Indian churches, at least that I've seen on trips to Mexico, do represent a form of an expression of ecstasy, of closeness to God. I was filming jazz funerals in the late nineties on the road that gradually ended many years later with the film I have out now, and you know at the time, I was deeply disillusioned with the Catholic Church, and I was getting a lot of information that made me pretty upset, and yet I would go to funerals and I would watch these rituals with a certain awe because I think they do express a reach toward God, a closeness in the danced memory that you don't ordinarily find in . . . what's a good term . . . garden variety churches?

GHH: Or people who have been conditioned by, for good and bad, what I would call "enlightenment thinking."

JB: Yes, that's another way to spin it. There's obviously a great interest now with identity politics, in where people come from and how the personal narrative reflects the voyage through social and political changes. I don't know if I'm the victim of a happy childhood or merely the product of one, but I keep going back to the relationship I had with my grandmother and of course my mother and dad and other friends.

GHH: I love the way you describe it as Victorian.

JB: Well, it was! You know in the 1950s, who would have ever thought that we would have Mardi Gras Indians, as just one example, becoming cult figures in the popular culture. I don't think I was aware of Black Indians until my twenties when I was working with Jon Foose and Ted Jones on *Up From the Cradle of Jazz*. The oral histories that we did focusing on the Black Indians really signaled a much deeper narrative, only parts of which we got. The idea that the Black man on the symbolic stage of Carnival would embrace the Indian as a symbol of resistance at a time when people were playing Dixie at upscale Carnival balls— hold those two in in either hand, either pole, and then try to kind of bring them together, and I think that's where we are today. The Indians represent a counter narrative to the Lost Cause.

GHH: [*To Adele*] Do you know Michael P. Smith?

AL: Yes, the photographer.

JB: I met Mike in the early seventies. It may have been '73, in fact I met him at the apartment on the top floor of the Cabildo, this huge attic apartment of Clarence John Laughlin, the photographer, who, well I have two of his photographs in the kitchen now. Clarence was a surrealist in his approach to the city, and Mike was intense, purposeful. . . . I think the first night I met him, he told me Richard Nixon was a war criminal. That was sort of the beginning of our dialogue, and I said, "Yeah I'd go along with that." This was during Watergate. Mike was a wonderful guy. He for many years funded his cultural work by being a commercial photographer, going out on oil rigs and things like that, but I really discovered the Spiritual churches through his work, and I went to a couple of services. When Jon and I began raising funds to do the documentary *Up From the Cradle of Jazz*, the book grew out of the film, usually it's the other way around, but Mike was very helpful. In fact, we licensed probably a dozen or so of his photographs for a montage in that film. I think they are all a part of the Historic New Orleans Collection archive. In the conversations I had with him, I think it's fair to say that I absorbed his point of view. Let me back up a moment and say, when I was in Mississippi in 1971 working out for Charles Evers, many of the campaign rallies were in Black churches. I'd never been to one until then, and just time and again my moorings just kept shifting with the beauty of those gospel choirs and the power of the singing. The two people I kept thinking of were Aaron Neville and Irma Thomas, who sang at the dances and proms when I was in high school, and I began to see their intonations and the way in which they sang. I began to see where that came from. So you know here it is probably seven years later, probably in '78, when Jon and I began going to Deacon Frank Lastie's church, the Guiding Star Spiritual Church, I heard those echoes from Mississippi and more so I think because of Mike's close eye on how the people in the altar dressed, the fact that women were bishops, the presence of Catholic icons, of Michael, St. Peter, and then of course the mysterious figure of Black Hawk, who is a guardian, a protective figure, all of that you know created a circle of figures of veneration and it fascinated me to no end.

GHH: Can you talk a little bit about the cultural Renaissance in New Orleans and also south Louisiana in the 1970s that not only were you part of, but you were one of the people who defined it.

JB: I did a big article in *Figaro*, I think it was 1979, called "The City's Cultural Awakening." Well, understand that when I got back from Mississippi, I finished the book toward the end of '72. I got an advance, and I went to Europe for I think seven months. I saw the Old World, and often when I traveled, you know Europe, backpacking that kind of thing, and people would say "Where are you from?" and every time I said New Orleans people's eyes would light up, and I started to think of the city in a different way. I had no idea of the culture that nourished jazz. I liked Louis Armstrong's music, but I didn't know that much about it. So when I got back, the book came out in '73, and I decided to live here and freelance. In doing so, I was planted in this rocking bohemian culture where young Black people, young white people were . . .

GHH: I was going to say you were really all about the same age. . . . Mike Smith was a little bit older.

JB: He was a bit older, but Dawn DeDeaux, for example, was editing *Museum Magazine*, the New Orleans Museum of Art's magazine, and of course doing her own work. Dalt Wonk and Josephine Sacabo the photographer, his wife, were people I knew. Valerie Martin, who was teaching at UNO (University of New Orleans), and I think had published two novels by the time she had left, among many other people, Chris Wiltz being one of them. If I go on, I'm going to have to decide when to stop. There were a lot of people doing different things, and you know Bunny Matthews's cartoons in *Figaro* I think captured a certain folk mentality. It was quite pronounced. The exhibitions for example at the CAC (Contemporary Arts Center), which I think came into existence in '77, were all about this bicultural heritage of the city. You can't deny the beauty of the architecture or the fact that the Confederate Museum stood there. . . . On the other hand, there was this rising voice in the Black community. I mean, when the Neville Brothers band came together in 1977, Professor Longhair was still performing at Tipitina's, those were some of the most ecstatic nights of music I've ever experienced. So with all of that going on, I felt a kind of hope and optimism for the city and the state, because the zydeco musicians, the Cajun musicians, Jazz Fest was a catalytic presence in all of this, there was now this kind of road between Lafayette and the outlying towns and the city. You could go to the Maple Leaf, you could go to Tipitina's or the clubs . . .

GHH: And you wrote about it.

JB: I did. I was there. I was kind of an eyewitness. It was a wonderful thing to write about. I remember George Landry was the chief of the Wild Tchoupitoulas. Big Chief Jolley: He insisted that I should spell it j-o-l-l-e-y, which I still do to this day, and see how many other people spell it the other way, so you know who holds the reins on this. But I remember one night at Tipitina's, maybe the Nevilles were playing, that was packed and that guy lit up a joint about six inches long, and people just parted you know, and then everybody watched him, and he's just taking it and then passing it to someone, and then the circle closed and life went on. The city certainly moves to its own beat.

GHH: I think you had the oil crunch in about '87, but even before that, New Orleans and south Louisiana were kind of becoming a thing culturally. I mean BeauSoleil was on Prairie Home Companion.

JB: So was Spencer Bohren. I think Dr. Michael White was on *Prairie Home Companion* and a couple others. Well, you know before Katrina, the city had a sort of rising cultural identity, so did Acadiana, and that's not to minimize the poverty, the racism, and the drugs and crime—that was part of the city for reasons of history that I think we understand rather well today, sadly so. I think Katrina changed things so dramatically, not just because of people who lost homes and couldn't come back. It was obvious that Nagin and the city council wanted to do everything possible to close some of the housing projects to keep people from coming back home. I remember interviewing the Episcopal bishop of New Orleans, Charles Jenkins, who was deeply involved with Jerome Smith and other people in trying to create affordable housing. I sat in his office, and he said, "I don't know how to prove it, but it's obvious that someone or some group of people don't want poor people to come back." You know, the city went almost overnight to being a disaster on Dateline, and although the music and the culture have now sort of returned in the lens of feature writing and cultural pieces, I think the struggle with sea rise, subsidence, and just the continuing plague of crime and poverty has colored the image of the city if you will, much more so than at least in the seventies and eighties when I was doing that kind of cultural writing.

GHH: I remember after Katrina, there was a sense that we can do it right this time. What were some of the opportunities that have been lost?

JB: Well, let me first say that I never bought that mantra.

GHH: Okay, good.

JB: I heard it often enough. I remember when *New Orleans Magazine* finally republished, I think it was November, Errol Laborde put the Joan of Arc statue on the cover, and the logo said, "And now the Renaissance." How do you have a Renaissance when the school system was in such terrible shape? Basically, the state taking over the school system ended up depriving teachers of pensions. This went all the way to the state Supreme Court which overturned a verdict for these teachers. To blame teachers and cut them out of money that they had justly earned seems to me the wrong way of going about a renaissance. Fortunately, because my house didn't flood, at least inside, I was back fairly early, in October. I went to some of the Bring New Orleans Back hearings in the Sheraton Hotel, and I could see the developers and the people at the Urban Land Institute, and I understood where they were coming from. Their idea was we can rebuild the city, we can make it a Paris on the Mississippi, if only we do medium rise and just let the Ninth Ward become a kind of garden that will flood whenever these terrible things happen. Well I understood the logic behind that, but what do you do with the people who've lost all these homes? I remember I was there when one of the guys from New Orleans East said to Joe Cannizaro, "I don't know you Mr. Canizaro, but I hate you." Look, Canizaro is an extremely conservative person . . .

GHH: Donald Trump was a guest at his house . . .

JB: Yeah, I know he gave a lot of money to Donald Trump . . . so did Boysie Bollinger, but you know I've known Cannizaro passingly for years, he's a very pleasant guy one-on-one, it's hard to feel any animus toward him even though I don't agree with his politics. The great problem was that we did not have someone who could pull the society together in 2006. When Nagin ran for reelection, Nagin, who really had been anything but a mayor for the poorest people in the city, suddenly ran, "Well, we've got to beat the man I've got to go back to city hall," and Jesse Jackson and Al Sharpton flew into the fray helping to get Black people who have been displaced back to the city to vote, and when he gave the Chocolate City comments on Martin Luther King Day, it was a clear signal to Black people that "we've got to hold on to our city." Mitch Landrieu did not run a very good campaign. He was reluctant to go after Nagin. He lost it, he came back four years later, and won by a landslide. I think if Landrieu had won in 2006, he has the temperament and personality and credibility in the Black community so that we probably would have seen a stronger comeback much earlier. I mean this is all second guessing, but by the time he became mayor and started accessing the federal spigot, he was rebuilding the city because he knew how to do it. It was part of his skill set. Nagin didn't have that ability, and I think Nagin. . . . He clearly had a breakdown of some kind. I'm not sure what the exact diagnosis would be, but he did it on the Garland Robinette radio program, practically sobbing. And I remember Susie Terrell, who had run for the Senate against Mary Landrieu a couple years earlier, but anyway she was working in Washington, I believe in the Commerce Department under George W. Bush. She told me that she had a conversation with Nagin saying, "Look we've got funds, we can help out," and he said, "We can't do that yet. We don't have the grant writers, we're not ready to get those projects in motion." And yet he loved going on national television. He thrived on that. He was a narcissist, and as we know he ended up going to prison, so when you think about the delayed recovery. . . . The charter schools have had some success, I'm not opposed to them in a knee-jerk way, but I think that the core problems of poverty and drugs are not going to go away without a policy that has the right intervention approach and a way to give young people alternatives to what they see in the street.

GHH: You were really the only public intellectual who came out against tearing down the projects.

JB: Maybe I was. I don't know.

GHH: I think you were pretty much alone in that. Would you still agree with that now?

JB: Well, I don't know, as buildings those brick structures were fairly sturdy. They needed work. . . . Obviously you have to upgrade any building every twenty to twenty-five years. What bothered me was that people who had legitimate leases could not return to their homes, and to blame the pathologies that did certainly exist in those places on all the people who live there I think was a gross mistake. I don't know. . . . I see the townhouses in those areas. They're certainly more handsome. I don't know if they are as well built . . .

GHH: . . . or sturdy.

JB: I don't know, I'm not saying they aren't. . . . That whole post-Katrina experience, and how it was such bitter divisions, and it was clear that what they were trying to do was just dump a whole bunch of poor people on Houston or Atlanta—I thought that was awful. I thought the people had a right to come back.

GHH: Let's go in this direction for a little bit. . . . What drew you to Earl Long? And when?

JB: My first memory of politics came in 1959. I was ten years old, and my father summoned me to the living room, and he said, "I want you to watch history in the making." I'll never forget that phrase. He said, "Look at that. That's your governor. His name is Earl K. Long. Three state troopers are taking him off to a mental hospital and Channel 6 is beeping out the curse words." And this is live TV, and I was just fascinated. First of all, that a governor could go crazy on the evening news, and later I came to see it almost as a metaphor of the state and the absolute disaster that democracy has become where we live. As time passed, of course I read A. J. Liebling's book, which is a classic, and then later I read the biography that Peoples and Kurtz wrote. When I read that book and learned that the FBI was tailing him for years, but never indicted him, and then the more I learned about how he had registered 100,000 Black people to vote in the late 1950s at a time when all of these other Southern states were trying to get Black people off any road toward voting, and of course bearing in mind that he had a major meltdown, he just became fascinating to me as a character doing the right thing in the worst possible way . . . carrying on with Blaze Starr the way he did. The idea just came to me: Why not do a one man play and put the guy in purgatory, trying to figure out where he's come from and where he's going? I wrote it toward the end of 2001, I think I wrote it in two or three months. I just literally sat at the computer screen and talked out the words, I mean I was talking all day long, I was talking it out, and then Perry Martin, who had directed John "Spud" McConnell in *The Kingfish*, I knew and contacted him. So the three of us had a meeting, I think it was October of '01. Perry was living on Crete Street near Grand Route St. John. We sat in his backyard on a fall day, and Spud read the script slowly, and I was taking notes. Perry is legally blind—smart as a fox—but has severe vision problems, and he would every now and then stop and say, "Okay wait, let's go back on that one," or he said, "I don't think that line works," and I'm writing all this down. And so we went through several more rehearsals, and finally I asked Perry, "I mean how much money do we need to do this?" I think he said $30,000, and of course, I blanched at that. Where am I going to get thirty grand? So I called Rob Couhig, who had recently run for mayor. He and I have been friends since high school, we went to Jesuit and Georgetown together. We got together and I told him what I wanted to do, and he said, "what's the most I can lose on this?" I said, "Well Rob, you're not going to lose money on this. Should be. . . ." "What's the most I could lose?" "Well, maybe ten to fifteen. . . ." "I'll do it." So I was giving these talks for Elderhostel at the time on literature and politics in Louisiana, and I asked Barbara McCurdy who ran Elderhostel, "Would you mind if I just did a straight read-through of this play?" She said, "No, that'd be great."

GHH: Wait a minute, go back, who were you doing this for?

JB: ElderHostel.

GHH: What was that?

JB: ElderHostel, I think it still exists, it was a company that was about cultural tourism for people say over sixty. So they would come to town and instead of "Here's your night on Bourbon Street," or "We're going to go to the Superdome," they have lectures by different people.

GHH: Where were they?

JB: Hotels, usually local hotels. So she (Barbara McCurdy) rented the upper floor of Ralph and Kacoo's Restaurant. I told Couhig, "Okay I've got the director and I've got the actor, they are going to come here and I'm going to read the play. Please come. I said, "Do you wanna see the script?" "Nah I'm not interested in the script." I said, "Please come." Okay so I got up and I read the play.

GHH: And you had the people there

JB: I had the people there. I had about fifty people there, and a lot of them were from places like New Jersey and New York and Chicago, shall we say educated sophisticated people, and oh they were all coming up, this is great you got to get this to Off Broadway and this is lovely, we love it, and I'm just beaming. I went over and Perry's just sitting there, Spud's sitting there, and there's no Couhig. So I said, "Well, why don't we go get a drink downstairs." In walks Couhig, "So good to see you guys hell of a script don't you think?" Of course, he never read it, so we went down, we had oysters, we had beer, and we cemented our agreement and the play opened I think it was March of 2002. By that time, the two sides of my life were like tectonic plates starting to hit each other. *The Boston Globe* series had begun, and I was going on national television giving interviews. I think I had the proposal in New York, but I don't think I'd signed the contract for *Vows of Silence*. And the play opened. Southern Rep at that time was at Canal Place, and I did an interview with Anderson Cooper from a satellite link on the corner of Canal and Peters streets. My grave muckraking self—this is a serious crisis, Anderson, and then I walked in and saw my play open. It was, I guess, an ironic experience. We got good reviews, and then after a month, we had to move because there was a problem with the lease and another play coming in. So we ended up at the True Brew café, which is no longer there, but it was right off Fulton Street, and they had a wonderful little space. One Sunday afternoon a woman came up to me and she said my father is that elderly gentleman over there. I see this guy, he's got a cannula and an oxygen kit, he's waving over to me, and she says please come say hi to him after the play. I said "Of course, I'd be happy to." So the play ended, I walked over to the guy and he said, "I knew Uncle Earl, and I'm the one who had $14,000 in a paper bag [*laughs*]."

GHH: There was something else you wanted to say about Elderhostel.

JB: Wait, Elderhostel, part two. AJ Loria was a wonderful lounge lizard. He played piano and he was just a terrific guy. He was very good friends with Allen Toussaint and they would go cruise, go eat, and go around seeing music. So AJ had done several CDs and I told the Elderhostel folks, you know I got this friend who just does wonderful music and we could probably do a show where I give these little vignettes of history and then he does a song. We did it and people loved it.

GHH: Well, that must've been great.

JB: I've even got a video of it!

But it got to the point where AJ lived on Grand Route St John at that time of the morning when you began at 9:00, only about ten minutes at most from the Royal Orleans parking lot. But there was always a problem getting him up. I can't tell you how many times I would go over and he was married to a very sweet Japanese gal who actually predeceased him. So I'd go over there and I'd knock on the door, and there'd be no answer, so I'd go around the alley and I'd knock on the back door, and I'd see this little face and she'd go, "Ooh, Jason" and "AJ JASON'S HERE," and I'd hear "Agghhh" and I'd say, "AJ, you gotta come." He smoked cigarettes and other cigarettes too. He would come and look at me smelling of nicotine and other things, and he would say, "I just got up," and I'd say, "Look man, we've gotta leave in five minutes." "Let me take a shower!" "No just put on Bay Rum, come one, we gotta go," and so this became a real struggle. We'd drive over there and come in at two minutes of 9:00 and the woman who was in charge of the event was just almost apoplectic. We got there late a couple of times and they're all these people sitting there and I'd just come in and say, "Well good morning, I'm sorry we're a little bit late, the traffic was terrible, blah blah blah," and I would start doing my vignette. AJ ceremoniously took out all of his CDs that he's going to sell, I usually had copies of *Up From the Cradle of Jazz*. We had a great roadshow going and it ended when one of the Elderhostel people called me and said look it's a great show, but we just can't do it with AJ not being on time, and so that was it. When he died, I hadn't seen him that often in the last few years, I think he died about a year and a half ago. And I went to his funeral. He used to make the Saint Jude Novenas, as Aaron Neville did, as Big Chief Tootie did, in that belief in the saint of hopeless cases. AJ was a daily communicant, he went every day to mass, and he was right out there on the bohemian edge most of his life, but did all right, he made a living, and I don't mean that in a condescending sense. He really had talent and sitting there in that church realizing how much the church meant to him was rather moving.

GHH: I guess my only reservation about Uncle Earl was that the 1948 deal that he didn't make with the federal government on oil revenues was absolutely disastrous.

JB: It was, although somebody did a paper or a big article disputing that he had had the power to do that. But you're right, and the book that deals with it is by the guy who had been lieutenant governor Bill Dodd, *Peapatch Politics*. And he says that basically he traded with Leander Perez for the support for his nephew Russel Long. I don't know whether that has stood up factually, but it does make sense to me.

GHH: You have often defined New Orleans as a duality of a city of laws and a city of spectacle and that these forces often collide. I'd like for you to talk about that.

JB: Well, you know growing up if you're only among white people for the most part and you gradually have a realization that most of the music you love and dance to is by Black people. You begin to get some inkling of a duality, and for me it really grew after I got to Washington and went to Georgetown and began to understand the civil rights movement and how little I had learned about it in high school. So after a lot of the writing I did about neighborhoods and for *Figaro*, *Gambit*, and other outlets, I really began to see the Black city for lack of a better term, as this powerful force of memory that came out particularly during Carnival season. I'll never forget something that Bill Fagely told me. He was a curator of African Art at the New Orleans Museum of Art and he wrote a great book, a memoir, before he died. Bill told me that you cannot understand New Orleans without going deep into Carnival. And in understanding Carnival on the surface, you've got Rex and the old line parades and balls, and on the other hand, you've got Zulu and the Young Men's Illinois Club who form a sort of a counter establishment, so to speak. And then you've got this powerful force of music and energy that has come out, songs like "Go to the Mardi Gras" by Professor Longhair and "Carnival Time" by Al Johnson creating a massive stage for the society to enact its myths, and I over many years, came to see these identity myths as happening sort of simultaneously. The more I studied and read about early New Orleans history, say the first century, Congo Square just overwhelmed me in its meaning. It was not just a place where the enslaved danced, but it was also a place where memory rituals were transplanted and reenacted. And to me that is really the foundation, the undergirding of this culture of spectacle. Now it's true that at the same time the planters would go into their New Orleans townhouses and have lavish balls, small though they may have been compared to the ones we have today, given the baroque nature of Carnival. But I think the Black cultural memory and the idea of resistance that manifested itself through these various rituals gathered strength and momentum across the twentieth century and really became a force unto itself by the nineties. I kept following these funerals, and the Indian processions and dancing, particularly with a sharp eye on the beaded artistry and what those breastplates were saying. I mean Big Chief Alfred Doucette had one with a lynching and people on the bottom of it watching it, we have that in the film, so there's a symbolic language one comes to realize in any city. I think this city, because it so prides itself on being unique, on being different, on being Creole, you find these identity pageants, whether it's Sicilians or African Americans or the Krewe of Rex. The idea of culture and the law in constant tension really began to crystallize for me when Landrieu announced that he had the legal authority, which he did, to remove the statues. I was starting my deadline on the book I think it was 2016, and I had to deliver the book I think it was middle of '17 or the end of '17, and I realized, well here's the city on this issue coming over to the side of the culture acknowledging that these symbols of white supremacy did not belong in the places where they were, and I think that tension between culture and the law will probably define the city for years to come.

GHH: I think of spectacle as something where the line between performing and the observer withers away. For example, I think you articulated that very well with the funeral procession of Carlos III. That was spectacle I would say.

JB: Oh absolutely. I mean here was a city that had practically burned to the ground less than a year before and when they get word that the king is dead, well, we have to celebrate the death of the king, the life of the king, and of course, long live the new king. How many people in the royal chambers of Madrid had any idea that in this far away backwater town there was a great funeral procession?

GHH: Would you say *City of a Million Dreams* is a culmination of all your life's work?

JB: Well . . .

GHH: Or a lot of your work?

JB: Certainly, the strand in my life of researching and writing and producing films or video pieces on the city and the culture are so dear to me I would say it is a culmination of sorts. It's not to say I wouldn't be opposed to going further, but I'm at a point now where I don't really have an outlet to do the kinds of interviews and writing that I did back starting in the 1970s and '80s.

GHH: Is that because of the demise of publications?

JB: Well, the main reason is that *New Orleans Magazine* has really moved away from journalism. It's become entirely commercial. I did the music column for twenty-five years, and it reached a point where it was not a comfortable fit and so I simply did my last call. You know, I've had the luxury to work on long-term projects for quite a while. The film has taken a long time and I'm going out on the road a lot now for screenings. The city is to me beautifully tragic and elusive all at once. There's so many dimensions to it I would never say I will never write about it again.

GHH: When you think about your work, writing about music and history and politics and religion, in many ways, I think it all came together with *City of a Million Dreams.*

JB: I was able to draw on a lot of the work I've done in several different streams so to speak, and in writing this book, I made a mistake frankly in pitching it as a tricentennial history. I don't think the tricentennial made much difference, yeah it was very well reviewed, but if I had had another six months, it would have been a longer book. I don't know whether that would have affected the sales, but I really wish I'd been able to do the 1884 World Exposition. It's a huge topic with all kinds of dimensions to it.

GHH: In your film you talk about European and African influences creating a culture that is essentially *sui generis*. Any thoughts on how New Orleans will evolve as a cultural force?

JB: Let me answer that this way, and I don't know if it really goes to exactly what you're driving at. But even with the depth of poverty and the issues of social justice and climate change that altogether bedevil this city, I do think that the future of New Orleans is that of an entertainment mecca if there were more money for theatrical productions to actually compete with other cities. For example, Louisville has the famous theatrical festival every year and the Alabama Shakespeare Festival is very well marketed. But you know the pandemic pretty much killed Southern Rep. I'm a bit out of school on this, but I think that La Petite now has Actors Equity performances. Somehow, if the city could sustain two or three top theatrical venues, I think it would go a long way to attracting more people and give us a greater identity as a cultural mecca. The jazz festival here has now become an economic powerhouse, but theater will draw people and for kids who are coming out of NOCC (New Orleans Center for Creative Arts), theater becomes a place for them to perform or at least aspire to perform. Somehow or another, I think if the money is there, the potential economic engine I think lies in entertainment.

AL: I just wanted to add that the film industry here as well could be great in terms of getting young people interested in acting and entertainment.

JB: Forgive me, I should have mentioned the film industry which is now a multimillion-dollar industry. In fact, my daughter Simonette is an official with IATSE (the local union of film set and theatrical workers). She was a coproducer along with Tim Watson on *City of A Million Dreams*, but she is also assistant business manager of the Local, and of course, every year they have to go to Baton Rouge to lobby for the film tax credits, which I think have proven effective, even though the *Picayune* editorials don't agree with that, but it's not the first time the *TP* has been wrong.

GHH: You've been an investigative journalist, a writer, independent scholar, and historian. How have you managed, because most people can't even fathom trying to make a living in any of these fields?

JB: I have to say that were I starting out today I would probably be looking for a regular paid outlet. But when I started freelancing in 1973, I moved into an apartment in the Irish Channel, and rent was $75, gas was 29 cents a gallon and my dad still carried me on his Blue Cross until I was about twenty-six. I was writing for the local outlets like *Figaro* and the *Vieux Carre Courier*. Ultimately, *Gambit*, which came along about 1980, and *New Orleans Magazine* were the major local outlets. I managed to start doing book reviews first for

The New Republic then the *Nation*. There were more alternative weeklies and newspapers with Sunday editions than there are today. The alternative weekly has practically been wiped out. So it was a struggle but if I could generate five to six hundred bucks a month, I could cover my needs. I wasn't going to Antoine's for dinner; I might go to Parasol's and have an oyster poor boy, but I was fortunate in developing outlets that took my work and I started getting grants in 1974. The first one came from the Fund for Investigative Journalism when Charles Evers got indicted for income tax evasion. When Charles Evers got indicted, I got on the phone and called some of the other Black leaders and I soon learned that there was a long list of people who had been in the movement with him, all of them having been audited. In the end, I found there were twenty-seven people like that in Mississippi and so the two papers that ran it were Hodding Carter's *Delta Democrat Times* in Greenville and the *South Mississippi Sun* in Biloxi. Those two articles had quite an impact on the, for lack of a better term, civil rights establishment. I soon got into a long conversation by phone with Roger Williams, who was quite an author in his own right. He'd done a biography of Hank Williams, but he was also a grant officer at the Southern Regional Council in Atlanta. He said why don't you make some calls and see if you can find out if other states have this phenomenon, and all the signs were there, and so I got an assignment from *The Nation* with a grant of $1,800, which in my life was a lot of money. So I went out on the road for almost two months, and I had friends in most of these places so I didn't have big hotel expenses. I did two long pieces for *The Nation* on this. That led to another assignment with the Fund for Investigative Journalism, a two-part series for *The Washington Star* on the same thing. The IRS audited the NAACP and a gun control group which I discovered after was the first series of the articles in Mississippi. I don't know who sent it to him, but Charles Rangel the congressman from New York opened a committee hearing on this and got the GAO to do an investigation of the Mississippi IRS field offices. They were eventually absolved of any guilt, and I wrote an op-ed attacking the report, but you know it did have something of an impact.

GHH: You thought of yourself as a jazz writer, right?

JB: Well, I just thought of myself as a writer, and I was working on fiction, the brilliance of which eluded New York publishers. I had one novel that did not get published and in retrospect, I'm glad it didn't, it might've kneecapped me out of the gate. But I ended up doing another one which was better but did not make the grade, and during that time, I became more and more deeply involved in interviewing musicians, getting to know the city, and by 1978, Jonathan Foose and I had landed the grant to start filming.

GHH: How much was that?

JB: It was $36,000, which back then was a lot of money. We did that film for $50,000 and that included paying ourselves I think $900 a month. I'd like to go back and reedit it, certainly color correct it and get a female narrator. We had a woman DJ from WBOK who had this wonderful voice, but she moved to Houston, and we had to get the thing done and so I did the narration. I'm chuckling because the fundraising was really surreal. I remember Jim Glassman, the editor of *Figaro,* said I know this guy named Mike Rapier and he went to Jesuit High School and he's older than you. I had done a piece on Jesuit High School for *Figaro* that attracted attention at the time. So I wrote the guy a letter and I think he was with *First NBC* and he wrote back and they pledged $500. So that's what we did, I mean we had fundraisers, and I scraped together another I don't know, $10,000, and finished the film. When I look back you know, one could live in this town on a modest income and still have a pretty good time. It is a very expensive city today. The rents are much higher and there are not the outlets that we once had.

GHH: What did you get the Guggenheim for?

JB: Jazz funerals. I had I had really come to see by that time [2001] that the funerals held a mirror to the city that were almost like nonfiction short stories of where the city was at a given point in time, tracing it back to the funeral of Carlos III. This was the first example of a funeral with music. Which is the term that the early jazz men used before television. I wish I could have gone back farther. At the same time, I was reading about the way Iberville and Bienville and the other French and French Canadian voyagers who originally came here viewed the Indians and their burial traditions. This was a real part of the way they interpreted this place because they were accustomed to funerals that for prominent people that were quite the pageants through the streets. There is a good deal of literature on that, which I quoted from Phillipe Aries's book, *The Hour of Our Death.* That's how I got the Guggenheim. I persuaded them that there was a great book with jazz funerals at the center and I think I got it in the field of folklore even though I applied as a historian.

GHH: So journalist, novelist, playwright, historian—which one do you like the best?

JB: I think my epigram should be "he wrote well, and he lasted" [*laughs*]. Hoping that I have a few more chapters ahead.

GHH: That's a silly question but I think perhaps at certain times in your life there's someplace where you land.

JB: Well, yeah, I'm entertained when people call me a filmmaker since I've made two.

GHH: I describe you as a documentarian.

JB: Well, I think that's closer to the mark. Tim Watson, my editor, is a key part of that, and I cannot let this interview end without giving great credit to Tim who is an artist as an editor. Simonette was very important within the sort of internal dynamics of how the film got made. The three of us for a better part of a couple of years just went through the script over and over, trying to see how different scenes and different episodes work. And of course, when Deb Cotton, God rest her soul, died, the narrative structure had to spend a great deal of time working on that. Every narrative I think has its own momentum and whether you're writing a long article or a book of fiction or nonfiction, or working on a film, the key is having characters who drive the narrative and take it to a place where the reader/reviewer doesn't expect to go.

GHH: What would you describe as a Catholic intellectual lens? I'm going there because I think that's what brings your work together.

JB: Well, if you let me cut the word intellectual from the question.

GHH: Okay sure.

JB: I think if one comes up with a certain degree of reverence about the rituals of the church and the beauty of the art that one is exposed to through the stained-glass windows, the frescoes, and in such churches the paintings, it gives a certain aesthetic sensibility to the mind of faith and as you go through life. I think there is a kind of ritual imagination that becomes a part of the working process of writing or creating a film. For example, we were deep into the editing of *City or Million Dreams*, which uses a series of funerals as a kind of moving viewfinder on the history of the city, and I kept thinking that I want people to understand the sacred nature of this tradition. Because when they see a saxophone player honking in front of an open coffin they're going to go, what is this about New Orleans? How did they get there? So we had begun our three-day filming of the Congo Square dances with Father Jerome LeDoux, one of the more legendary figures in the Treme neighborhood, having been pastor of St. Augustine Church for many years. He wrote a very interesting book as well, and he and I had been pals. I called him and asked if he would come give an invocation because when you're a white director and you have Black musicians and Black dancers who are reenacting the world of the enslaved, I wanted to get some grace note in the beginning. LeDoux and I went to the side and he said, "Well, what do you want me to say?" and I said, "Well, Father LeDoux, I don't want to script your prayer but you know we are reenacting what the ancestors did and paying homage to them." So he nodded and he went out and he gave the most beautiful invocation—we thank you for the beauty of the earth, for bringing us together, and we are remembering what our ancestors did. Anybody who comes to that film for the first time and sees that understands there's a reenactment that is going to happen, but more so, here is a Black Catholic priest performing a blessing for the film crew and the dancers and the musicians. So I think something like that springs to mind when you ask about the influence of Catholicism. You know another scene comes to mind in the novel *Last of the Red Hot Poppas*, which is going to be released next year in a new paperback edition. The moral intelligence of that novel is the undertaker Reverend Christian Fraux. Many undertakers are also pastors in the Black community and there's a scene about two-thirds through the novel where they're gathering in the state capital and are having a wake for the deceased governor and the way in which Fraux uses the line from the Psalms, I have to tell you I got from the funeral for Raymond Miles, the gospel singer. This was out in New Orleans East before the flood and Bishop Paul Morton was presiding and Morton got so exercised, he was jumping up and down. Raymond was a very popular gospel singer, and he was murdered, and Morton talked about the Israelites having to go across the river and having to leave their harps in the trees and I put those lines as the speech of Christian Fraux. Would a non-Catholic writer have had that insight or inspiration? I don't know, but I think when you have a sensibility about art and narrative and how they come together—

GHH: It's a Catholic worldview.

JB: Well, I'm not sure it's a Catholic worldview, but [it's] one [that] goes back to memories that shape your sensibility and your artistic slant. I mentioned earlier the choirs I saw in Mississippi and how deeply moved I was because they reminded me of the music I had grown up with here. But that sort of dynamic tension between art and narration or between ritual and expression—to plagiarize Hemingway—is a feast you carry with you and it's there when you want to fall back on it.

Index

About the Editor

Photo © Barry Kaiser

Howard Hunter is a native of New Orleans and a history teacher of forty-two years. He is coauthor with James Gill of *Tearing Down the Lost Cause: The Removal of New Orleans's Confederate Statues*, published by University Press of Mississippi; has published articles on New Orleans and the Civil War for both academic and general audiences; and is past president of the Louisiana Historical Society.

www.ingramcontent.com/pod-product-compliance
Lightning Source LLC
Chambersburg PA
CBHW020613030726
47497CB00007B/2215